Young Black Changemakers and the Road to Racial Justice tells the stories of how Black youth become changemakers and speaks to researchers, educators, community organizations, and the public. Through many kinds of civic actions, Black youth are driven by a larger purpose to improve the world for Black people. Black families and Black-centered organizations support and sustain Black youth's civic engagement. Investing in community-based organizations can benefit young Black changemakers, and Black identity and community can offer belonging and joy. Black youth's stories call us to root out anti-Blackness in schools, on social media, and in public discourse. Black youth bring society hope for the future and point the way forward on the road to racial justice.

Dr. Laura Wray-Lake is Professor of Social Welfare at the University of California, Los Angeles (UCLA), USA. She has conducted research for over a decade on youth civic engagement. As an author and lifelong learner, she has over 90 publications that document young people's power to contribute to their communities and to create social and political change.

Dr. Elan C. Hope is Director of Research and Evaluation at Policy Research Associates, USA. She is an expert in youth development, racial justice, and well-being. She is an award-winning author of over 60 articles that explore how young people challenge oppression and create positive change in their communities.

Dr. Laura S. Abrams is Professor of Social Welfare at UCLA, USA. She is a youth justice expert and an award-winning author of five books and over 100 articles. She is a member of the American Academy of Social Work and Social Welfare, and recipient of the 2021 UCLA Chancellor's Public Impact Award.

T0384707

Contemporary Social Issues

General Editor: Brian D. Christens, Vanderbilt University

Contemporary Social Issues is the official book series of the Society for the Psychological Study of Social Issues (SPSSI). Since its founding in 1936, SPSSI has addressed the social issues of the times. Central to these efforts has been the Lewinian tradition of action-oriented research, in which psychological theories and methods guide research and action addressed to important societal problems. Grounded in their authors' programs of research, works in this series focus on social issues facing individuals, groups, communities, and/or society at large, with each volume written to speak to scholars, students, practitioners, and policymakers.

Other Books in the Series

Developing Critical Consciousness in Youth: Contexts and Settings
Erin Godfrey and Luke Rapa, editors

Critical Consciousness: Expanding Theory and Measurement
Erin Godfrey and Luke Rapa, editors

Young Black Changemakers and the Road to Racial Justice

Laura Wray-Lake
University of California, Los Angeles

Elan C. Hope
Policy Research Associates

Laura S. Abrams
University of California, Los Angeles

CAMBRIDGE
UNIVERSITY PRESS

CAMBRIDGE
UNIVERSITY PRESS

Shaftesbury Road, Cambridge CB2 8EA, United Kingdom

One Liberty Plaza, 20th Floor, New York, NY 10006, USA

477 Williamstown Road, Port Melbourne, VIC 3207, Australia

314–321, 3rd Floor, Plot 3, Splendor Forum, Jasola District Centre, New Delhi – 110025, India

103 Penang Road, #05–06/07, Visioncrest Commercial, Singapore 238467

Cambridge University Press is part of Cambridge University Press & Assessment, a department of the University of Cambridge.

We share the University's mission to contribute to society through the pursuit of education, learning and research at the highest international levels of excellence.

www.cambridge.org
Information on this title: www.cambridge.org/9781009244220

DOI: 10.1017/9781009244190

First published 2024

A catalogue record for this publication is available from the British Library

Library of Congress Cataloging-in-Publication Data
NAMES: Wray-Lake, Laura, author. | Hope, Elan C., author. | Abrams, Laura S., author.
TITLE: Young black changemakers and the road to racial justice / Laura Wray-Lake, Elan C. Hope, Laura S. Abrams.
DESCRIPTION: New York : Cambridge University Press, 2023. | Series: Csis contemporary social issues series
IDENTIFIERS: LCCN 2023019019 (print) | LCCN 2023019020 (ebook) | ISBN 9781009244220 (hardback) | ISBN 9781009244213 (paperback) | ISBN 9781009244190 (epub)
SUBJECTS: LCSH: Racial justice–California–Los Angeles. | Racism–Prevention.
CLASSIFICATION: LCC HT1581 .W63 2023 (print) | LCC HT1581 (ebook) | DDC 305.8009794/94–dc23/eng/20230518
LC record available at https://lccn.loc.gov/2023019019
LC ebook record available at https://lccn.loc.gov/2023019020

ISBN 978-1-009-24422-0 Hardback
ISBN 978-1-009-24421-3 Paperback

CONTENTS

9 Freedom Dreaming   160
   Laura Wray-Lake, Elan C. Hope, Laura S. Abrams, Mariah Bonilla,
   Domonique Kianna Henderson, Elena Maker Castro,
   Channing J. Mathews, Dominique Mikell Montgomery,
   Victoria Millet, Jason Anthony Plummer, & Sara Bloomdahl Wilf

ILLUSTRATIONS

TABLES

CONTRIBUTORS

MARIAH BONILLA is a 2023 graduate from UCLA with a BA in Public Affairs and Chicanx & Central American Studies Minor. She was a policy fellow within the UCLA Latino Policy & Policy Institute Programs' department. Bonilla is passionate about abolishing structures of inequality.

ELENA MAKER CASTRO received her PhD in human development and psychology from UCLA in 2023 and is an assistant professor of psychology at Bates College. A former high school teacher, Castro considers how we can understand and support youth's developmental processes as they navigate and transform oppressive systems. Her dissertation was funded by the National Institute of Minority Health and Health Disparities.

DOMONIQUE KIANNA HENDERSON is a graduate of Howard and Baylor Universities and a current doctoral student of social work at UCLA. Her research focuses on gendered racism and its implications for the mental health of Black women and girls. She is a firm believer in merging research and community work, and founded a nonprofit organization called CRWND, Inc. in 2021, which focuses on mentoring Black girls while centering mental health, academic excellence, and leadership. She is an honor minority doctoral scholar with Casey Family Programs and a Frank D. Gilliam Jr. Social Justice Award winner.

CHANNING J. MATHEWS is an assistant professor at the University of Virginia. She has authored over 20 works highlighting intersections of race, identity, and social inequity. Currently, Mathews examines Black and Latinx youth's positive connections to their racial groups and their association with activist engagement in sociopolitical and Science, Technology, Engineering, and Math-based contexts.

DOMINIQUE MIKELL MONTGOMERY is an assistant professor in the School of Social Work at the University of Nevada Reno. Her research agenda is informed by her experiences as a member and supporter of communities surviving and thriving despite state-sanctioned oppression. Competitive funding sources, including the Stoneleigh Foundation, the SPSSI, and the Edward A. Bouchet Graduate Honor Society, have supported Montgomery's work.

VICTORIA MILLET is an art and culture project coordinator at Community Coalition. She received a master's degree in social welfare from UCLA and a bachelor's degree from the University of Wisconsin.

JASON ANTHONY PLUMMER is a political social worker and an assistant professor in the School of Social Work at California State University, Long Beach. His research focuses on identifying the ways in which racism prevents society from having nice things like a functioning democracy, high quality of life, and a socially just society.

SARA BLOOMDAHL WILF is a doctoral student in social welfare studying youth sociopolitical development and civic engagement, with a focus on social media as a context. Previously, Wilf worked as a researcher and program evaluator with nonprofits in India and the USA.

1

Introduction

LAURA WRAY-LAKE, ELAN C. HOPE, & LAURA S. ABRAMS

> You can't be . . . intellectualizin' the Black experience. Like, we're also human beings . . . it's more so a human experience that's just particular to Black individuals, you know, because of our Blackness.
>
> Joe Cornell

Joe Cornell (he/him) is a young Black changemaker. Like other Black young people whose stories appear throughout this book, Joe Cornell shared his human experience as a young Black person fighting for racial justice. As a 17-year-old Black boy, he was actively committed to bettering the lives of Black people and challenging racial injustices. As one of few Black students in a predominantly white school, Joe Cornell's changemaking focused on "improvin' the experience of Black students and POC [people of color] students and students that belong to marginalized communities – within predominantly white institutions and private institutions in particular." He actively participated on his school's Diversity, Equity, and Inclusion Committee and led a coalition that works to hold private school administrators accountable to their espoused racial justice policies. Joe Cornell is making real change in his school, making it more welcoming, safe, and equitable for Black students and other students of color.

Changemaking is personal and deeply meaningful for Black young people. Joe Cornell shared that his Black identity makes his changemaking around racial justice policies especially powerful, saying "as a Black individual, not only am I bringing, you know, the concept . . . but I'm also bringing a lived experience of things they . . . wouldn't necessarily know about the Black experience for obvious reasons." The obvious reasons? Non-Black individuals are not targeted by anti-Black racism in the United States. Joe Cornell, like many other young Black changemakers, realized that he is building on a historical legacy of Black people's fight against racism and for liberation. He put it this way: "What sort of ties us together as Black people in general is that shared history, that of not only, you know, pain and suffering, but also the resilience and the accomplishments." As a young person, Joe Cornell recognized that he is on a journey in identifying his power and developing his abilities as a changemaker. His experiences helped him to realize that "social justice" was "where my heart was," and to solidify his identity as a changemaker. Another signature element of young Black changemaking is looking toward the future. Joe Cornell envisions a future where Black people are in more leadership roles in the country: "I feel like it's gonna be the responsibility of . . . the next generation of Black organizers and, you know, adults that are . . . in this world, and they're in this country and, you know, movin' into these leadership positions."

This book tells the stories of what it is like to be a young Black changemaker through the words and lived experiences of Black young people. If you conduct research related to, organize with, teach, parent, or care for Black youth in any capacity, this book is for you. We provide recommendations drawn from young Black changemakers' own words and experiences in every chapter for educators, parents, practitioners, and scholars to better support young Black changemakers. We interviewed 43 Black young people, between the ages of 13–18 years, to learn how and why they engage in changemaking and to document their journeys to becoming changemakers. Some people already deeply understand young Black changemaking in its historical and contemporary forms, including scholars of the Black experience, civic leaders in Black communities, activists in Black-led social movements, and those who were and are young Black changemakers themselves. At the same time, many people do not understand or acknowledge young Black changemaking. Too often, people engage in negative stereotyping of Black youth, and Black youth are misunderstood, misrepresented, and mistreated. We wrote this book because we want more people to see and value Black youth for who they are and what they bring to society. Our purpose aligns with Joe Cornell's quote that opened this chapter, as we aim to not intellectualize the Black experience, but to portray young Black changemakers' humanity by sharing their stories in their own words.

And who are "we," the authors? We are a multiracial and multigenerational group of scholars who came together with a shared passion for amplifying the voices of young Black changemakers. Our authorship team includes three more established scholars at the helm and eight students and new professionals, including doctoral students, master's degree students, one undergraduate student, and a postdoctoral fellow and three doctoral students who became professors during this project. Six members of our team identify as Black, one as Latina, and four as white. Most of us are women, and we have one man among us. We share these details to clarify at the outset that we bring different perspectives and backgrounds to this book. To ensure that we interpreted Black youth's experiences appropriately, we collaborated as a team every step of the way. We provide more detail about our methods in Appendix A, and in the final chapter, we each reflect on what we learned from our unique positions on the team.

THE BACKDROPS FOR THIS BOOK

This study of young Black changemakers took place in Los Angeles, California between February and August 2020. What an important time and place that was for capturing Black youth's experiences! The COVID-19 pandemic altered life as we knew it beginning in mid-March, 2020. We interviewed most of the youth during the onset of the global COVID-19 pandemic at a time of unprecedented lockdown – when school was held virtually and face-to-face contact with people outside of one's household was limited or non-existent. Despite these unusual circumstances, the COVID-19 pandemic was not a major theme in young Black changemakers' stories. Our interviews had a broader focus on youth's changemaking over time, and the study was conducted in the early months of COVID-19, when the longer-term nature and impacts were still unknown. We did not ask much about COVID-19, and some young people definitely mentioned it, but most did not discuss their pandemic-related experiences in detail. The same could not be said for the other major historical event that occurred during our study. The murder of George Floyd by police on the public streets of Minneapolis, Minnesota occurred on May 25, 2020, which ignited uprisings against racial injustice and police violence that continued and amplified the ongoing movement for Black lives. We added interview questions to give youth space to talk about this event, which had a major impact on their lives, as we detail in Chapter 8. These youth were living through major social and historical events and witnessing a large-scale movement in their own neighborhoods and on a national and global scale. Although the pandemic may not have played a central role in the interviews, the global movement against anti-Black racism certainly did.

With nearly 10 million residents and over 4,000 square miles, Los Angeles is the most populous county in the United States, and the major city within it is the second largest in the United States. While considered by many to be socially and politically progressive, Los Angeles also has a long history of anti-Black racism and was an epicenter of racial protest in summer 2020. The city has a history of stark residential segregation, mass incarceration, and racialized poverty (Hernández, 2017). The Los Angeles Police Department (LAPD) is notorious for racialized violence and a lack of accountability for use of force against Black and Brown residents (Felker-Kantor, 2018). The Watts Uprising in 1965 and the 1992 Los Angeles Uprising following the innocent verdict for officers who brutally beat Rodney King, an unarmed Black man, situate Los Angeles as a city with a history of protest against racism and police violence. In summer 2020, Los Angeles was home to large-scale protests around police brutality; the protests pointed to a groundswell of momentum for the Black Lives Matter Movement. The 2020 protests sparked more police violence against protesters, and according to the New York

Times, a Los Angeles City Council commissioned report concluded that the LAPD had "severely mishandled protests, illegally detaining protesters, issuing conflicting orders to its rank-and-file officers and striking people who had committed no crimes with rubber bullets, bean bags and batons" (Bogel-Burroughs et al., 2021, par 1). Even after this widely supported protest movement and widespread calls to defund the police, in 2021 the LAPD shot 38 people, killing 18 of them (J. Ray, 2021). Individuals shot by police in Los Angeles are disproportionately Black and Hispanic or Latino/a/x/e. Bunn (2022) analyzed national fatal police shooting data collected by the Washington Post and found that Black people are twice as likely as white people to be shot and killed by a police officer.

Some progressive change was achieved in the wake of the summer 2020 protests. Los Angeles County includes 88 cities, and change was enacted through local elections, ballot measures, and direct advocacy to policymakers. Black youth were on the front lines of many of these change efforts. For example, in February 2021, the Los Angeles Unified School District's Board of Directors voted to cut one-third of the school district's police force, a $25 million funding cut, ban the use of pepper spray by officers in schools, and redirect funds to promote Black student achievement (Gomez, 2021). This achievement was the result of a yearlong campaign led by students, some of whom participated in our research study. Additionally, Culver City passed a resolution acknowledging a history of racism, police violence, and exclusion (City Council of the City Culver City, 2021). In Manhattan Beach, the deed to a beachfront property that was unjustly taken from its Black owners was returned to the family's heiress, a model upheld as a form of meaningful reparations (Ross, 2022). On November 3, 2020, Los Angeles County voters passed Measure J, allocating 10% of the county's general fund to "address the disproportionate impact of racial injustice through community investments such as youth development, job training, small business development, supportive housing services and alternatives to incarceration" (County of Los Angeles, n.d. par 1). Thus, Los Angeles was an ideal place to learn from Black youth who were actively involved in changemaking.

As we mentioned, COVID-19 is not a major theme in this book. Still, the early days of the pandemic exposed our society's pre-existing racial inequalities. Black and Latino/a/x/e communities were at higher risk of COVID-19 exposure and death from the disease (Reitsma et al., 2021). Lee (age 18, he/him), a young Black changemaker in our study, described the COVID-19 pandemic as an additional burden that Black people must face, remarking, "we already got a lot of stuff to be scared of and now we are scared of the 'Rona too." Police violence and COVID-19 became dual pandemics. As Dr. Janine Jones (2021, p. 427) stated, "The COVID-19 pandemic shined a magnifying glass on racially based structural inequities in a manner that was impossible to unsee or to look away." Young Black changemakers in our study were actively addressing socioeconomic and racial inequalities – including homelessness, gentrification, everyday racism, and school and health inequities – in their Los Angeles neighborhoods well before the pandemic. They were and are leading our nation on the road to racial justice, through everyday acts of helping as well as through social movement participation and leadership.

These were the contexts in which we found the young Black change-makers; these are the backdrops for their changemaking journeys. In the next section, we provide background on what it means to be a "young Black changemaker."

WHAT IT MEANS TO BE A YOUNG BLACK CHANGEMAKER

The concept of changemaking is known by many other names, and broadly falls under the umbrella of civic engagement. So, what is civic engagement? This term has not completely taken hold in the public vernacular, and academics have put forward various definitions. Put most simply, the American Psychological Association (2009, par 2) defines civic engagement as "individual and collective actions designed to identify and address issues of public concern." This definition emphasizes civic actions, but civic engagement more broadly includes values, attitudes, knowledge, and skills (Wray-Lake et al., 2017). Public conversation about civic engagement tends to focus on specific forms of civic action, such as voting, protesting, political campaigning, volunteering, or community service. There is not "one way" to be civically active – individuals engage in many different forms of civic actions. What we consider actions to address issues of public concern, or as others have put it, actions that contribute to community or society (Wray-Lake et al., 2017), can vary depending on an individual or community's culture, norms, and values and the larger political context of a region or country (Wray-Lake et al., 2021). This book shares what civic engagement looks like for Black youth in Los Angeles. In the chapters to follow, Black youth tell us how they are civically engaged and why. Their perspectives and experiences are shaped by their contexts, and their civic actions may look similar to or different from civic actions of youth in other communities and contexts.

So, this book is about Black youth's civic actions, but that is not all. Changemaking is not simply synonymous with civic actions. We use the term "changemaking" to capture civic actions that are connected to a higher purpose. Individuals can engage in civic actions for a host of different reasons (Ballard et al., 2015), and civic actions are not always aligned with a larger vision or goal for better communities or a better future. For Black youth in our study, civic actions are purposeful and intentionally aimed at positive change for their community and for Black people in the United States. These Black youth are changemakers, taking part in and leading many efforts to ensure that the world is a better place in general, and for Black people in particular. These youth are envisioning a future without racism and without economic inequalities, and they are working now to make real changes toward this future. To use a phrase coined by Dr. Robin D. G. Kelley (2002), these Black youth are "freedom dreaming," meaning that they are imagining a future that guides their struggle and their quest for justice. Black people have long had to struggle against racial oppression, and Black youth's civic actions are a response to that struggle. Black youth also have big dreams for a better future – a future where there is equality and freedom from suffering. We share the stories of young changemakers, so that they can help us all imagine a better future. As Kelley (2002, p. 10) wrote in *Freedom Dreams*:

In the poetics of struggle and lived experience, in the utterances of ordinary folk, in the cultural products of social movements, in the reflections of activists, we discover the many different cognitive maps of the future, of the world not yet born.

In our book, young Black changemakers poetically share their struggles and lived experiences as well as their reflections and visions for the future. It is important for the world to listen to young Black changemakers – to hear and reflect on their journey, experiences, and struggles – and let them inspire us to work toward a world where everyone is free from oppression. In this book, we will say much more about young Black changemaking, positioning Black youth as experts on their own experiences who are agents of change in their communities and society.

We have good reasons for focusing on *young* Black changemakers, meaning those who are in their adolescent years. Adolescence is considered a unique age period where young people experience many different developmental changes simultaneously (although this period may look different across different contexts and cultures). Adolescents experience dramatic physical growth during puberty and beyond, which coincides with rapid brain development, sexual development, and social and identity development (Crockett et al., 2023). Adolescence is a time when youth are actively figuring out who they are, who they want to be, and what they stand for, at the same time as they are developing the cognitive abilities to understand society's problems on a deeper level (Flanagan, 2013). They often bring energy, passion, and new ideas to address social issues. Sociologist Karl Mannheim (1952) called youth's interface with society and culture "fresh contact" and argued that young people's fresh, new perspectives on long-standing societal issues are essential for making social change. We agree. Because young people are less entrenched in "the way things are" in society, young people can better envision new futures that break old cycles.

Black youth may be among the most active freedom dreamers. Black young people, and young people in general, continually reimagine what it looks like to be civically engaged. For today's youth, social media is part of the civic commons, or public spaces in which they gather and act to challenge oppressions and create change (Wilf & Wray-Lake, 2021). Young people are creatively reimagining how to engage in online civic actions so rapidly that research struggles to keep pace. Young people find new and creative ways to act civically across many different settings, and some youth act civically amid substantial barriers to civic participation. Adolescents are legally excluded from some types of civic action such as voting and are often systematically excluded from many other spaces where decisions are made including political parties, local councils, and school boards. Young changemakers are determining ways they can make change in the contexts they are in and with the resources they have. When looking at the experiences of young Black changemakers, it is especially important to broaden our perspectives beyond traditional ideas of civic engagement, because Black youth may turn to creative strategies for civic action, informal modes of participation, and other ways of building individual and collective power to resist systemic racism (Watts & Flanagan, 2007).

YOUNG BLACK CHANGEMAKING IN THE CONTEXT OF RACISM

In the United States, Black changemaking takes place in the context of systemic anti-Black racism. Given the realities of anti-Black racism, Black youth's changemaking is often aimed at eradicating racial oppression. Joe Cornell's work to stop racism and strive toward racial equity in his predominantly white school exemplifies young Black changemaking and illustrates how Black youth resist racism and freedom dream for a better future without racial oppression.

Systemic racism refers to "forms of racism that are pervasively and deeply embedded in and throughout systems, laws, written or unwritten policies, entrenched practices, and established beliefs and attitudes that produce, condone, and perpetuate widespread unfair treatment of people of color" (Braveman et al., 2022, p. 171). Anti-Black racism is systemic racism that is directed specifically toward Black people. Anti-Black racism is a form of oppression: Oppression includes prejudices and institutional power that create systems that benefit dominant groups and discriminate against others – whether by race, gender, social class, immigration, language, sexuality, or other factors (Palmer et al., 2019). Oppressions co-exist in different ways for different people. Scholars call this intersectionality, a term coined by Black legal scholar Kimberlé Crenshaw (1991) to describe inequalities faced by Black women due to sexism and racism and embodied in the work of The Combahee River Collective (1977), an organization that advocated for Black queer women whose rights were not fully represented by the civil rights or women's movements.

In understanding Black young people's experiences of anti-Black racism, it is important to recognize that anti-Black racism occurs at interpersonal, cultural, and institutional levels (Jones, 1997). Interpersonal racism is the most studied and understood form of racism, consisting of direct interactions with people who enact bigotry, prejudice, microaggressions, and other unfair treatment. Research conducted by Dr. Anna Ortega-Williams and colleagues (2022) pinpointed everyday spaces such as schools, buses, and streets where Black youth experience interpersonal anti-Black racism. Dr. Devin English and colleagues (2020) asked Black youth about their daily lives for two weeks and found that they experience racism online and in person on an average of five times every day.

Racism is also embedded in our institutions and culture. Institutional anti-Black racism consists of policies and practices within institutions such as schools, the justice system, or health care that systematically disadvantage Black people. Cultural racism is the predominance of a majority racial group over other racial groups. Cultural anti-Black racism includes the negative stereotypes about Black youth that pervade media and everyday narratives. Dr. Elan Hope and colleagues (2021) found that 72% of Black adolescents experienced institutional racism and 93% experienced cultural racism in their lifetime. The harms of racism for Black youth are indisputable: Many studies have documented the tolls racism takes on Black youth's physical and mental health (Trent et al., 2019; Williams et al., 2019).

For as long as racism has existed, there has also been active resistance to this oppression. From the rebellions of enslaved Africans in the Americas to the Civil Rights Movement to the Black Lives Matter Movement and so much in between, Black resistance against racism through civic action has a long, rich history (Frey, 2020; Taylor, 2016; Webster, 2021). Resistance is a response to systems of oppression that are marginalizing and harmful and can be broadly defined as actions undertaken to undermine power and domination (Johansson & Vinthagen, 2020). Resistance may be more or less explicitly aimed at restructuring power in ways that reduce oppressions, but it is almost always about reclaiming humanity and exercising control in the face of discrimination, disregard, mistreatment, or dehumanization (Tuck & Yang, 2014; Wray-Lake et al., 2022). For example, during the period of chattel slavery in America, enslaved Africans engaged in collective rebellion to fight for freedom, and through everyday actions, resisted systems of oppression in many ways such as slowing down work, feigning illness, and sabotaging equipment or goods (Frey, 2020).

Although protesting may be the most visible and recognizable way of challenging racism, today's Black youth engage in many different forms of resistance. For example, some Black youth challenge anti-Black stereotypes by achieving excellence and giving back to their communities (Carter, 2008). Black changemaking is often a response to oppression, but Black civic life is about much more than a struggle against racism; it is also rooted in rich cultural strengths, traditions, and Afrocentric values such as helping and

uplifting family and community (Boykin, 1986). Black civic life also encompasses spirituality and joy.

In the stories within this book, being an adolescent, being Black, and
being highly civically engaged are merged in youth's lived experiences. Black
youth are navigating multiple layers of racism and experiences with other
marginalizing systems as they engage in changemaking. This book tells the
stories of how Black youth are navigating these contexts and doing this work,
where anti-Black racism is a backdrop and Black culture and community are
sources of support. No single story can encapsulate young Black changemaking, as Black youth have very different backgrounds, experiences, and journeys into changemaking. Yet, at the same time, some consistent influences
show up in their stories, such as experiencing racism and drawing strength
from identity, family, and community organizations.

SOCIOPOLITICAL DEVELOPMENT THEORY

To situate Black youth's civic engagement in prior research, we turn to
sociopolitical development theory, which is a model to understand how
Black youth become changemakers. Developed by Black community psychologist Dr. Roderick Watts, sociopolitical development is "a process of growth
in a person's knowledge, analytic skills, emotional faculties, and capacity for
action in political and social systems" (Watts et al., 2003, p. 185). Watts
developed this model from community-based programming with Black boys
and young men, and also drew from the work of other Black scholars and
activists as well as Paulo Freire's (1970) closely related concept of critical
consciousness (Watts & Halkovic, 2022).[1]

Civic action, critical reflection, and agency are three main components of
sociopolitical development. Sociopolitical development encompasses many
civic actions, and what binds them together is an emphasis on challenging
oppression. The way we define changemaking – as actions with a higher
purpose for creating social change – aligns with sociopolitical development
theory and helps clarify the civic actions most relevant to the pursuit of racial
justice for Black youth. Critical reflection and agency are essential ingredients
of sociopolitical development that inform and are informed by civic action.
Critical reflection is defined as awareness and analysis of inequities in society,
such as racism and other systems of oppression. For example, when Joe
Cornell conveyed his understanding of how racism is perpetuated in

---

[1] For our academic readers, we recognize there are various terms to describe the sociopolitical
development process. Debates and precision about terms for these components can be an
interesting academic exercise, but we do not engage the debate in this book. For simplicity in
this book, we use a single term for each major component – critical reflection, agency, and
civic action.

predominantly white institutions, his deep awareness and critical thinking illustrated critical reflection about inequities. Civic agency, which we simply call agency, involves perceived capacity and motivation to challenge oppression and create positive change in communities and society. When Joe Cornell described a "power moment" in recognizing his capacity to have his views reflected in school policy, this was an excellent example of a young person naming their agency. Sociopolitical development theory originally posited that critical reflection and agency lead to action, and studies have found evidence for this idea among Black youth (Hope, Smith et al., 2020) and youth more broadly (e.g., Bañales, Mathews et al., 2020; Diemer & Rapa, 2016; Plummer et al., 2022). However, this process is not a one-way street; civic action can also inform agency and reflection (Heberle et al., 2020). Throughout the book, we illustrate how Black youth are developing agency and critically reflecting on injustices as they engage in changemaking.

Sociopolitical development theory and evidence points to four main influences on Black youth's civic actions, critical reflection, and agency to challenge oppressive systems. These four influences are: experiences of racism, social identity, early influences, and opportunity structures (Anyiwo et al., 2018; Watts & Halkovic, 2022), and we introduce them briefly here because they are central topics in the stories to come of young Black changemakers.

First, Black youth who experience interpersonal, cultural, or institutional racism may use civic action to actively cope with the trauma of racism and feel compelled to change the unjust conditions that harm them and others. In a review of 26 studies, Dr. Elan Hope and colleagues (2023) documented considerable evidence that experiencing racism at any level (whether it be institutional, cultural, or interpersonal) is related to more civic action to challenge these injustices among Black youth and other youth of color.

Second, Black youth's racial identity – or how being Black matters to who they are as a person – is increasingly recognized as central to changemaking (Anyiwo et al., 2018; Mathews et al., 2022; Watts & Halkovic, 2022). Dr. Channing Mathews and colleagues (2020) laid out processes by which youth's exploration of racial and ethnic identity overlaps with their development of critical reflection and action. Yet, much more remains to be learned about racial identity and changemaking, including the role of collective identity (feelings of solidarity and belonging to a social identity group; Watts & Hipolito-Delgado, 2015) and intersectional identities (Godfrey & Burson, 2018; Santos, 2020).

Third, early life experiences, including family upbringing and other influential relationships and cultural experiences, shape Black youth's change-making. Research shows how Black families' conversations about race and racism inform Black youth's civic engagement (Bañales, Hope et al., 2021; Christophe et al., 2022), and that Black music, Black joy and community, and Black history shape Black youth's sociopolitical development (Anyiwo et al., 2022; Davis et al., 2021). Early influences on changemaking that go beyond family influences have not been comprehensively examined for Black youth.

Fourth, opportunity structures – including schools, organizations, and programs – provide access and opportunity for Black youth to develop critical reflection, agency, and civic action (Watts & Hipolito-Delgado, 2015). Research has emphasized how community-based organizations, such as community organizing groups, support sociopolitical development (Fernández & Watts, 2022; Ginwright, 2010a; Terriquez, 2015). Research has also shown that school curricular and extracurricular activities that spark critical reflection and prioritize youth voice and agency offer valuable opportunities for youth to grow as changemakers (Cohen et al., 2018; Hipolito-Delgado et al., 2022; Seider & Graves, 2020).

Sociopolitical development theory and related research have yielded valuable insights about Black youth's experiences of changemaking that inform and help to structure the work presented in this book. Our work builds on this theoretical tradition, and we point out ways that our work supports and extends this theory throughout the book.

THE MAIN IDEAS FOUND IN THIS BOOK

In the next eight chapters, we bring to life the stories of 43 young Black changemakers living in Los Angeles, California in 2020, in the context of major social upheaval and the possibility for change. Youth chose their own pseudonyms for the book, and we report their age and preferred pronouns when we quote them. To help readers get to know these young people further, we provide a profile of each young person in Appendix C. We also invited Black youth in our study and in organizations around Los Angeles to submit art to be featured in the book. We selected five outstanding pieces from two young Black artists – Zoie Brogdon and Meazi Light-Orr. Four drawings and a poem are interspersed between the chapters. Featuring this art was another way for us to uplift Black youth's voices and showcase their talents.

As a preview of what is to come, we share 10 main ideas that emerged from these youth's stories. These ideas cut across the book chapters and form the core of this book's contributions to theory, research, applied work with Black youth, and public discourse about Black youth.

(1) **Young Black changemakers are fighting for racial justice in different ways.** Black youth engage in many different civic actions and envision different types of change (Chapter 2). They passionately and purposefully pursue racial justice through civic action for their own safety and survival

(Chapter 3), for their families (Chapter 6), and for other Black people (Chapter 8).

(2) **Young Black changemakers are future-oriented.** Black youth are taking actions now (Chapter 2) and envisioning bold changes (Chapter 9) to create a better world for their own family members and future generations of Black people. This future orientation toward racial justice embodies Black youth's freedom dreaming and continues a legacy of changemaking from their families, communities, and Black resistance that goes back generations (Chapter 4).

(3) **Experiencing anti-Black racism is a catalyst for changemaking.** Black youth face interpersonal and institutional racism in non-Black school spaces (Chapter 3) and contend with many forms of racism in everyday life, including cultural racism (Chapter 4) and police violence (Chapter 8). Even while facing the harms and substantial emotional burdens of anti-Blackness, young Black changemakers resist multiple forms of racism through civic action.

(4) **Black racial identity motivates Black youth's changemaking and offers tools to cope with and resist racism through changemaking.** Understanding oneself as a Black young person, and the history of being Black in the United States, is informed by changemaking and shapes future changemaking (Chapters 4 & 8). Black youth's personal and collective identities, as well as intersecting identities related to gender and social class, shape changemaking (Chapter 4).

(5) **Black families encourage changemaking in multiple ways.** Black youth's families, and especially mothers, connect youth to changemaking opportunities and communicate values that support changemaking, and Black youth seek to honor and protect their families through their changemaking (Chapter 6).

(6) **Black community spaces are safe havens for Black youth and incubators for their changemaking.** Black spaces in schools offer safety from racism (Chapter 3). Black civic organizations offer critical education about Black history (Chapter 7). Black youth need community support, given that changemaking to resist anti-Black racism comes with substantial emotional burdens (Chapter 3). Black community members inspire Black youth to launch into changemaking (Chapter 5). Black communities offer spaces where Black youth can feel like they belong, experience joy and pride, and build solidarity for collective action (Chapters 3, 4, 5, 8).

(7) **Access to civic opportunities enables Black youth to begin and sustain their changemaking.** Black youth benefit from family members and other adults who connect them to opportunities and encourage them to participate (Chapters 5 & 6). Fun experiences and community building

opportunities also draw Black youth to civic actions (Chapter 5). Community-based organizations offer opportunities for Black youth to see impact from their civic actions, take ownership of their civic work, gain critical knowledge, feel encouraged by adults, and be in community with other Black people. These experiences build agency, increasing youth's skills and power to sustain their changemaking over time (Chapter 7).

(8) **Black youth exert agency to forge their own paths toward impactful changemaking.** Agency is a launching point for young Black changemaking, as Black youth seek ways to pursue their passion for racial justice (Chapter 5). Black youth show agency to help and protect their families through changemaking (Chapter 6). Youth develop agency over time through civic opportunities and support from others (Chapter 7), which is further activated by racial justice movements (Chapter 8).

(9) **The racial justice movement of summer 2020 activated young Black changemakers.** Summer 2020 was a pivotal moment when Black youth recognized their role in the larger social movement, drew from past legacies of Black changemaking, and deepened their agency, reflection, and action, all while continuing to grapple with systemic racism and its emotional toll (Chapter 8).

(10) **Young Black changemakers give us hope for a better world, and we must follow their lead.** We hope this book offers a sense of hope from the ways that Black youth are working to create change locally and nationally. In Chapter 9, we look to the future, sharing how these young Black changemakers describe the better world they envision. Youth's messages are calls to action for those committed to working with and supporting Black youth in their quests for justice.

Up Next

In Chapter 2, we document the range of civic actions that Black youth take and the purpose they are aiming for through these actions. This alignment between young people's civic actions and purpose is the epitome of changemaking. Our emphasis on changemaking recognizes that why young people are engaging in civic actions is as important or more important than the specific actions they take. We present a contemporary portrait of today's young Black changemakers. As young people continually update their ways of being civically engaged, including using social media alongside in-person actions for change, and respond to momentous times in history like the racial reckoning of summer 2020, it is important, as Joe Cornell expressed, to keep knowledge of young Black changemaking current and centered on human experiences.

Untitled by Meazi Light-Orr

2

Civic Actions with a Purpose

ELENA MAKER CASTRO, LAURA WRAY-LAKE, &
DOMINIQUE MIKELL MONTGOMERY

> I am a young 16-year-old Black girl just striving to make a change and make a
> difference in, not only my community, but my family's life, and make an
> impact on the world.
>
> Layla

When we interviewed Layla (she/her) in July 2020, a Black, 16-year-old rising
high school junior, her involvement in many different civic actions blew us
away. She participated in the dance ministry at her church. She watched the
news daily. She actively shared her views on issues via social media. She strove
to do her best in school, as a dancer and a track athlete, acted as a mentor to
her younger sister and cousin, and aspired to start a nonprofit organization to
mentor Black youth. What inspired us most about Layla's story was not just
how she was civically engaged, but *why*. Every action had a larger purpose,
which she summed up as "to make a change and make a difference in, not
only my community, but my family's life, and make an impact on the world."
In describing her current and future actions, Layla emphasized uplifting Black
children and her Black community. Based on her observations that
"gentrification has, you know, taken over" her neighborhood, she was passionate about building capacity for Black-owned businesses and helping Black
young people, who look up to her "for information and ask questions" about
life. She believed that her own hard work to achieve in school and beyond
provided a model for Black children around her and provided a foundation
for her future plans to give back to the Black community. Her actions were
also driven by the grim reality that "there is still racial injustice going on."
Layla's daily news watching was an intentional habit she cultivated because,
"being a young Black girl, it helps me navigate the world" and "keeps me
informed on what I should be doing to make a change in the world."
Especially in summer 2020, as the deadly brutality of police violence against
Black people was on full display, Layla joined other Black youth in "fighting
for the younger generation or my generation . . . to be in a world where things
are equal." Layla believed that for her and other Black youth, it is "our duty to

carry the torch and pass it on to future generations. And then also in the midst of carrying the torch, making more differences at the same time." Layla is clearly highly civically engaged. She is impressive but not unusual among her Black peers. Through Layla's story and others that we share, the first central message of this chapter is that Black youth are civically engaged in many ways.

If we had simply asked Layla to list her various civic activities, we would have missed the larger purpose driving these actions, which was a passion for creating a world where Black people have equal chances to succeed and thrive. This intertwining of civic actions and larger purpose is precisely why we call the youth in our study "young Black changemakers." We define changemaking as a set of civic actions that serve a larger purpose of improving something about community or society. The second central message in this chapter is that young Black changemakers take many different actions that have larger purposes, and these purposes boil down to wanting a better world for Black people. Many forms of young Black changemaking are efforts to resist and challenge anti-Black racism. The study of young Black changemaking is not new: A long legacy of Black changemaking is documented in the writings of Black liberation scholars and activists such as James Baldwin, Angela Davis, and bell hooks, and among contemporary scholars of Black youth liberation such as Drs. Roderick Watts, Shawn Ginwright, and Cathy Cohen.

To build on this scholarship and further understand what young Black changemaking looks like, we center the stories and voices of Black youth in Los Angeles. Youth self-selected into our study from recruitment materials seeking "young Black changemakers" between the ages of 13 to 18 years who identified as Black, lived in Los Angeles, and were highly civically engaged. A major goal of this book is to center Black youth's voices and experiences, and so it is only logical that we would let them educate us on what young Black changemaking is. We start by describing the array of civic actions taken by young Black changemakers, to convey the point that young Black changemaking is not singular. We then name several larger purposes that drive youth's specific civic actions to demonstrate that young Black changemaking, regardless of specific actions, is purpose driven. For Black youth in this study, their overarching purpose was to create a better world for Black people.

THE MANY WAYS OF MAKING CHANGE

This study builds on Drs. Laura Wray-Lake and Laura Abrams' (2020) study of civic engagement among youth of color (who were primarily Black) in the urban center of Rochester, New York. There, we spent considerable time listening to and documenting young people's definitions of civic engagement. This youth-centered analysis resulted in a robust way of thinking about civic engagement that went beyond how youth civic engagement is traditionally defined. We used this prior work to inform the starting point for this study. Instead of starting from scratch in asking young people to define civic engagement or changemaking, we started with a checklist of 21 possible civic actions that came from our previous qualitative work (Wray-Lake & Abrams, 2020). This list (shown in Appendix B) provided examples for young people and represented a jumping off point for them to reflect on their many ways of engaging in changemaking. We emphasized that youth were experts and should define changemaking in their own words, and we asked young people to add to the list by considering any of their civic actions that would expand the list further.

This is the only time in the book we present youth's responses in numeric form to provide a snapshot of Black youth's civic actions. By looking at young people's responses to the checklist, it is obvious how varied youth's civic actions are. Each civic activity was endorsed by 32% or more of the youth. The number of civic activities young people reported ranged from 2 to 21, with an average of 13 activities. Most activities were endorsed by 40% or more (often much more) of the sample. The most frequently endorsed activities were helping family (82%), helping others in need (82%), mentoring children or peers (82%), participating in a club or team (84%), and following the news and staying informed on social issues (82%). Young people were least likely to report campaigning for a cause or candidate (32%), or organizing or advocating for policy change (37%). From our observations, Black youth were just as likely to engage in these different activities across ages and genders.

THREE DOMAINS OF CIVIC ACTION

Possibilities for civic action are diverse and ever-changing, especially among young people, given changing technological innovations and platforms, shifting political landscapes, and human creativity (Levine, 2022). Because of the large and growing sea of potential civic actions, it is useful to have a way of organizing the many types of civic activities. Here, we take a deeper look into three domains of civic action: community helping (e.g., helping family, neighbors, and others); activism and organizing (e.g., campaigning, organizing, and protesting); and interpersonal civic actions (e.g., expressing opinions, posting, and educating others). These domains are a heuristic that offer a shorthand way to describe many different civic actions. All three domains were fairly highly endorsed across our sample of young Black changemakers, and community helping (69%) and interpersonal action (73%) were more common than activism and organizing (58%).

Another set of activities reflected participation in school or community-based organizations such as clubs, religious groups, the arts, and service or advocacy-focused organizations. We see these organizations as spaces where changemaking is facilitated and where youth access opportunities to support their changemaking over time. Many civic activities take place in organizational spaces, although other actions are youth led or occur outside of formal structures. We focus on organizational contexts of youth civic actions in Chapter 7.

Before we explore Black youth's own descriptions of community helping, activism and organizing, and interpersonal action, we offer a few more numerical observations to help further contextualize these three dimensions of young Black changemaking. Young people can and do engage in civic actions across more than one domain. Over half the youth (55.8%) reported engaging in all three domains of community helping, interpersonal actions, activism and organizing; and additionally, nearly one-third (27.9%) engaged across two domains. No one behavior dominated these domains; instead, each behavior was relatively equally endorsed within each domain. Sometimes, civic actions that fell into different domains were closely connected. For example, speaking out against injustice, which we categorized as an interpersonal action, was also associated with behaviors in the activism and organizing domain. The fact that behaviors often work in tandem across domains shows how the three domains are not completely distinct categories. Rather, young Black changemakers utilize multiple forms of changemaking to achieve their larger goals. This quantified look at civic behaviors aligns well with youth's stories, showing that young Black changemaking is purposeful and includes many different civic actions all aiming to positively change the world for Black people.

Community Helping

Young people provided help for those around them in many ways, ranging from formal service through organizations to more communal activities and informal helping. Often their helping behavior was embedded in everyday life. Tom (age 17, he/him) helped his community by doing "just the small things, like [if you] see somebody who needs help, packing their groceries or something like that, you know, just making your community a better place to live." Some Black youth described helping as inherent to who they were as a person, conveying that they have always been helpers. T (age 17, he/him) shared about helping, "I've been like that forever." Similarly, Mia (age 16, she/her) articulated that helping is part of who she is: "Yeah, so I consider myself to be a really helpful person. I love to help people. A lot of the activities I do along with [a health equity organization and youth wellness program] really stem from my need to be an aid to others." Harvey (age 18, she/her) also felt like she had been a helper all her life, starting with family roles, saying, "I think that I just always had a role of responsibility just throughout my life, because I'm like an older sibling throughout my whole family." Helping is intrinsic to these youth's identities, including how they see themselves, and how they interact with the world. Past research has shown that Black youth's helping behavior is often informal and deeply rooted in their local community (White-Johnson, 2012; Wray-Lake & Abrams, 2020). Some Black youth help their community to resist and challenge racial oppression (Lozada et al., 2017), a topic we return to later in this chapter.

Interpersonal Civic Actions

In interacting with peers and others in day-to-day life, Black youth are civically active through interpersonal actions that may go unnoticed. Interpersonal civic actions include expressing opinions, sharing information, and having conversations to spread awareness and educate others. For youth in our study, the main issue of focus was anti-Black racism. Thus, these actions align with what Drs. Josefina Bañales, Adriana Aldana, and others call *anti-racist interpersonal actions*, which are individual acts that occur in everyday contexts that respond to racism by challenging the words or actions of others, defending targets of racism, and creating dialogue about racism (Aldana et al., 2019; Bañales, Aldana et al., 2021). Interpersonal civic actions also include spreading awareness of racism to non-Black peers. These exchanges happen in person and on social media. Using social media, O.A. (age 15, she/her) raised awareness of racism in summer 2020, sharing, "I basically described how I felt about this racial injustice and ways that . . . my platform – basically my followers, something that they could do to help since this is something that really affects me as a person." Sean (age 16, he/him) took opportunities through class assignments to raise awareness about racial injustice to his peers, saying, "I made a Google slide presentation for my college summer school class about injust justice systems . . . if you committed the same crime, it shouldn't matter what race you are, the punishment should be equal."

Some youth worked to spread awareness and educate others about Black history. Mea (age 16, she/her) was passionate about informing other Black youth on racist current and historical events and engaged in these interpersonal actions "because we need to be in the know, we got to know, man." Similarly, JD (age 13, he/him) spread awareness on a range of topics to his Black community members to get people "woke," saying, "I look up things that help out the South Central areas to get people woke up and see what's going on in the real life . . . it's like artifacts and websites for people to read about the community and how to make their life and their community better." Amir (age 13, he/him) spent time educating primarily non-Black peers and school administrators about Black history. In explaining why, he shared, "We need to inform the students about Black history because in our school, we don't really learn about Black history and if we do, it was very minimal. And in our Global Studies term ..., Africa was the last section to read about, and we didn't even have time to go through the whole thing."

We observed that through these interpersonal actions, Black youth are playing the role of de facto educators to fill the gaps left by their school curricula. Evidence shows that US school children are woefully undereducated about the country's history of racism. According to a 2018 Southern Poverty Law Center Report on "Teaching Hard History," a dismal 8% of high school seniors surveyed knew that slavery was a central cause of the Civil War, and only 32% of high school seniors surveyed knew it took a constitutional amendment to end slavery (Shuster, 2018). These statistics may not be all that surprising given that education on civil rights is not required in a growing number of states. Moreover, due to the attack on "critical race theory" by Republican elected officials in states across the country, since January 2021, 42 states have introduced legislation and 17 states have imposed bans or restrictions on teaching about racism and sexism in schools (Schwartz, 2022), with 84 other bills pending at the time of this writing (Johnson et al., 2022). Given this alarming situation, increasing numbers of Black youth are taking on the daily burden of educating peers about Black history and racism.

Activism and Organizing

Youth took part in national protests for racial justice as part of the Black Lives Matter (BLM) Movement and for other social justice issues such as women's rights and Lesbian, Gay, Bisexual, Transgender, Queer (LGBTQ+) pride. Tom described his experience of going to a BLM protest shortly after police officers murdered George Floyd, saying:

I was ... tryin' to finish strong in my classes. But I felt like there was so much more important things goin' on in the world ... I was literally writing essays in the car on the way to a protest. 'Cause I felt like I needed to be there, you know. I knew if I didn't go to any protests, I'd feel like I missed the opportunity to really be engaged in my community and really use my voice to create change.

Youth also participated in marches to speak out about local issues. Destiny (age 16, she/her), who lived in the Crenshaw neighborhood of Los Angeles, protested gentrification in her community: "We walked to the Crenshaw Mall ... a different set of people were about to buy out the Crenshaw Mall. It was very powerful, us walking to the Crenshaw Mall and speaking up there and just speaking up – speaking in our community that's being gentrified." Youth led or engaged in grassroots organizing campaigns, often to advocate for much-needed school or community resources.

Through community-based organizing efforts, youth sometimes had opportunities to advocate directly to local or nationally elected officials.

Cory (age 15, he/him) went with his organization "up to the LAUSD [Los Angeles Unified School District] headquarters. And I went, and I spoke to some board members on defunding the school police and puttin' it more into . . . more . . . counselors and things like that." Youth-led policy change in schools through school clubs such as Black Student Unions. As part of a healthy equity club, Mia led efforts to have menstrual products made available in school restrooms, saying, "We do lots of fundraising to make sure that we can fund the projects that we're going towards, for example, getting the down payment for any period dispensers and making sure that we have the funding to present to our administrators to . . . back up what we're advocating for." Youth organized for electoral campaigns, such as voter registration and mobilization, and many expressed how voter drives and winning campaigns advanced community interests and larger movement goals. Kevin (age 17, he/him), in discussing his involvement with a multi-organization collaborative, shared, "We come together and work to . . . achieve plans . . . throughout the voting and to improve our community efforts." As our quantitative analysis also showed, activism and organizing overlap with interpersonal actions, as online civic actions are part of both domains. Youth often used social media as a space for movement mobilization, particularly during the COVID-19 pandemic when in person activities were limited. Drs. Roderick Watts and Carlos Hipolito-Delgado (2015) make the distinction that interpersonal actions are aimed at seeking justice via everyday interactions with others, whereas collective actions, which include activism and organizing, aim to change policy or institutional practices. Scholars and activists alike recognize the value of collective action for collective liberation (Freire, 1970; Garza, 2020; Taylor, 2016), and for Black youth, collective action toward racial justice deepens youth's sense of community and Black identity development, topics we emphasize in Chapter 4.

ACTING WITH PURPOSE

Purpose can be broadly understood as a person's guiding reason or objective for doing something, and developmental scientists also consider "purpose" as a key part of positive youth development. Dr. William Damon defined purpose as "a stable and generalized intention to accomplish something that is at once meaningful to the self and of consequence to the world beyond the self" (Damon et al., 2003, p. 121). Having a purpose means having a lasting goal that is pursued over the long term. Youth with purpose look to the future and are propelled to act in ways that make progress toward their larger vision. A purpose must deeply matter to oneself and be meaningful to the larger society. Civic action is a useful strategy to progress toward meaningful long-term goals that matter for society. Dr. Heather Malin coined the term civic purpose to refer to "sustained intention to contribute to the world beyond the self through civic or political action" (Malin et al., 2015, p. 103).

Civic purpose became clear in our conversations with young Black changemakers. As we saw in Layla's opening story, young Black change-makers are not just remarkable for what they do but also for why they choose to engage. Young Black changemaking is rich with purpose and entails many different civic actions aimed at making positive change in the world. Three main purposes of changemaking reflect many young Black changemakers' experiences and encompass multiple domains of action: (1) redistributing resources for racial justice; (2) navigating an anti-Black world; and (3) giving back to the Black community. These are not the only civic purposes that guide young Black changemaking, just the most salient in our study. Some young people emphasized a single purpose, whereas for others, more than one purpose figured in their larger vision for the future. Across the three civic purposes, there was a common thread: Black youth seek change in different ways, but they share a passion and commitment for creating a better world for Black people.

Redistributing Resources for Racial Justice

A 2021 report by the University of California, Los Angeles' Center for the Transformation of Schools examined data from 14 school districts in Los Angeles County and found that compared to other students, Black students in Los Angeles experience disproportionate rates of poverty, are more likely to reside in neighborhoods with polluted air and water, and have much higher rates of contact with school police (Johnson et al., 2021). Young Black changemakers keenly observed the stark inequities between schools and neighborhoods in Los Angeles, which reflect deeply rooted and enduring racial and economic divisions. To catalyze change for the Black community, Black youth understood that they needed to redistribute resources for them-selves and for their Black peers and community members. Thus, youth often took action through local grassroots efforts to convince policy makers that investment in Black youth and communities is an essential priority. To illustrate this purpose in action, we share Quinn's story. Her changemaking to redistribute resources for racial justice included activism and organizing as well as community helping.

Activism and Organizing Quinn (she/her) was a 16-year-old eleventh grader attending a large public school in South Los Angeles. As a resident of a majority Black and Brown LA community, Quinn witnessed firsthand that her public school lacked resources compared to neighboring, wealthier, and whiter communities. Based on her experiences, she believed "we could, we should just do better" to rectify these inequities. When Quinn was in ninth grade, she became involved with a grassroots organization in South Central LA with a deep history of community organizing. At this organization, Quinn cultivated a passion for improving educational equity and opportunities for her peers and for future generations. She explained:

I want to be able to have the same opportunities as everybody else. And I want people in my younger generation status, same opportunities too ... I don't want us to go through all these budget cuts and we not have books and all this stuff ... so we have a better chance at doing what we want to do in the future.

To pursue this vision, Quinn worked closely with the organization to advocate for local policy change. Through an organizing campaign, she and her peers tried to convince elected officials to invest in local schools to address inequalities. She recounted one episode from spring 2020:

We went to LAUSD to protest .... There was a board meeting, and our group went and gave our speeches and ... talked to the whole board about the way they spend their money and how ... the new rule they're trying to put out would take money from, you know, schools in not as good communities and give it to you know, the wealthier schools.

Black youth like Quinn advocate for school funding redistribution as a larger racial justice goal, in part because of their personal experiences of contending with unequal resources. Success with Lex (age 18, she/her) emailed the LA mayor because "I just see so many other communities that have what I would like my community to have." Through an English class assignment, Cory wrote to a local official "about how schools in my area, they get less resources than schools like Palos Verdes and how it was unfair." Collectively, this group of youth saw contacting elected officials as a route to achieving a more equitable distribution of resources in their schools and communities.

Black youth also described challenges to their advocacy that are rooted in structural racism and ageism. Quinn explained how young Black change-makers constantly contend with negative stereotypes that shape elected officials' and societal views of Black youth. For example, in advocating to the LAUSD school board, Quinn reflected:

Well, I feel like, honestly, we didn't impact the person that we were aiming for, because she kind of took us as a joke, but I felt like we got our voice out to the community, to everyone else. So they know that we actually care. And that we're not just trying to go to school just to go to school.

In part due to these types of setbacks, these youth emphasized that change-making is a long-term endeavor. One's civic purpose is not achieved overnight, and young Black changemakers such as Quinn remained committed to racial and economic equity, regardless of setbacks. As a testament to her long-term vision, Quinn aspires to be President of the United States. Young Black changemakers were driven to activism and organizing to fulfill their hope and desire for racial justice for all Black people. These young Black changemakers understood that protests, organizing, and other advocacy strategies of racial justice movements are effective ways to create societal change. As Dr. Daniel Gillion (2020) argued in his book *The Loud Minority*, social movements such as BLM and others have changed policy through influencing elected officials as well as voters.

Community Helping In working toward racial and economic equity through resource distribution, Black youth also engaged in community helping, which sometimes intersected with activism and organizing. Quinn intertwined community helping with organizing, describing how both support the community: "We do a lot of protests. And then we go out to festivals and other group activities. We'll go to schools and talk about what we do and try to find ways to fix the school or the community. [We do] a lot of outreach programs." Quinn found great meaning in helping as part of her activism, sharing that "I'm really all about helping, fairness and stuff." For Quinn, it was not always easy to disentangle specific efforts to help the community from organizing to create policy change on behalf of her community. These actions are connected by a larger purpose of redistributing resources to improve the world for the Black community now and for future generations.

Some young Black changemakers channeled their desire to change racial and economic inequities into directly helping people marginalized by these inequities. Youth primarily did this work through formal and organized volunteer activities, and most commonly, by volunteering to help people who were unhoused. The number of people who are unhoused has become a crisis of epic proportions in Los Angeles. Amid the COVID-19 pandemic, over 66,000 people were counted as without housing in Los Angeles County; the second largest number of any major area next to New York City (Chan & Maxouris, 2022; City News Service, 2021). By engaging in this type of community helping, young Black changemakers in Los Angeles are focusing on one of the most pressing community problems facing the city. James (age 16, he/him) was compelled to help people who were unhoused in LA because it was such a salient local issue, saying:

Living in LA, there's always been just a sight of seeing homeless people . . . I just found myself always curious as to how they're treated and why they live the way they are . . . . Being there was something I wanted to do. It was a chance for me to show that I care for another group of people.

Youth's reflections on helping unhoused community members were often lengthy – they described their contributions in detail and reflected on the meaning they derived from their work. For example, Tom discussed how he volunteered at a shelter as part of a Black leadership group:

We would work at homeless shelters . . . and we were serving food. But I remember we split up into groups and like, I remember my job was like, going through the food and seeing . . . what food is bad and what food is good and we were having to sort food and throw it in the dumpster. And we were helping people. It was a place … homeless people could come in. And they had a shop for them where they could come, just have clothes. And it was really cool … .. So, it was kind of giving them a place where they could feel, you know, like, normal … and it was … really good. I really enjoyed [it].

Tom also recounted a specific time when he remembered "seeing this home-less lady wearing my sister's jacket. And she was like, so happy." Tom goes on to say that it made him realize "it's not that hard at all to change somebody's life, you know, because for us that was just like an old coat but for her that's … something that was really important." Tom further reflected on his own socio economic advantages and how important it was to use his advantages to help other individuals in need, saying: "I'm using my talents, using my abilities and my position in life, to, you know, help others. [It] makes me feel like I'm really taking advantage of the position I'm in, you know, because I am blessed to have these opportunities to … help other people." Community helping was a tangible, concrete way of seeking to redistribute resources to communities in need.

Activism and organizing and community helping are different ways of changemaking that can align with the same overarching purpose. Black youth like Quinn who engaged in organizing to redistribute resources were seeking to change the systems that harm Black youth. They are pursuing lasting policy change, and this work is difficult and comes with many setbacks. They do not often see immediate results and must rely on a longer-term vision and hope for the future. Quinn, Tom, and others engage in community helping to distribute needed resources to people, seeking change in the lived experiences of people who are suffering. They see more immediate impacts of their helping behavior when individuals get much-needed resources, and, as we describe further in Chapter 7, seeing the impacts of civic actions propels Black youth to continue changemaking over the long term.

Navigating an Anti-Black World

Black youth are growing up in a deeply antagonistic racialized society with constant affronts to their humanity. Based on youth's personal experiences with anti-Blackness, many chose changemaking actions that helped them-selves and their peers navigate contexts of racism, minimize the burdens of anti-Black racism where possible, and rewrite negative narratives about Black youth. We highlight how interpersonal civic actions and community helping advanced this civic purpose, starting with Destiny's story of striving to help peers navigate the anti-Black world through interpersonal civic actions.

Interpersonal Civic Actions Above, we shared Destiny's deep commitment to her community through protesting gentrification of the Crenshaw Mall. Destiny channeled this same commitment to racial justice into helping her peers navigate anti-Black racism through interpersonal civic actions. Like many Black youth, Destiny's purposeful commitments to changemaking are rooted in her personal experiences of racial injustice and racial trauma. Destiny was once held up at gunpoint by police officers in her neighborhood, which is why she felt strongly about protecting Black youth from police violence. Destiny recounted how the police "... pulled a gun on me ... and my cousin and my friend – we were just walking – goin' to school in the summer." For many Black youth, the threat of police violence is ever-present: According to a national study, Black youth experience alarming rates of police contact. Nearly 42% of Black boys and 20% of Black girls have been stopped by police; 80% and 79% of Black boys and girls, respectively, have witnessed police stops; 43% of Black boys and 37% of Black girls have been searched by police; and 15% of Black boys and 14% of Black girls have personally experienced the use of police force against them (Del Toro et al., 2022). As we will further describe in Chapter 4, this is one of many forms of racism Black youth endure, and these harmful experiences can lead to changemaking for racial justice.

Destiny's experience with police violence compelled her to educate young Black people about their rights and how to protect themselves from the police by organizing "Know Your Rights" workshops to educate Black and Brown children about "what happens if a police pulls you over." When asked why she did this work, she succinctly responded, "Because I'm a Black girl in America, and that's my community that I'm standing up for." Destiny believed that this work was vital because her peers "don't learn about it. Their parents tell them, maybe, but they don't learn about it in schools . . . . They don't teach you about Black rights." In pursuing this civic purpose, Destiny had a long-term vision, seeking to "educate kids on that and educate my own kids on that when I get older." The "that" to which she is referring is both knowing your rights as a Black young person and also, "valuing Black lives. A lot of kids don't understand how precious a Black life is or how precious their life is." Looking to the future, Destiny talked about how she intends to raise her children. Destiny emphasized how important it is to prepare youth for "some bad things going on." Destiny does not want her own kids to grow up thinking "the world is all sunshine." For Destiny and other youth in this study, helping Black youth navigate hostile climates and policies are long-term commitments that can benefit current and future generations.

Community Helping In working to help Black youth navigate an anti-Black world, some young people prioritized helping other Black youth break out of a cycle of disadvantage or injustice. For example, Sa'Myah (age 18, she/her) was actively engaged in helping members of her community daily, such as by looking out for elderly neighbors and younger children. Sa'Myah referred to her neighborhood as "messed up," and said that "stuff can be dangerous," but she tried to help others as much as possible. Helping Black youth get on a different path, for her, was aimed at navigating the anti-Black world and was part of a larger goal of pursuing justice: "Everybody thinks the gangbangers be wrong and stuff. But you know, they don't always be wrong. I'm not gonna say I fittin' to help everybody get out but, you know, just need some type of justice."

Some young Black changemakers engaged in community helping to disprove stereotypes about Black youth, which is part of navigating an anti-Black world. KJ (age 16, she/her), who participated in a service organization for Black youth and families, reflected that civic engagement for Black youth is distinct because Black youth need to show that they can help others rather than receive help: "So, I feel like for other races, they're probably thinking that the only people who need help is African American people ... well, that's not true because we're going out to help other people who aren't just African American people, but people of many colors, shades." She further referred to how:

Everything portrayed on the media, really ... what happens with ... Pop Smoke, XXXTentacion, Nipsey Hussle. All of those deaths ... the Black community in the Crenshaw area ... when you go down there, it's not just everybody there is Black. There's all types of races. But what's portrayed on the media isn't that there's all types of races. It's, "Well, let's help our African American group who is in poverty." And I'm like, "That's not necessarily true."

KJ and other youth see and hear the portrayals of Black youth and Black communities as impoverished and needing help. Through their community service, these youth are working to change these narratives, rooted in anti-Blackness, by helping improve the lives of other Black people and by demonstrating that Black youth help others in their communities regardless of their race or ethnicity.

Negative stereotypes about Black youth, rooted in racism, are perpetuated in different ways across many contexts of everyday life, producing almost inescapable injustices for Black youth. For example, in 2020, a National Public Radio poll of 1,400 diverse US residents between the ages of 18–54 years found that 66% of individuals believed that the media portrayed negative stereotypes of Black people, and 83% of Black people surveyed felt that way (Variety, 2020). Previous research has documented various ways that Black youth challenge and resist negative stereotypes (Rogers & Way, 2016; Smith & Hope, 2020). Young Black changemakers are battling to transform narratives of Black youth and help their peers navigate this anti-Black world in the meantime. Seeking a world where Black youth are safe from anti-Blackness – whether through community helping or interpersonal actions or other actions – illustrates how young Black changemakers take many different civic actions in striving for racial justice.

Giving Back to the Black Community

Another civic purpose for young Black changemakers is giving back to the Black community. This purpose, like others, manifests as a longer-term vision for change. Although many civic actions advance this purpose, here we focus on a civic action we have not yet discussed: bettering oneself to better one's community. Bettering oneself to better one's community is a form of community helping. This action, however, only becomes understood as a civic action when done in pursuit of a civic purpose. Youth make personal investments in building their own strengths and skills to reach their maximum potential. Typically, this means striving to do well in school and beyond. What makes this activity a form of changemaking is that youth see these actions as advancing the larger purpose of giving back to the Black community; they hope to gain education and skills to enable them to offer substantial support and resources to their community. When enacted with this larger purpose in mind, bettering oneself also helps one's community over the long term. Doing well in school and planning for a career are important in themselves and well-studied by researchers. Yet, rarely do scholars or others consider academic success and career goals to be part of civic engagement. Nonetheless, for some Black youth, these activities can be a core part of their changemaking (Wray-Lake & Abrams, 2020). Bettering oneself to give back to the Black community represents a unique intertwining of civic action and purpose, and we share several youth's stories to illustrate this.

Phea (age 17, she/her) engaged in many civic pursuits including informal helping, volunteering, electoral campaigns, and protesting. A thread that wove together Phea's activities was her passion for becoming a businesswoman. In fact, Phea already ran her own nonprofit where she created t-shirts and donated the proceeds to a tree-planting organization in Africa. This cause was personally meaningful, as Phea's mother was born in Senegal. About the funds she raised, she shared, "I would . . . take it over there to Africa, and they were doing a little organization thing where they were helping plant some trees, so $1 would be like a tree." Phea's goal was to be a Black woman with a business degree, and with her business degree in hand, Phea envisioned, "I'll be able to . . . serve my community also, actually help my community by having that degree, being in school, and graduating as a Black woman." Phea further contextualized her personal educational pursuits as part of the purpose of shifting narratives about Black people: "Black women . . . are the most, you know, educated now, when it comes to . . . going to school and stuff like that. And I'm really proud about that, too, and I wanna, you know, add more onto that statistic." Phea aspires to become a successful businesswoman to give back to the Black community and change narratives about Black women, demonstrating that civic purposes can be intertwined.

Other youth shared their visions for future impact, aiming to be successful financially and give back to the Black community once they've established themselves. Kobe (age 17, he/him) envisioned himself making money as the boss and "giving out backpacks ... cars and shoes and stuff like that," and Sean similarly envisioned a time when he could give back to his community through "charities" and "school giveaways." Youth explained that their self-betterment could create broader community change by inspiring others. According to Bree (age 15, she/her), focusing on being her best self inspired others to follow her example: "I like to focus on myself a lot because I feel like if you better yourself, then other people will look at you and then better themselves, and then it just builds. Like, it just gets bigger and bigger... and then it just ... makes your community better." Returning to Layla, she emphasized working hard to get good grades and stay focused to serve the larger purpose of starting a mentoring program to give back to the Black community. For Layla, these were smaller steps she could take on a long-term path toward addressing bigger community issues like gentrification:

For me to really better my community, because ... where I live, it started off as, you know, a Black community. And then ... gentrification and everything has brought other races into the community. So, it's kind of hard to really help where I live, personally ... because gentrification has, you know, taken over ..., it's not much I can do. But – where my church is and stuff – if I better myself with getting good grades and staying focused and on track ... and I start this mentoring program, it can show people like no matter where you come from, you can always succeed, and no matter what the color of your skin, you can always succeed no matter what anybody tells you.

By developing skills and resources in the short term, Black youth like Layla and others are positioning themselves to give back to and uplift the Black community over the long term.

THE TAKE-AWAYS

Young Black changemakers are civic actors with purpose. Their changemaking is aimed at long-term, big picture visions for a racially just future. Changemaking is not fleeting or spontaneous, but rather thoughtful and purposeful. Changemaking for racial justice is a big tent, and within it, Black youth have different visions for changemaking that can improve the world for Black people, ranging from resisting and seeking to change unjust systems to uplifting Black youth and communities now and into the future. Black youth are not siloed into one domain of civic action or one way of changemaking. Instead, there are overlaps and complexities across the ways of changemaking, which serve as powerful reminders that each young Black changemaker is charting their own path.

Contributions to Research

This study illustrates the value of considering civic actions in tandem with civic purpose. We not only need to know what civic actions youth undertake, but why. Researchers must more deeply consider whether to study, support, and encourage civic actions undertaken for any purpose, or to focus more specifically on actions that uplift communities and seek justice and liberation from oppression, which were these young Black changemakers' big picture goals. Changemaking, as we described it for Black youth, aligns well with sociopolitical development theory's description of actions youth take to challenge oppressions they face (Watts & Halkovic, 2022). Our study shows that this model can be even better represented by research that examines youth's civic actions in the context of their civic purpose.

We also expand the conceptualization of civic purpose in a way that better captures the experiences of Black youth. Previous theorizing and research on civic purpose, which has not focused on Black youth, emphasized that purpose must "go beyond the self" (Damon et al., 2003; Malin et al., 2015). In contrast, we found that for Black youth, civic purposes can center the self while also extending to communities and to future generations. Indeed, in racial justice pursuits, personal liberation from oppression is and must be bound together with the liberation of the collective. A stark distinction between individual and collective goals is not needed – and not appropriate – for characterizing Black youth's civic purpose. Notably, research has been documenting the civic purposes of Black youth – and their social responsibility, communalism, and racial justice motivations – for a long time without using the term (e.g., Ginwright, 2010a; Watts et al., 2003).

Our work continues to highlight what is unique about civic engagement for Black youth. Research has recognized the importance of understanding what civic engagement means and how it is expressed in different racial and ethnic groups and community contexts (Gordon, 2007; Hope, Cryer-Coupet et al., 2020; Wray-Lake & Abrams, 2020). Our qualitative methods revealed under-recognized forms of changemaking for Black youth, such as bettering oneself to better the Black community, which was only identifiable by examining action alongside purpose. Our findings also show how strongly racial justice and equity guide how Black youth think about and make choices concerning civic actions. Not all Black youth express the same civic purpose; for example, some youth are more explicitly justice-seeking than others. Yet, young Black changemakers framed their civic actions and civic purpose from their personal and collective experiences of being a young Black person. Other scholars have similarly noted that individual and collective experiences of oppression are drivers of civic action (Anyiwo et al., 2018; Hope, Smith et al., 2020), and this is a principal idea of sociopolitical development theory (Watts & Guessous, 2006). We will continue to explore how racism, racial identity, and changemaking are linked in Chapters 3 and 4.

Finally, we name what may have appeared to be lacking in this chapter, which is the term *political*. Our team had some internal disagreements about whether and which of these youth's civic actions fall under the category of political actions. On the one hand, scholars of civic engagement and political science generally agree that political behaviors are actions that pertain to exerting power or influencing people or institutions with power to make decisions about social issues (Hope, Pender et al., 2019; Wray-Lake, 2019). Thus, scholars might understand many of the youth's interpersonal civic actions, activism, and organizing as political. Yet, others on our team asked whether it was fair or right to politicize actions Black youth were taking to ensure their own survival and humanity. Often, these youth were fighting for themselves and others to be safe from harm and treated with respect and fairness. We pondered whether Black youth themselves used the term *political* to describe their actions. Some did, but many did not. We also recognized that racial justice efforts are political in our society whether we – or Black youth – want them to be or not. It should not need to be a power struggle to ensure Black people in the United States are treated with dignity and equality across societal institutions, but unfortunately, that struggle has persisted for centuries. As the classic mantra from the feminist movement says, *the personal is political* (Hanisch, 2017). Political actions become necessary when individuals personally experience injustice and dehumanization. As long as white supremacy and racism pervade the institutions of our society, racial justice work will include a political agenda. Yet, it is vital to not forget that these are people's lives we are talking about. Black youth are more than simply political actors or objects; they are people who deserve much better.

Practical Insights

Understanding Black youth's civic actions and purpose can help dispel assumptions and stereotypes of Black youth. Public discourse about Black youth's civic engagement is often fleeting, narrow, and largely negative – attending to certain actions at certain points in time that uphold a racist narrative about Black youth, which is often a narrative about deviance and violence (Kilgo, 2021). Not recognizing or understanding Black youth's civic actions is another way in which society silences Black youth. Our findings present a different, youth-driven narrative of young Black changemaking. Black youth engage in many forms of changemaking, spanning from helping as a core part of how youth define themselves to involvement in organizing and activism; from informal everyday actions to formal civic spaces in schools and community-based organizations. Their purpose-driven civic actions deserve to take center stage in media messaging and public discourse about Black youth.

Young Black changemakers are doing critical work to move us toward a better world for Black people, and they should not have to do this work alone. Anyone reading this book can look for ways to support and be authentic allies on the road to racial justice with young Black changemakers. One step is to learn and practice how to be an anti-racist, and for this wisdom, we recommend the seminal work of Dr. Ibram X. Kendi (2019). Another avenue to support young Black changemaking, for those with the resources, is financially supporting community-based organizations that serve and support Black youth. These include organizations focused on service, mentoring, educating for social and racial justice, and grassroots organizing. Investing in initiatives led by Black youth would be particularly valuable, whether through supporting a young entrepreneur, donating to Black youth-led efforts, or attending protests, marches, or events organized by Black youth.

Community-based and school-based organizations can create rich opportunities for Black youth to pursue their civic purposes through offering varied opportunities for community helping, organizing and activism, and interpersonal civic actions. Such opportunities will likely appeal to Black youth if they align with youth's guiding purposes such as redistributing resources for racial justice, navigating an anti-Black world, and giving back to the Black community. Black youth must be viewed as visionaries and capable leaders within civic spaces. In Chapter 7, we offer more insight about how community-based organizations can support Black youth.

Finally, it takes only time and openness to appreciate and celebrate Black youth's accomplishments – in civic action and otherwise – and to listen to and value Black youth's perspectives in school, community, and civic spaces. We hope that hearing Black youth's stories of purpose-driven civic actions can inspire others to do their part to improve the lives of Black people and challenge racial injustices.

Up Next

A central idea of this chapter was that Black youth's civic action is driven by the pursuit of racial justice. Young Black changemakers are future oriented and are fighting for racial justice in different ways. Sociopolitical development theory tells us that experiences of racial oppression often drive the process of becoming a changemaker who challenges racism and seeks racial justice (Anyiwo et al., 2018). In the next chapter, we delve into Black youth's experiences of racism and resistance to anti-Black racism. Schools were a salient context for experiencing racism for these young Black changemakers. Thus, Chapter 3 focuses on schools – and particularly non-Black school spaces – as sites of racial oppression and resistance for Black youth.

3

Changemaking in Non-Black School Spaces

JASON ANTHONY PLUMMER, DOMONIQUE KIANNA
HENDERSON, & LAURA WRAY-LAKE

And so, I was like, 'Okay, well, we can start a group.' And I was like, 'Black Student Union. duh.' And so, we started Black Student Union . . . and we were talking with everybody about situations that they've experienced. And I had asked the question . . . 'Has anybody on campus ever experienced anything that happens to do with their race that's not in a beneficial light?' Everybody raised their hand.

KJ

KJ (age 16, she/her) was a rising eleventh grader with a passion for helping others. For years, she had been active in community service to help others and mentor younger children, and she recently accepted a role as a regional youth leader in a Black service organization. In contrast to her long-running experiences of helping, her passion for directly challenging racial injustice was activated by an encounter with racism in school. According to publicly available data, students at KJ's public high school identified as 45% Latinx, 35% white, and 3% Black or African American (California Department of Education, 2019). Clearly, KJ and her classmates attended school in a non-Black space. Non-Black spaces are settings often predominated by whiteness (numerically or culturally) and where Black youth experience racism and exercise resistance to this racism. KJ recounted the powerful story of how she started the Black Student Union at her school, which we share here in its entirety to illustrate how Black youth experience and react to non-Black spaces:

So, it all started in experience. My ninth grade year I was in French class and I was sitting in class – it was me and two other girls – they're twins – and they were African American. Everybody else in the class was Caucasian and it was a couple Hispanic children, but everybody else there was Caucasian. And it was one boy and he had said the N-word, so everybody looked over like, "What?" and whatnot.
So, I told him – I was like, "You can't just go around saying that type of stuff." And he was like, "Or, what?" And I was like, "Oh, okay." So, I went up and I brought it up to the school and everything and they were like, "Oh, well, we've never had to experience this, and we've never had, you know, a child of color come out and speak out about this." And I was like, "Really?" And she was like, "Yeah."

So, then I was like, um – I asked some of my friends around lunchtime. I was like, "Do you guys ever – ?" Because it happens all the time. So, I asked them if they've ever experienced stuff like that and they were like, "Yes." And I was like, "Okay. So, why don't you guys say anything?" And they were like – majority of them said that they felt – not scared to say something, but they just didn't feel comfortable with saying anything because we only have one other Black teacher staff on campus.

So, a lot of them were like, "Oh, well, we don't feel comfortable talking to them about this because the one time that we did say something, nothing happened." I was like, "Okay. Well, what if we try – since you guys aren't comfortable – we can go there as a group together and speak out about it?" And I was like, "There is other African American children at our school," because out of 3,000 of us, I would say ... it's kind of a sad number – it's at least 60 of us on campus.

And so, I was like, "Okay, well, we can start a group." And I was like, "Black Student Union. Duh." And so, we started Black Student Union and whatnot, and we were talking with everybody about situations that they've experienced. And I had asked the question – 'cause I was like, "Has anybody on campus ever experienced anything that happens to do with their race that's not in a beneficial light?" Everybody raised their hand, and I was like, "Wow."

So, we sort of talked about it in class and the Black teacher staff – Mr. T. – he's ... the person that oversees it 'cause you have to have a teacher .... And he was like, "Okay. Well, we can all maybe go talk to the staff about this." And we were like, "Mr. T., have you ever experienced anything like this?" And he was like, "All the time." And so, we were like, "Wow." And that's sort of what started our group, I guess.

KJ's story vividly captures several major ideas in this chapter. First, non-Black school spaces create discomfort and can silence Black youth. KJ and her peers were well aware that Black students and staff were in the minority at their school, and for that reason, her peers did not feel comfortable speaking up about their experiences. Second, Black youth encounter every-day racism from peers and school administrators in non-Black schools. KJ and other Black youth were exposed to a classmate saying the N-word in French class, and then experienced their school administrators' denial and disregard of how such racist incidents affect Black youth. Third, Black youth engage in various forms of resistance to challenge racism and create spaces where they are fully valued. KJ resisted by creating a Black Student Union (BSU), an organization where Black students gather to create a safe space away from racism and collectively challenge racism at the school. Fourth, Black youth seek out allies in non-Black school spaces who can support their efforts to resist racism. KJ and her peers sought out Mr. T, the only Black teacher on campus, to be the sponsor of the group, and he supported the students' efforts by encouraging them to address the administration and by validating their experiences of racism by sharing his own. Finally, Black youth experience the burdens of the emotional labor that this changemaking work requires of them. Although KJ did not express these experiences as part of this particular story, other Black youth describe the exhaustion and emotional toll that can result from having to educate others about racism and its harms.

WHAT ARE NON-BLACK SCHOOL SPACES?

The school still caters mostly to those white students and their needs.

Camille

Non-Black spaces are most simply defined as settings where Black people are in the numerical minority. Without any specific prompting from interviewers, at least 20 youth in our study (around half) shared the challenges of everyday racism in non-Black spaces and the ways they confront these challenges. Their stories overwhelmingly focused on schools, which is not surprising given that adolescents spend many hours per day in school settings. Of the 43 youth in our study, six attended a predominantly Black school, with 55–92% of the student body identifying as Black; 13 youth went to predominantly white schools (3–5% Black students); 12 attended predominantly Hispanic or Latinx schools (3–34% Black students); seven attended multiracial schools, where no racial or ethnic group was clearly in the majority (9–40% Black students); and the remaining five students attended schools with no demographic data available from the National Center for Education Statistics. Regardless of the racial and ethnic composition of the student body, Black students' school administrators are overwhelmingly likely to be white. According to the National Center for Education Statistics (2020), 79% of public-school teachers identified as white in 2017–2018. Further, the nature of public-school curriculum, instruction, and policy is overwhelmingly rooted in whiteness and white supremacy that denies or undermines the humanity of Black people in the United States (Gray et al., 2018; King, 2006). In this chapter, we focus on a subset of young Black changemakers who shared salient descriptions of and experiences in non-Black school spaces.

Black youth often feel like outsiders and feel unwelcome in non-Black schools. Non-Black spaces are not just non-Black numerically, but also tend to culturally uphold the norms, rules, and expectations of whiteness. Non-Black spaces often operate as environments where Black youth are silenced and feel they cannot fully express themselves. James (age 16, he/him) felt "split with two separate worlds" in attending a private predominantly white high school and living in a majority Black neighborhood. He described his school experience by saying, "In my surroundings, my opinion is very unheard. I feel like my opinion and my thoughts are often not neglected, but not listened to …. It causes me to kind of doubt myself and belittle myself." Joe Cornell (age 17, he/him), who described himself as "the only Black male" in his predominantly white private high school, shared a similar experience of being unheard and having self-doubt when he transitioned to high school. Without "any interactions really with any white people" before high school, at first, Joe Cornell experienced "not wanting to rock the boat too much or to cause too much disturbance. But then, also, you know, feeling like maybe I was making these sort of things up, and maybe I was being too sensitive about certain issues." By "these sort of things," Joe Cornell was in part talking about the experiences of discomfort and alienation that can come with being Black in white spaces. In worrying about rocking the boat or being perceived as too sensitive, he was also describing the challenges of speaking up about racism when you are the only Black person in the room. Similarly, KJ's peers expressed to her that they "didn't feel comfortable talking" to the administration about negative experiences they had as Black students in their school. NA (age 13, she/her) felt the same way about her private predominantly white middle school, saying:

I feel just overpowered, and ... I know that's the case for a lot of the Black youth. A lotta the times, we are the minority, and it feels that way a lot, and we feel all alone and overpowered, so yeah, so youth engagement really helps to make us feel like we have a voice, and we can make a change.

Like NA and KJ, the young Black changemakers were able to find their voices in non-Black spaces; many joined with other Black students to collectively resist racism in their non-Black schools. Even so, these youth shared sentiments of discomfort and isolation, which reflect the realities of the "white gaze."

A phrase originally coined by Toni Morrison, the "white gaze" captures the idea that most spaces and perspectives in society are white by default (Morrison, 2019). In navigating non-Black spaces, Black people often feel constantly judged and evaluated by the white gaze, which is a major obstacle to feeling comfortable to be oneself (Banaji et al., 2021). Through the white gaze, white race and white privileges are rendered invisible, while other racial groups and their differences from white people are hyper-visible. White perspectives are the normative standard, and other perspectives are silenced (Sue, 2006). A few youth named the culture of whiteness specifically, such as Tsehai (age 14, she/her) who attended a predominantly white private school. When describing dynamics of race and social class in her school, Tsehai shared:

There's a lot of conversations about like, wow, these white kids are really thoughtless. Oh my god, these white kids don't realize, you know, how privileged they are and they get up and defensive because of, you know, when they recognize areas of privilege, people get defensive and there's a lot of those ... conversations about frustrating topics and stuff.

Scholars of whiteness document that white people become highly fragile and defensive in conversations about race and racism (DiAngelo, 2018) to avoid confronting their privileges or admit holding any racist beliefs (Helms, 1990). Joe Cornell also described one way that white privilege operates in his private school: "If a student has a problem you know, they bring it to the educator with the understandin' that it's gonna be fixed because – it's a teacher that they're payin' to go to. And ... to be frank, the sense of entitlement a lot of my peers, you know, have." At first, Joe Cornell "didn't understand" how to navigate the power structures of the school to have his voice heard as a student, but over time, he worked to develop his voice and learned how to "take up space" in the school like the white students did naturally. Tom (age 17, he/him) explained how learning to take up space in non-Black spaces can be a valuable skill. As a biracial Black and white student at a predominantly Latinx charter school, Tom experienced his school environment as "very different," but felt like his school prepared him to operate in a white world "where you know it's mainly white men ... I'm gonna have to know how to be taken seriously and, you know, communicate what I want to say, in a way where they're listening."

In schools with a strong culture of whiteness, teachers and administrators may strive for a so-called *race-neutral* environment where people claim to not see color or claim that race does not matter. Yet learning from these young Black changemakers and a larger body of literature (e.g., Carter Andrews et al., 2019; Sondel et al., 2019; Tatum, 2003), we know that Black youth often do not experience these white-centered environments positively. As Amir (age 13, he/him), a student at a predominantly white private school shared, a white environment can be "really overwhelming at first" and "it put a lot of pressure on me." In addition to the stressors of navigating white-centered spaces, Black youth also experience explicit racism in these spaces.

EVERYDAY RACISM IN NON-BLACK SCHOOL SPACES

During an incident, one kid said the N-word. Like everyone heard about it, but nobody heard how it was resolved and like the school didn't really address it, you know?

Tsehai

Anti-Black racism is ordinary and common, playing out in the everyday interactions of Black adolescents' lives. When peers use racial slurs and when teachers or school staff treat Black students unfairly, these are examples of interpersonal racism (Brooms & Davis, 2017). When school policies and administrators fail to respond to racism, disregard racism, or deny Black youth safe spaces free from racism, these are examples of institutional racism. The young Black changemakers' stories illustrate how institutional and inter-personal racism operate in schools, spaces in which we require young people to spend abundant amounts of time and that, in theory, aim to support the healthy development of all students. Racism operates to prioritize the needs and comfort of white people, especially in predominantly white spaces (Anderson, 2021; DiAngelo, 2018). When Black youth are recruited and made visible in non-Black spaces while being dismissed or tokenized, this is an example of what sociologists call a white centering logic, valuing diversity or multiculturalism as an educational experience only, rather than as a pathway to achieving racial justice (Hagerman, 2018; Mayorga-Gallo, 2019). Here, we highlight two particularly pernicious experiences of everyday racism faced by young Black changemakers in non-Black school spaces: (1) the double whammy of interpersonal and institutional racism; and (2) the tokenism experienced by Black students in non-Black schools.

Double Whammy of Interpersonal and Institutional Racism

In the stories of young Black changemakers in our study, we recognized a pattern where an experience of everyday racism among peers often turned into a larger experience of institutional racism due to the school administration's response to such incidents. We call this experience of both interpersonal and institutional racism a double whammy because the school's response magnified the harm of the initial incident by refusing to address it. Tsehai, Amir, KJ, Joe Cornell, and Ray were among the young Black changemakers in our study who recounted hearing racial slurs from their peers in school. Amir's story illustrates what it is like for a Black student to encounter racism from peers, followed by disregard from the school administration:

I was at school . . . I was playing basketball with my friends. And then, one white kid walked up to me. And his whole group walked up to me and they're like, "Oh, can we have the N pass? Can you have the N-word pass?" And I told them, no. And then I walked off. I left the basketball court. And then after school, they walked up to me again, and was begging me for it [the N-word pass]. And so, then I just left and I went to the counselor and talked to him about it. And he was just like, "Oh, do you know who these kids are and blah, blah, blah." And so I told them who they were. And . . . I was expecting to not see them the next day like they got suspended or something, but they didn't. They just came to school like nothing happened. And one of them walked up to me and was like, "Oh, why'd you snitch? Why'd you snitch?" . . . I just never talked to them again . . . . It made me notice how much of a difference it is from where I come from and where they come from. It's not that many Black people at the school, it's only like, in my grade, out of about 200–300 there's only about 12 Black people in my grade. It's not that many people to talk to, and to . . . connect with. And so it made me realize how much of a difference . . . both of our worlds are.

The N-word pass refers to permission from a Black person for a white person to use the N-word. Amir, upset by this request from a white student to use a racial slur, sought accountability from the school counselor. Judging from the white peers' questions to Amir of "why'd you snitch?", it appears that the school discussed the incident with the white youth, but the school's actions did not seem to have the desired effect of having the white teens understand why their actions were offensive and how to repair the harm done to Amir. The lack of consequences upset Amir further: "I was a little mad. I was even more mad at that time. Because I was expecting for them to get at least suspended. Because . . . that's like a big deal [calling someone the N-word]. And for them, they didn't get their parents told about this. It's like . . . they [the school] don't even care. So, it's frustrating." The experience also made Amir realize that Black youth live in a different world from white youth. Amir's story also highlights that when Black youth challenge racism by seeking solutions at the institutional level, this form of changemaking may lead to heightened experiences of discrimination. This pattern is found in some research where youth who engage in actions to challenge oppression sometimes report more racial discrimination at a later point in time (see Hope et al., 2023). In Amir's case, the lack of accountability for the students was also a reminder of how school administration and policy act to uphold white supremacy.

Success with Lex's (age 18, she/her) experience also shows how interpersonal experiences are intertwined with institutional racism. We do not know the demographics of her school, but she highlighted multiple types of racism she experienced in a single story:

> My family would have to come up to the school all the time confronting the administration because they messed up my schedule. I even had an altercation, which almost went into a legal thing because my teacher, I didn't wanna participate in an activity – and he basically pushed me into the circle with his hands. . .. And I was one of the only Black students in there. And it was voluntary, so it wasn't mandatory to participate in anything, but he still forced me to. So it was just this big thing, and my four years at that school, it was just very hard trying to get the classes that I wanted. . .. And as far as the college-application process, I saw my counselors, you know, helping non-Black students more, giving them outside resources . . . "Oh, you should join this program to put on your resume." Or, "Oh, you should contact her. She'll help you with getting into this university.". . . but they never brought the African American kids in to get that information – so it just felt like I was trying to really work three times as hard just to get the resources I need to go off to college.

Success with Lex described an act of violence by her teacher – he physically pushed her in response to her disinterest in participating in a voluntary activity. She attributed this mistreatment to her race, emphasizing that she was "one of the only Black students in there." Moreover, Success with Lex connected this incident to a larger pattern of Black students being ignored and denied the same resources as non-Black students to prepare for college. Success with Lex's story is an example of how schools can often hyper-focus on Black students when it comes to classroom behavior and disciplinary action, but Black students are often invisible when it comes to additional resources and support for academic advancement (Annamma et al., 2019; Bell, 2020; Scott et al., 2017). Success with Lex's experience is also an example of evaded racism, a type of racism that often occurs in schools where concrete discourse about racial inequities is avoided and unexamined at the institutional level, which serves to perpetuate deficit-oriented views about and mistreatment of students of color (Kohli et al., 2017). This type of racism can increase racial inequalities in educational attainment and college attendance for Black students (Offidani-Bertrand et al., 2022). Applied to Success with

Lex's example, if Black youth at this school have lower rates of college acceptance than their white peers, the school might interpret this as a problem of the Black students, rather doing an institutional analysis of their college counseling practices.

Camille (age 15, she/her), a Black and white biracial young person, further illustrates how Black youth in non-Black school spaces experience individual acts of racism in a larger context of institutional denial of racism. Camille shared this story as part of a larger discussion of how she challenged racism in her school and advocated for a BSU:

My parents have been calling school, emailing them, pushing for them to allow us to kind of have a place in our school because my school is very diverse. We have every kind of people at my school for the most part, but a lot of the minorities exist in small numbers and they're minorities, and it is mostly white students . . . . Even when in one of my meetings with administrators during my freshman year, they tried to tell me that it wasn't majority white students. And they tried to show me the percentages of each different race but it was majority white students and . . . even if it wasn't, which it is, the school still caters mostly to those white students and their needs. And there's a lot of unfair treatment. There was one day during this school year where we had a class color day and my class color was red. So one student came to school with a MAGA [Make America Great Again] hat on. And so . . ., I don't know if she could have even gotten in trouble for that. But, anytime we try to talk about it, they just told us, don't worry about it. Don't talk about it. Don't make a big deal about it. They just kind of silenced us whenever we try to speak up about it, because even though technically it might not be against school rules . . ., it still is hurtful to us.

Camille and her parents requested that Black students have their own space, a club, at the school. In response, the school administration denied this need based on their school's racial and ethnic demographics. According to public records, the student mix at Camille's private all-girls school was 31% white, 26% Hispanic or Latinx, and 16% Black. Yet, rather than acknowledge Camille's and others' views that they felt in the minority and that the school catered to white students, they used data to make an argument for multiculturalism. The language of multiculturalism in education may have originally been intended to challenge inequalities, but is more often used to evade discussions of power and racial hierarchy. As Dr. Sadhana Bery (2014, p. 334) stated in her analysis of multicultural frameworks in education:

When led and controlled by Whites, and in the absence of collective struggles to dismantle the apparatus of white supremacy, multiculturalism can reproduce dominant racial/racist ontologies, epistemologies, and practices, albeit in new dis/guises . . . multiculturalism, when combined with color blind ideology, results in a reassertion of racism and racist hierarchies. . . . Multiculturalism is simultaneously the consequence of and embodiment of white supremacy.

Thus, perhaps not surprisingly in a context that espouses multiculturalism, when a student wears a MAGA hat to school and Camille expresses to the administration how hurtful it is, they not only deny her feelings but also ask her not to discuss it, emphasizing that a dialogue about race and racism has no place in this school context. Camille recognized the school was trying to silence her and her Black peers. She continued to challenge this culture of white supremacy that was hidden under the guise of multiculturalism.

Although interpersonal acts of racism are already understood to be everyday occurrences, the stories from these young Black changemakers also show how institutional racism in non-Black schools is pervasive and recognizable in everyday experiences. These examples underscore young Black changemakers' awareness of institutional racism and how it operates in their lives. According to sociopolitical development theory and research, this critical awareness of racial inequality can often fuel Black youth's actions to challenge racism (Hope, Smith et al., 2020). Notably, just as with Success with Lex, Camille's parents were also involved in challenging the racism that their Black children experience and advocating for Black students' needs at their schools, which underscores ideas from Chapter 5 that families play an influential role in supporting young Black changemaking.

Tokenism of Black Students in Non-Black Schools

Many schools say they value diversity and often include diversity as part of their mission statements. Supreme Court decisions have reaffirmed that schools have a compelling interest to create a racially diverse learning environment, from outlawing racial segregation (Brown v. Board of Education, 1954) to upholding the constitutionality of race-conscious admissions' policies in university settings (Fisher v. University of Texas, 2016). Research has shown that a diverse student body can promote intergroup dialogue and help to reduce stereotypes (Rivas-Drake & Umaña-Taylor, 2019). Dr. Margaret Hagerman (2018) noted that white parents value placing their children in diverse school settings, in part to affirm white supremacist logic that we live in a post-racial world where racism no longer exists and where people of all races have equal chances to succeed. Black youth in non-Black school spaces sometimes experience this focus on diversity as tokenism. Tokenism refers to the practice of accepting a small number of a minority group – in school admissions, scholarships, hiring, or elsewhere – to give the impression of being welcoming and inclusive to these groups when in reality, the setting is not inclusive (Ruby, 2020). In effect, tokenism is the result of diversity initiatives that do not include meaningful inclusion of those who enhance diversity.

As one experience of tokenism, young Black changemakers in non-Black school spaces described being repeatedly photographed for school materials. Camille, who felt continually silenced by the school when bringing attention to Black student experiences, also noted that she has "been chosen for multiple photoshoots to go on the school website and school pamphlets and stuff like that. And it just feels like they don't really care about us or listen to our voices unless they're trying to show off for other prospective students and people who fund our school." Indeed, the school's desire to show Camille off in promotional materials starkly contrasts with how they responded when she expressed concern about the classmate wearing a MAGA hat or wanted to start a BSU. Tsehai, who also attended a predominately white private school, also experienced tokenism in being photographed to promote the school's diversity:

I was walking down the alleyway with one of my Black friends – she happened to be Ethiopian as well and then one of my Indian friends. And this woman just stops us with the camera and she's like, "Is it alright if we take a picture of you and interview you and ask a question or something?" And we're like, "There are so many other students here." It doesn't have to be me every single time and stuff. So, this school has also fostered a bit of an uncomfortable environment for students of color.

Camille recounted another story of tokenism, which consisted of the school quite literally selecting tokens of different racial and ethnic groups to be part of a student leadership group. Camille shared:

The woman who runs [the student leadership group] is white. She has to pick a variety of students to show the diversity we have at school. Yeah, but it's always . . . kind of nerve racking, I guess. Telling your friends like, "Hmm, we have this number of Black students already. So I don't know if you'll be let on or not because, just there's a certain number."

Although many students were interested in this leadership opportunity, the selection process appeared to function by fulfilling diversity quotas rather than being based on students' qualifications for leading and representing the school. In fact, Camille described the group's function as "focusing on recruitment. [W]e host all the events with incoming families, students, and parents." This experience of tokenism was another impetus for Camille and her peers to advocate for a BSU, because, rather than wait for a selective opportunity where only a certain number of positions for Black students were available, Camille wanted to "create a community where everybody is heard and welcomed and feels safe."

A superficial value on racial diversity appears to reward schools in making Black students more visible; for private schools in particular, this tokenism may benefit their recruitment efforts. Again, attention on Black youth when it benefits the school contrasts with these students' experiences of the school administration's denial or disregard of racism. Black youth in our study understood that this momentary attention to diversity did not translate into equity or inclusion of Black students in the school environment.

Another aspect of tokenism is featuring Black youth in ways that uphold racial stereotypes. As Dr. Megan Ruby (2020) stated regarding tokenism in the media and elsewhere, "Men and women of color are used as tokens by perpetuating a stereotype of the white imagination of how people of color act in the ways white people expect them to." Tom (age 17, he/him) had attended a private, predominantly white middle school and recounted this experience of tokenism:

When I was at [school], I remember I was failing, straight up. . ... But I was talented in track. So, they had a rule there where if you got below a certain GPA [grade point average], they're not going to let you play a sport. I had way below the GPA that I needed, but at the end of the day, they still let me and my friend JJ, who was also Black, they still let us play because we were talented and they needed us to win. They need us on the team, but it kind of showed us, well actually me, not at the time, but looking back. . ... That was where their mind was at, that was where they really saw us as going, to help us win in sports. They didn't really value what we were doing in the classroom as much. Because if they did, then they would have taken that as priority. So, that's when I realized . . ., it's really us out here as young Black men . . . if we're not fighting for ourselves . . . if we don't want it, no one's going to give it to us.

Tom and his friend were seen and valued solely for their athletic abilities, a way of tokenizing them that upheld stereotypes of Black males as athletes rather than all around students. The school's rules were selectively applied to enhance the sports reputation of the school, and this framing commodified the Black athletes, disregarding their academic needs and dehumanizing them in the process.

The everyday nature of racism that Black youth face is interpersonal, institutional, and sometimes hidden like tokenism. Everyday racism is normative in non-Black school settings and exists because school policies and practices allow it (Solórzano & Perez Huber, 2020). Without active resistance, these social norms of disregarding the humanity of Black youth are reinforced. Ideally, we would hope that adults in non-Black spaces would disrupt anti-Black racism in schools. Yet, young Black changemakers exercise agency in taking matters into their own hands.

RESISTANCE TO RACISM IN NON-BLACK SPACES

For as long as there has been anti-Black racism, there has been Black resistance. Black youth resist racism and white supremacy in their non-Black school spaces in many ways. Resistance is broadly defined as behaviors enacted to undermine power and domination, whether from racism or other forms of oppression (Johansson & Vinthagen, 2020). Resistance is a useful term, serving as a reminder that some civic actions are a direct response to racial injustices that are experienced and observed. Resistance can be more or less explicit about reclaiming power in ways that reduce injustice, but is almost always about reclaiming humanity in the face of discrimination, disregard, mistreatment, and dehumanization (Wray-Lake et al., 2022). Here, we highlight three resistance strategies of young Black changemakers in response to everyday racism in schools: creating safe spaces, holding administrators accountable, and raising awareness about Black experiences.

Creating Safe Spaces for Black Solidarity

In response to racism, Black youth often seek out and create spaces to share with other Black youth where they can feel safe and empowered. In these Black spaces, Black youth find validation, social support, and space to process racism experienced in the larger school environment. NA captured this sentiment when she reflected on the value of the Black student club at her school:

It was a gathering of all of us together in our community, and we all came together to support each other in a safe space. And whenever I was there, I felt really comfortable and inspired that all of us were there together, and we all had each other's backs, so it was a really great experience.

Other young Black changemakers felt similarly about their Black student club, which was usually, but not always, formalized as a BSU. O.A. (age 15, she/her), who attended a predominantly white public high school, appreciated the safe space of the Black student group at her school "since there's a small minority of Black students that go to my school. And so it creates a safe environment for those minorities to just come around and become equals." Tsehai, a student at a predominantly white private school, described the empowering nature of Black spaces in non-Black schools and her commitment to strengthening this community space, saying:

Seeing all these other Black kids from different grades and stuff and talking about the shared experience that we have that … no one can really relate to except them … it's super empowering and it's nice to have a safe space. So I want to strengthen that community. So that the other Black kids that don't really participate in BSU and stuff can also have that space … I definitely think that they deserve it. They should have it.

Research on BSUs supports the value of these spaces for Black student belonging and as spaces to build solidarity around experiences of racism as well as visions for anti-racism (Harrison et al., 2020). These spaces are often called counterspaces, which Dr. Micere Keels (2019, p. 11) defined as "spaces where those of a similar social identity gather to validate and critique their experiences with the larger institution." Case and Hunter (2012) described counterspaces as spaces that promote wellness of a marginalized group, challenge negative stereotypes and cultural narratives of the group, and allow the group to collectively carry out acts of resistance to challenge oppressions they face. These counterspaces for Black students are more often institutional-ized in predominantly white college or university settings and are less often built into the fabric of high schools by default. Unfortunately, some Black youth experience substantial administrative opposition to having BSUs or similar counterspaces for Black students. Camille had to fight to convince her school's administration to see the value of a BSU, saying:

It was like everything that we said, every reason that we gave, there would always be some pushback for it. And there was one big argument: How would white students feel if Black students had a group that was just for them? And that was just always a really weird question to me because the whole school is just for them. The white administration just doesn't understand that.

Camille was directly confronting white supremacy culture in her school. Settings like Camille's school do not recognize racism as a larger systemic problem, and the feelings and comfort of white people are prioritized in a way that reasserts white dominance (Bonilla-Silva, 2018; DiAngelo, 2018). This is precisely the dynamic at play when the school administrators asked Camille to account for "how white students would feel" about the BSU. Despite this major obstacle, Camille and her peers eventually succeeded in convincing the administration to allow a BSU. She achieved this changemaking success by waging a social media campaign that included voices from Black youth at the school and beyond, and the administration could no longer deny the request. Camille shared: "When everybody was commenting on the Instagram post . . . there were so many people sharing their experiences . . . there was a point where . . . they [school administrators] couldn't just ignore us anymore, so that felt really good. And [we] finally got to make our voices heard."

Similar to Camille's experience, Black youth often work hard to create safe spaces for other Black students, often viewing this work as an important responsibility they had as Black students in non-Black spaces. Mia (age 16, she/her), a student at a public predominantly Latinx high school, described the fear and discomfort she had experienced in going to club meetings when "there's not one other Black face in there." Through leadership in a health equity club, Mia strived to be "that force of comfort and reliability for other Black youth who may not . . . feel comfortable getting involved in an activity that's 98% white." Similarly, Joe Cornell shared his sense of responsibility to create safe spaces for Black students, "It . . . felt more like a responsibility to create a space where they could, you know, be the best versions of themselves and not . . . have to feel so not supported, so alone." These youth's pursuit of safe spaces for Black youth contributes to the civic purpose of navigating an anti-Black world that we described in Chapter 2. Safe spaces for Black students give them a setting and a network where they can feel seen and valued, which is especially important in non-Black school contexts that often deny Black youth this sense of belonging (Keels, 2019). Black spaces also operate to build communities that support further acts of collective resistance, such as holding the school administration accountable for perpetuating a climate of racism.

Holding School Administration Accountable

When young Black changemakers challenged racism in schools, they often directed their resistance efforts toward the system by holding school administration accountable and challenging school policies rather than focusing on individual perpetrators of racism. These systems-level solutions were more likely to bring about the change they sought – dismantling racism in the school context. In the stories we already shared from KJ and Camille, their efforts to create safe spaces for Black youth required them to challenge school administrators and hold them accountable for ensuring Black students' safety and well-being. As another example, Amir was the leader of his predominantly white private school's Black Student Alliance (BSA). He lamented that "it's not that many Black kids" in the school, "so it's not much we can do." Although Amir and his group experienced obstacles to feeling heard as a group, they "try and talk to the principal about certain things" and in gatherings every week with the BSA "we'll talk about a new topic about injustice to Black people." Thus, Amir and his BSA were engaging in conversations with the principal to raise awareness of Black student experiences and see what changes they could initiate.

As a member of the Diversity, Equity, and Inclusion Committee at his predominantly white private high school, Joe Cornell helped to write policies to address racism. He shared the rationale for having such policies in place:

I first started getting' into . . . the policy and procedures for acts of discrimination or acts of bigotry within school . . . especially private institutions that don't have a lot of Black students, where the policies that are holding non-Black students or white students, in particular, accountable, you know, for certain actions. And even educators, you know, when they make an inappropriate comment or if they witness or, you know, hear inappropriate comments, what policies are holdin' that teacher accountable for addressing it and insuring, you know, that it doesn't happen again. Followin' up with the student, makin' sure that that student feels, you know, seen, heard, safe, represented, all the things that a student in a school should feel.

As part of this role, Joe Cornell often found himself in the role of spokesperson, sharing his experience as a Black male in a predominantly white school and explaining to administrators why racism is hurtful. Joe Cornell recounted an event "involving students participating in Blackface at my school and sendin' Snapchats with racial slurs." After talking with the Dean of the school, "she cleared me to be the first person to be able to share [the incident] with educators at my school." In communicating about this event with the school staff, Joe Cornell shared that his goal was:

To not dilute how graphic all of it is and . . . the effect that it has on a Black student, especially, I'm the only Black male in my entire grade – one of maybe two or three in the whole entire high school. So, being able to share that, I feel like was an important moment, you know, for my educators or at least for myself to be able to let them know . . . how I feel . . . when I see something like that . . . . To be frank, the result of not callin' out specific things, like you let that sort of thing accumulate or you let those sort of behaviors go unchecked. And then . . . this is what happens and what type of effect is that gonna have on a Black student who has to continue to go to classes potentially with these sorts of students.

Obviously, for Joe Cornell, the Blackface incident was personally painful, and he used this incident as a teachable moment for the entire school staff, so that they could better understand how harmful these experiences of racism are and the implications of letting racist behavior go unchecked in the student body.

Others similarly felt a responsibility or obligation to speak up against racism, because there were so few other Black students or staff to do so. H.E.R. (age 13, she/her), a student at a public predominantly white high school, shared that she was "very shy" and typically would "probably want to stay quiet." Yet, because her school is "predominantly white . . ., I know they won't talk about it . . ., there's very few kids that will." By "it," H.E.R. was referring to racism and Black youth's experiences in the school. Despite her shyness, H.E.R. became an advocate for Black students to the school administration, saying: "I have to be one of those people that'd step up and be like, 'Okay guys, so something has to change because it's not a lot of Black teachers here. It's not a lot of Black activities that we can do as a group.'" Similarly, James, who attended a predominantly white private high school, felt like he "had to" step up to write statements about George Floyd's murder and the protests that followed, because "my school had not released any statements at that time" and statements from other classmates were "one-minded and one track." Thus, James felt an obligation to speak out, which led to him being "forced to take action and lead an initiative" as a leader of his BSU. His further actions were successful in holding the school administration accountable for change to make the school a more positive place for Black students:

I've had to release many statements for my . . . school just so that they can understand. And then in that same school, I've had to also kind of demand . . . it wasn't sent as a demand but it was a demand. We've kind of politely asked that they change the school, the headmaster change specific things . . .. The BSU leaders have . . . made lists about the things we've had to do. Things we want changed. And so we met with our headmaster . . ., and we kind of told him this list. And that's happening. So he's actively changing the way the school works, so that's good.

Some youth noted the significance of impactful discussions in educational settings about racism. Joe Cornell explained the importance of schools taking preventative measures through actively educating students about "diversity" and anti-racism and called for schools to take action to challenge anti-Black racism:

I wanna be proactive in dismantling it. You know, and I feel like schools should do the same in the way that they – you know, they shouldn't have a diversity conversation after Blackface incidents, you know, happen at their school. It should be somethin' that's, you know, actively taught . . . that's where the whole entire anti-racist conversation comes into play.

Some youth's efforts to hold their school administration accountable for addressing racism occurred in the aftermath of George Floyd's murder and the racial reckoning that followed. As we describe in Chapter 8, Black youth became even more activated in fighting for racial justice during this time. Yet,

Black youth were also fighting racism in schools well before May 2020. In holding school administrators accountable for how Black youth are treated, these young Black changemakers, in the words of Camille, are "creating a school environment where we feel like we are actually loved and cared for other than just meeting a diversity quota." The collective actions of these young Black changemakers were aimed at uprooting racism so that Black youth can thrive.

Raising Awareness of Black Culture and Experiences

Given that Black youth often feel disregarded and that few people understand their culture and experiences in non-Black school spaces, one way that Black youth resist this form of racism is by sharing their identity, culture, and experiences with classmates and administrators. Bree (age 15, she/her), who attended a large public school that was majority white (40%) and Latinx (35%), said, "I love being Black and I always tell people that." She described wearing her hair natural or in braids, "uplifting Black people … on social media," and wearing clothes like "Tupac jackets" that celebrate Blackness. Importantly, Bree had a clear purpose in wearing these styles to school, which was to get "other people's attention. It makes them wanna get involved in what you're involved in." By conveying her love of being Black to others, in part through her appearance, Bree sought to influence "my non-Black peers, even administrators to … see that I'm so engaged and focused, and I put my effort and time into Black things." She used this strategy to "get more attention and try to make other things we can do for the Black community." Scholars have described Bree's strategy as cultural resistance. For example, Dr. Leoandra Rogers and colleagues (2021) examined Black girls' narratives to show how Black hair can be part of their resistance strategy. When Black girls celebrate their Black identities, such as by wearing natural Black hairstyles, they directly challenge norms of whiteness and white standards of beauty. Rogers and colleagues stated, "The call is to accept and celebrate Black girls not because they fit society's mold but because they are accepting who they are, as they are. It is a powerful stance of resistance" (p. 14). Indeed, Black identity and changemaking are closely connected, as we further describe in Chapter 4.

Black youth in non-Black school spaces also engaged in cultural resistance by taking action to insert Black history and culture into the curriculum, where it was often absent. Ray (age 17, she/her), who attended a predominantly Latinx charter school, described how she and others collectively tried to raise awareness about Black history:

They do a little bit of stuff for like Black History Month, but if it's … the Hispanic month, they go all out …. So it was for Black History Month …, I was in Black

Student Union at my school, so I was like, "We have to do something big for Black History Month. This is our opportunity to do something big." So, for the whole week, we had Spirit Week of Black – we had a blackout day. We had, like you wear all black, and, the second day, it was culture day, and then the third day, it was '90s day, rep your favorite hip-hop artist.

Other youth took similar approaches to raising awareness about Black history and culture. KJ joined her BSU to organize "our first Black Student Union assembly." KJ and her peers wanted others to learn more about Black people's experiences and "the stuff that happens in the Black community." They invited members of the Divine Nine, the nickname for the nine historically African American fraternities and sororities of the National Pan-Hellenic Council. KJ shared that the assembly was "really good. And I feel like a lot of people were educated about stuff that happens" and began to reach out to her for "what they can do, how they can help." Through expressing Black identity and inserting Black history and culture into school events, Black youth are pushing back against the default context that does not acknowledge Blackness in positive ways and are trying to reshape students' and administrators' awareness about Black experiences.

ALLIES IN NON-BLACK SPACES

When resisting racism, Black youth benefit from the support of allies. There are different definitions for what it means to be an ally in racial justice work, and some prefer terms like accomplice or co-conspirator that convey a more active role of the supportive person in the struggle against oppression (Brown & Ostrove, 2013; Burns & Granz, 2022; Love, 2019). At a basic level, and in the context of anti-Black racism, an ally is a person who supports Black people in changemaking to resist racism and proactively works alongside others to challenge racism (Lamont, 2021). Young Black changemakers did not often use the terminology of allyship, yet their stories provide insight into how allies supported their changemaking, who served as allies, and when presumed allies were unhelpful or created obstacles to changemaking.

Black youth look for and sometimes find allies in school staff or administrators of color. Joe Cornell had two allies who supported him by validating his experiences of racism and the culture of whiteness. One was his adviser, about whom he recounted the following:

I feel very fortunate in the sense that, every year that I've been at school, I've had the same adviser, and he's a Black man. He's one of the few Black men on campus . . .. And I was telling him the things I was experiencing, and just sort of how I was feeling like I was making all these things up, and I didn't know how to pick apart the real from things I was being too sensitive about. And just hearing from him the words that "you are not crazy." That was a moment that gave me some sort of peace . . .. In a sense that, okay, if it's not me makin' it up . . . it's not a figment of my imagination . . . it's somethin' that's out there, and I can actively seek and, you know, work to dismantle. So, I would say that was an important moment for me, having him . . . as a resource.

Joe Cornell's adviser validated his feelings in confirming that the racism he experienced was real, not imagined, and helped him see a path to resistance through challenging racism at the school and district levels. Joe Cornell's other ally was the school Dean, who he described as a non-Black woman of color. He was grateful for the Dean because when he experienced racism, she was "right there to help me unpack it." Joe Cornell felt these meetings really helped him, and it was nice "not havin' to explain things as a concept that's foreign to her." Allies of color, like Joe Cornell's adviser and Dean, can play particularly powerful roles in validating Black youth's experiences of everyday racism because of their shared personal experiences with racism. With the Dean, however, Joe Cornell started to "feel like I'm, you know, becoming a bit of a burden when time after time, I'm coming to her office." But, as part of Joe Cornell's growth as a changemaker, he realized "I have to take up this space" and advocate for himself and other Black students. Even though his Dean was supportive, Joe Cornell still had to learn how to navigate the school power structures in order to utilize her as a resource.

Not all Black youth have Black school staff to support them in resisting everyday racism in schools. For example, Success with Lex shared, "I just feel like we need to get . . . more minorities in the school system – specifically African American counselors, African American teachers. More people that could relate to African Americans – because it was just really hard for me." Success with Lex's school demographics were not publicly available, but she had a difficult experience due to lack of representation of Black teachers and staff on her campus.

The presence of Black school staff alone does not mean that Black students will have supportive allies in resisting racism. In Camille and her peers' struggle to start a BSU at her high school, she shared that "one of those teachers – she does not want us to have one. She's a Black woman, but she doesn't want us to have one. And so, it's really hard to push for a BSU in a place where even some of the Black people don't support it." Although we know nothing else about the Black teacher at Camille's school or her experiences, one potential process at play is internalized racism, which is evident when a person of color accepts or upholds the racial hierarchy either consciously or subconsciously. Dr. Rita Kohli (2014, p. 372) explained how internalized racism comes about for teachers of color:

Building on the framework of internalized racism, being a person of color does not guarantee you immunity from seeing the world, or parts of the world, with a perspective that privileges white culture. Typically, many teachers of color themselves have been educated by an oppressive schooling system that promotes white cultural values, and oftentimes we are socialized to see non-white cultural knowledge as inferior to that of the dominant culture (Apple 1991; Clark & Flores 2001).

Also important is that Black school staff are navigating their own experiences of interpersonal and institutional racism, as well as more hidden forms of racism like tokenism and disregard. KJ, whose story opened this chapter, shared that the only Black male teacher, Mr. T, who had become the BSU adviser, himself experienced racism in the school context "all the time." When we asked KJ if things had gotten better with the racism in her school after establishing the BSU, she thought the climate had improved, but also reflected on the racial dynamics among the teachers, saying:

I would say yes, and especially talking with one of my history teachers [Mr. C]. My favorite history teacher in the world. And – well, we had a really, really, really long conversation about everything that happens . . ., he tells me about some of the stuff that he has heard. And he told me before – 'cause he is Caucasian – and he said, "It's sad to say, but when Mr. T brings up stuff that happens around campus or anything like that, the school – not necessarily dismisses him, but sort of dismisses him." And Mr. C was like, "Well, maybe I can use my skin color as something to be beneficial towards everybody." So, he speaks up about it. And it's sad that people listen to him – a white male – over Mr. T, a Black male, but he uses it for the betterment of the minority.

Based on KJ's story, Mr. C recognized and understood the racial oppression that Black students and his Black colleague Mr. T faced, and used his privilege to participate in the struggle, which according to Amélie Lamont (2021), is a key aspect of allyship. KJ found this form of allyship helpful to the cause *and* a disheartening reminder of the racial hierarchy in the school.

New-Black peers can also be allies to Black youth challenging racism in their schools. Tsehai gave a shout out to a senior who was "a really helpful white ally" and an active part of a committee to help meet the needs of students and parents of color at the school. O.A., who attended a predominantly white public high school, commented on an increase in peer support for racial justice in social media posts after George Floyd's murder in summer 2020:

I've been getting a lot of supporters that also agree with this because I've been seeing a lot of my friends . . . in my school that I didn't think would be . . . really open about this movement. But a lot of people from my school, especially non-Black people, are really talking about it every single day and really being open about it, just something that I really like about them, and it's gained my respect for them a lot.

Feeling this groundswell of support made O.A. feel that more people at school would "relate to her struggles" as a Black student.

Several young Black changemakers also described experiences with allies that presented challenges to their changemaking. Sara Vaughn (age 15, she/her), who attended a predominantly white private all-girls school, distinguished between an all-Black affinity space and her BSU, which is often "half and half – Black and non-Black." Sara Vaughn named several challenges to the multiracial BSU space. For example, while the non-Black students used the space to "process, you know, what it's like to discover police brutality, what it's like to become an activist," she had not been able to process what the moment meant to her as a Black person. Sara Vaughn felt that the BSU was not really a space for Black students, but rather "a space for other people to align themselves with Black students." These dynamics made "the conversations harder," and the conversations became "very much like, 'How do I become a better ally?... How do I learn more about the Black experience?'... that just makes it harder for me to, I guess, kinda figure out how I fit into that space." Thus, regardless of the good intentions behind the non-Black allies' participation in the BSU, they turned the conversations to their own learning and needs as allies, leaving Sara Vaughn to feel that her experiences were, once again, disregarded. Asking Black people to educate others about Black experiences places an additional burden on them. We next turn to the emotional labor that is inherent in young Black changemaking.

THE EMOTIONAL LABOR OF YOUNG BLACK CHANGEMAKERS IN NON-BLACK SPACES

> I feel like, just in general, as an individual, I've been overwhelmed a lot ....
> Toward the beginning of this ... of course before the burnout, it's like I really
> wanna be there, and I really wanna, you know, help out however I can ... it
> just was a really tough moment for me, especially when the protests started.
>
> Joe Cornell

For young Black changemakers, continual exposure to racism in non-Black spaces creates emotional burdens, and the constant nature of resisting racism can add to those burdens. The different emotional burdens that Black people and other people of color shoulder in non-Black spaces is often referred to as "emotional labor." Coined by Sociologist Arlie Hochschild (1983), the term emotional labor originally referred to a person constraining their emotions at work so that workplaces would be "suitable" and "professional." Scholars have adapted the concept of emotional labor to experiences of Black people, particularly Black women, in institutions of higher education. For example, Dr. Bridget Turner Kelly and colleagues (2021) offered a framework for understanding how and why Black female college students engage in emotional labor. They showed that Black students' emotional labor can take various forms, including suppressing emotions to acquiesce to a predominantly white environment and proactively engaging in emotional labor as resistance to racism. The young Black changemakers described experiencing both of these forms of emotional labor, as well as the burnout and need for healing that can result from these experiences.

One form of emotional labor is suppressing emotions. Black youth may avoid expressing themselves as a way to navigate non-Black spaces. Some of these experiences were already evident in earlier examples showing how Black youth experience non-Black spaces and feel unable to speak up and be fully themselves. Joe Cornell identified this feeling as "not wanting to rock the boat too much or cause too much disturbance." As he had explained to his counselor, he had the feeling that "maybe I was making these sorts of things up, and maybe I was being too sensitive," which led him to feel "like I had to push through" and "suppress a lot of the feelings and emotions I had about certain behaviors and certain things." As we described, the "certain behaviors and certain things" that Joe Cornell referenced here pertain to everyday racism. Suppressing emotions in the face of racism can impact Black youth in various ways. For Joe Cornell, he felt that his teachers only knew him as a student but not as "a human being but, also, a Black person existin' within this space." Similarly, as Dr. Fantasy Lozada and colleagues (2022, p. 13) stated in their review of Black youth's emotional development, "To feel and express one's emotions is a basic human experience" that is too often denied to Black students in classrooms and elsewhere.

The stifling of Black youth's emotions in schools can sometimes lead to withdrawing from school or community activities. Sa'Myah (age 18, she/her) noted that in general, "I'm such a social person," however, when it came to participating in a civic space where she was the only "dark skinned person," she stopped participating because "I don't like feeling like I can't talk or express myself." Nicole (age 18, she/her), who identified as Black and white, experienced racial discrimination in school in being "bullied by Hispanic children" for being "the white girl with cornrows." She described times when neither group accepted her, making it hard to engage. When non-Black spaces create a culture that limits the ability of Black youth to express their thoughts and feelings, Black youth get a message that Blackness is unwelcome and undesired. Some Black youth may withdraw from school or civic opportunities when they cannot bring their whole selves into these spaces (Gray et al., 2020).

Of course, as we have already shown, many Black youth do not disengage and instead actively resist racism in non-Black school spaces. Yet, resisting racism in non-Black spaces often means taking on the emotional labor of explaining racism and Black students' experiences to others. James noted that although he always saw himself as a leader, he felt "kind of thrown into new leadership positions" to represent Black students' experiences in response to George Floyd's murder and the racial reckoning of summer 2020. He was chosen "because I'm Black." As described earlier, James stepped up to write statements on behalf of the school, because the school-prepared statements regarding George Floyd's murder and their response were lacking. Although the efforts of James' student group were successful and the principal was "actively changing the way the school works," James felt exhausted because he "had put so much energy and time into, I wouldn't want to say force, but also forcing people to understand my opinions." As Tsehai explained, this process of sharing the Black experience with non-white peers and administrators can be exhausting:

> Some people don't want to educate themselves about what matters, you know, and stuff and so as a Black student, I have taken it upon myself to be . . . the person that, you know, advocates and stuff, which is, can be tiring. And . . . I don't want the . . . the rest of the Black community to be burdened with that because I know we all are, but it's . . . kind of how it is. So I want to promote a community so that they can be together in it and you know, like, share the weight of it.

Tsehai's comments also illustrate that when Black youth create safe spaces and build community with other Black students, the weight of emotional burdens can be shared with others.

As the stories of Tsehai, James, and others show, Black students are sometimes expected to educate their non-Black peers of the realities of racism. When Black youth educate their peers, real change can happen (Quimby et al., 2018). Joe Cornell noted that he has "white counterparts and white educators who are well meaning. But what they're bringing to the conversation is an understandin' of Blackness as a concept and not as a lived experience." The Black experience is humanized when Black youth share their lived experiences with others. Although many youth are encouraged by adults to engage in civic activities, Black youth often take civic action out of necessity to create safe spaces for other Black people, combat racial injustice, reduce burden while promoting equity and inclusion of Black people, and address social issues that are relevant to the Black experience. At the same time, in asking Black youth to become racial justice facilitators in schools, we cannot lose sight of what a heavy responsibility is being placed on their shoulders. Black youth's racial justice activism may be more emotionally taxing than when these actions are taken by non-Black peers (Gorski & Erakat, 2019; Jones & Reddick, 2017). As journalist and writer B. L. Wilson (2020) explained, "Asking Black people in the United States to discuss race is asking them to relive every moment of pain, fear and outrage they have experienced."

Like Tsehai and James, Joe Cornell felt the burdens of his emotional labor in continually resisting oppression. He named feeling "overwhelmed" and that "I can't handle it," experiencing "burnout" and feeling "worn out" from the constant need for actions to resist racism, which he called "a 24-hour situation for me." Yet, despite experiencing these burdens, Joe Cornell also illustrates how Black youth resist racism to fight for their own wellness and healing. When white teens zoom-bombed a dialogue about racial justice that Joe Cornell helped organize, Joe Cornell realized how proactively challenging racism supports his health. He shared:

> So that was sort of an epiphany moment for me in a sense that Black people, organizers in general I feel like, so often we play defense in a sense that just everything that we do is as a reaction to white supremacy or acts of bigotry. And I realized that

really influenced the way that I wanna move forward in this work. And I don't wanna play defense. I don't wanna wait for something' to happen to me or some sort of damage to be inflicted to me or my, you know, psychological-emotional mental health, you know, before I do something or say something.

As a Black person, I can't afford to have my mental health . . . just completely deteriorated, because I've been constantly waiting for, you know, something to . . . happen to me, you know, before I do something . . . figure out some sort of a recourse.

"I can't afford to have my mental health just completely deteriorated" is a powerful statement. It applies to Black youth organizers who fight against racial justice for their own and their community's well-being and it applies to Black youth in non-Black spaces who have to deal with everyday racism (Turner et al., 2022). Joe Cornell's recourse was to be proactive in dismantling racism through anti-racist actions to protect his own mental health. Joe Cornell's story also exemplifies how Black youth can promote their own wellness through finding solidarity with others who are advocating for racial justice. He attended a conference for other private school students from historically marginalized backgrounds that focused on racial justice organizing. He came back and felt "refreshed and . . . had a fresh mind in terms of . . . the work that needed to be done and, you know, just having that motivation . . . to continue to be a part of that change, you know, 'cause burnout is real." Black youth doing racial justice work engage in emotional labor, which can aid in developing emotional maturity but can also be exhausting (Fernández & Watts, 2022). Learning how and when to lean in and pull back is a part of the emotional dynamics of young Black changemakers who experience everyday racism in non-Black spaces.

THE TAKE-AWAYS

Black youth who attend school in non-Black spaces do not always feel welcomed or comfortable, and they regularly experience everyday racism that is interpersonal and institutional. Young Black changemakers use multiple strategies to resist racism, or in the words of Joe Cornell, "to persevere, to continue on, to feel like I have a place within the school to feel motivated." Resistance involved creating safe spaces in schools they could claim as their own, holding administrators accountable, and raising awareness of Black culture and experiences. Black youth noted the importance of authentic allies in non-Black spaces, and also shared the burdens that arise from the emotional labor of being in non-Black spaces and engaging in racial justice work.

Contributions to Research

These stories convey the power of all-Black spaces – whether a BSU or other Black affinity group – for creating safe havens free from racism, where Black youth can be themselves and find solidarity for resistance with other Black students. Scholars have mostly focused on the value of BSUs on college campuses (Lane, 2022; Thelamour et al., 2019). The voices of young Black changemakers underscore the value of BSUs in high schools. This finding aligns with the reflections of BSU members of Round Rock High School and their teacher Tiffanie Harrison, whose writing emphasized the sanctity of these Black spaces and their necessity for Black students' well-being (Harrison et al., 2020). More research should investigate the power of these Black school spaces and the multiple purposes that they serve in the lives of Black youth, from emotional safety to identity development, community building, and organizing for resistance.

These findings also illustrated how whiteness and anti-Black racism operate in non-Black school spaces, which ranged from everyday interpersonal racism to systemic racism. Sometimes scholars who study racism have difficulty pinpointing the effects of systemic racism in research (Greer & Cavalhieri, 2019; Williams, 2018), yet these Black youth vividly described experiences of school-level institutional racism and how institutional racism exacerbated the harms of interpersonal racism. Future research should continue to examine systemic racism and white supremacy culture in schools to better identify the often hidden or nuanced ways that whiteness operates – particularly in "liberal" spaces – such as through superficial use of diversity or multiculturalism that can lead to evaded racism, tokenism, and other forms of racism that de-emphasize or disregard Black students' needs (Assari & Caldwell, 2018; Kohli et al., 2017; Leath et al., 2019). Documenting these manifestations of racism and their pernicious effects on Black students, as well as other students of color, is an important step toward understanding how to dismantle racism in schools.

This study highlights the emotional labor inherent in resisting racism in schools. Youth's stories showed just how much daily resistance work young Black changemakers do in non-Black spaces to be seen, heard, and valued. These forms of resistance take considerable emotional resources that can leave some Black youth feeling overwhelmed and exhausted. The emotional labor of young Black changemaking should be more thoroughly recognized and documented in research (Linder et al., 2019; Maker Castro et al., 2022).

A caveat worth noting is that Black youth we interviewed focused on resistance as changemaking, but changemaking is not the way youth resist racism in schools. For example, Black youth in our study did not describe behaviors such as noncompliance with authority, which are resistance strategies often subject to overly harsh school discipline when enacted by Black youth (Sevon, 2022). Future research would benefit from using a resistance lens in understanding Black youth's varied school behaviors, rather than using the current default deficit-based framings (Wray-Lake et al., 2022).

Practical Insights

First and foremost, it is time for schools to take more responsibility, ownership, and accountability for anti-Black racism. Accountability requires educators to do the deep, difficult, personal work to root out white supremacy logics and behaviors, and also requires reexamining school policies and practices that create harm to Black students. To support this difficult work, we recommend Drs. Tehama Lopez Bunyasi and Candis Watts Smith's book *Stay Woke: A people's guide to making all Black lives matter* (2019) as a practical guide for educators and others engaging in anti-racist work. Anti-racist teaching practices in the classroom and restorative justice practices (Lodi et al., 2021; Schiff, 2018; Vincent et al., 2021) can be effective tools for reducing racism among students. After hearing these young Black changemakers' stories, we hope readers are convinced of the urgent need to eliminate racism from schools.

Yet, importantly, there are no quick fixes to this perpetual problem, and schools that aim to be anti-racist must engage in a continual, unending process toward that goal and face obstacles along the way. In a disturbing turn of events, since we began this project in 2020, many politically conservative states and school districts have banned books about racism and restricted teaching about racism in classrooms. As of this writing, 42 states have introduced legislation and 17 states have imposed bans or restrictions on teaching about racism and sexism in schools (Schwartz, 2022), with 84 other bills pending (Johnson et al., 2022). It is more important than ever to call for more teaching about racism and more confronting of whiteness in classrooms. Yet, as climates in some regions of the United States make this increasingly harder to do, schools face real challenges in how to engage in this work and support Black students. Our research cannot resolve or eliminate these obstacles to anti-racist practices in schools, yet hearing Black youth's voices speaks to the moral imperative of stopping the harm they face from racism in school settings. Stopping this harm necessarily requires educating people about racism.

Black youth need supportive allies in schools. Young Black changemakers spoke to the importance of having Black teachers and administrators on their school campuses. Black representation among the school staff is an essential investment for schools to make, because when Black students see people like them represented at the school, they feel a stronger sense of belonging and have people to turn to when experiencing racism in schools who are more likely to understand what they are feeling. Of course, schools need to recognize the additional emotional labor required of Black faculty and staff on school campuses. Black youth also need allies from any and all racial and ethnic backgrounds and ages who are willing to join this fight. As youth shared, not all allies are equally helpful, and Black youth need authentic allies who will shoulder some of the burdens of resisting racism in these non-Black school spaces. Black youth may also draw support from their families (as we describe in Chapter 6) and from civic organizations (as we describe in Chapter 7) that strengthen their resolve and efforts to resist racism in schools.

At a minimum, schools should have no barriers to allowing Black youth to have their own spaces to be themselves and find solace with other Black students. BSUs should be allowed in every school setting, and Black students should get to decide how these groups operate. The opposition that Camille and other Black youth faced in creating BSUs, however, underscores that allowing Black youth their own space in non-Black schools is not obvious to everyone. Black students' wellness should be a priority. Schools must take rapid steps to allow, protect, and invest in Black student spaces on campuses everywhere.

We should all better appreciate the remarkable power of Black youth to withstand and fight against the racial oppression they face in schools. The successes of these young Black changemakers in raising awareness of racism, creating safe spaces for their Black peers, and calling out the racism of their school administrators are incredibly inspiring. Black youth often engage in this resistance out of necessity to protect their community and to ensure generations of Black folks who follow them do not experience the same battles and harms. They are working hard to reclaim their humanity in school settings where being fully human should be a basic right and undeniable experience. Readers of any age, race, or profession can acknowledge the strengths of Black youth, recognize their full humanity, and follow these youth's leads to support Black youth's safety and fight to challenge racist systems.

Up Next

This chapter described how Black youth experience and resist racism in non-Black schools. According to sociopolitical development theory, experiences of racism and other forms of oppression initiate the process of sociopolitical development for Black youth (Watts et al., 2003). Scholars of sociopolitical development now recognize that identity development and changemaking are intertwined for Black youth, and both are shaped by experiences of racism (Mathews et al., 2020; Watts & Halkovic, 2022). As being Black is obviously central to being a young Black changemaker, Chapter 4 explores how changemaking and Black identity development are related for these young Black changemakers.

Melanin by Zoie Brogdon

Is it scary?
To me, the dark is beauty and acceptance.
To the world
Simply put, it's terrifying.

Why am I a threat?
Is it because my skin, my grace, my culture holds more power
Than the whip you crack over our backs as you tell us to build you the world?

Why are you kneeling on our necks?
Is it because you are afraid that if we breathe our toxic words
Will infect your soul and show you the truth?

I can't breathe.

My throat is closing, my body is limp, and I cry out for help
But you don't care.
All because my skin is the same color as the thing you were afraid of as a child.

The dark.

4

Identity and Changemaking

ELAN C. HOPE, CHANNING J. MATHEWS, &
LAURA WRAY-LAKE

For myself, and for my peers that are Black youth who are really civically engaged, it's just much more personal than it is for other people . . . . It's much more personal and it's deeper in a way.

Sara Vaughn

Black identity and changemaking are interwoven in the lives of young Black changemakers. Sara Vaughn (she/her), a 15-year-old Black girl who was a community volunteer and organizer, described the connection between identity and changemaking in her story of engagement. Identifying herself as Black with strong Cajun roots, Sara Vaughn was deeply involved in working alongside other Black people for positive social change. Being Black was integral to her changemaking; as she put it, "I just think [my Blackness] makes everything that I'm doing all that more important." For Black young people in the US, racial identity is a core part of growing up and figuring out who you are in the world. Racial identity is defined as the meaning and importance Black youth ascribe to being Black and the process by which Black youth find and create this meaning (Cross et al., 1991; Sellers et al., 1998). Healthy Black racial identity development includes feeling pride in being Black and being connected to Black communities (Butler-Barnes et al., 2012; Neblett et al., 2012; Pinckney IV et al., 2011). For youth in our study, being Black was overwhelmingly important for their changemaking, and being proud of being Black was one step more important than that. As Unique (she/her), a 17-year-old girl who was highly engaged in many forms of changemaking told us, "Being Black is lucky. But being unapologetically Black is a gift."

Racial identity for these young Black changemakers is more than feelings of pride. Black identity is also a collective experience. Changemaking is a bridge from individual identity to collective care in Black communities. Such collective care leads to forming collective identity, in which Black youth understand themselves not just as individuals, but in relation to a larger community with a shared history, struggle, and goals for liberation. Sara

Vaughn described how changemaking acts as a bridge between her personal and collective Black identity, saying, "There's more that I have to do, because I'm Black. Not have to do. It's more that I have to be able to do. And there's a community there. And I always have a community to come back [to]." We asked Sara Vaughn to talk more about her sense of duty to the liberation of Black people and Black communities, and she went on to say:

Well I think there's something historic there ... we've been fighting a long time. You know, you can't let that ball drop now. And we're still not there. And you know ... I don't know! ... I think there's a sense of community that I can feel that's with people that I've never met. And that way we're all fighting for the same thing. And we've been doing this for a long time, but we're going to keep doing it.

Sara Vaughn's sense of collective identity with other Black people, even those she had never met, stemmed in part from Black people's history of fighting racial justice. This collective identity also fueled her actions to challenge racial injustice and influenced her sense of duty to act given her personal identity as a Black young person.

Other aspects of Black youth's identities also shape their changemaking, particularly when they experience oppression related to these identities. Sara Vaughn talked about being a young Black person and a young Black queer girl:

Speaking in terms of my identity ... there's so many communities that I belong to. And as a woman or a girl, and LGBTQ, and Black ..., there's so much that needs to be changed. And yet, in the middle of that, being Black is probably the most influential part of my identity.

For Sara Vaughn and other young Black changemakers, experiences with oppression due to gender, sexuality, and class identities often strengthened, and sometimes complicated, the connections between identity and change-making. Sara Vaughn's experiences with gender strengthened her resolve to make changes that supported Black communities. She said:

Even with the attention around the murders of Black men, about how much less attention is coming to Black women ... I just been thinking a lot about how different pieces of my identity affect how people see me, you know, and how that affects how I conduct myself, I guess. But I don't think that that's changed my engagement. I think it just makes the work I do, for Black women's health in places where there is that intersection, more important to me.

Sara Vaughn's story is similar to the stories of other young Black change-makers. Her identity as a young Black queer girl and her connection to Black communities and the legacy of social justice action helped to sustain her changemaking.

This chapter explores the connections between Black identity and chan-gemaking. We share how Black youth discover, reconcile, and reimagine their identities in the contexts of the racism they experience and their community and historical legacy of social change. Changemaking can result from racial pride and care, and constitutes resistance against structural racism and oppressive institutions that stifle Black joy, creativity, and freedom. The relationship between identity and changemaking for Black youth also works in the reverse; changemaking can further develop Black young people's pride and joy in being Black. Identity and changemaking are tied together through historical legacy, active participation with a community collective, and envisioning a Black liberatory future.

PROUD TO BE BLACK AND PROUD TO MAKE CHANGE

For Black young people, it is generally a good thing to be proud of being Black. Racial identity is an integral part of human development, especially during adolescence (DeCuir-Gunby, 2009; Rivas-Drake et al., 2014). According to Robert Sellers and colleagues' (1998) Multidimensional Model of Racial Identity, racial identity includes how important race is to you, how you feel about being a member of your racial group, and how you think other people view your racial group. For Black youth, feeling a sense of belonging to their racial group supports many aspects of positive development from academic achievement to mental health and even civic engagement (Hope, Gugwor et al., 2019; Leath et al., 2019; Rivas-Drake et al., 2014; Seaton et al., 2006). The young Black changemakers in our study were proud of being Black, and their positive Black identity propelled their changemaking efforts. Zia (she/her), a 14-year-old biracial Filipina and Black girl described it plainly. She said, "Just being a part of the community . . . is what motivates me." She went on to say, "I'd say that I'm proud to be Black, and . . . it shouldn't be a problem with anybody else." Zia was proud to be Black and felt connected to her Black community; those parts of her racial identity motivated her to engage in changemaking to pursue racial justice through volunteering, helping others, speaking out against injustice, and protesting.

The connection between being proud of being Black and being a changemaker was shared by other young people as well. Harvey (age 18, she/her) shared a story about attending a Black Lives Matter protest with her cousin and then described what connected her to that experience. Harvey stated, "It [protesting for Black Lives Matter] connects to me because I know that I'm a Black person . . . I know that that's not just for other people. It's for me too. So you know, I just feel appreciative of something like that." Being a part of the Black community motivated Harvey's pursuit of racial justice, and as a Black young woman, she had a personal stake in the outcomes of the change she was a part of making. Civic engagement is not just for others; civic engagement matters for young Black changemakers personally as their identity is rooted in the communities they work with and fight for. Similarly, Unique told us, "Well for me . . . being Black and being civically engaged . . . it really comes from a place of passion for me like everything I do." For Unique, her racial identity – being Black – was central to her sense of self and to her changemaking.

Changemaking also reinforced positive feelings about being Black. For Quinn (age 16, she/her), collective gatherings to protest against racial injustices made her feel proud to be Black. She said:

> [Changemaking] made me feel more proud to be Black. Just like no matter what's going on. We're still gonna make it into something joyful . . .. The meetings always end in a joyful prayer type mode. You know they'll have somebody come in and sing something about what you're talking about, or at home or somebody will play music. Even at the protest. They had people singing, doing dances and stuff. It's always just, you know, some type of enjoyment no matter how sad or serious something is.

The way these young Black changemakers described the connection between Black racial identity and changemaking fits with previous research. The two develop in tandem as young people gain life experience during adolescence and the transition to adulthood. In a study of youth activism, Black identity – particularly beliefs about the importance and unique experiences of being Black – was associated with intentions to participate in future racial justice activism (Hope et al., 2019). In another study of Black college students, activism during the transition to college prompted youth's continued exploration of their racial identity (Mathews et al., 2022). Racial identity and changemaking are closely connected; though this link may shift over time, identity and civic actions catalyze one another in the lives of Black youth.

CHANGEMAKING WITHIN AND BEYOND BLACKNESS

For some young Black changemakers, their racial identity and changemaking were nuanced by other identities they held. Intersectionality is a concept first named by legal and critical Black studies scholar Kimberlé Crenshaw (1991), who argued that Black women have unique experiences of structural oppression due to being both Black and women. Likewise, young people have different experiences with oppression and privilege that are related to their multiple, overlapping identities, and these experiences shape their civic actions (Godfrey & Burson, 2018; Santos, 2020). In our study, some changemakers described how gender and social class intertwined with their Black identity to influence their changemaking.

Blackness across Gendered Experiences

Some girls described experiences at the nexus of race and gender. These girls did not just talk about themselves as Black, but named themselves as Black girls or females. These identities do not exist separately; they are intertwined into Black girls' lived experiences. They often remarked about their pride in being Black women, but named the struggle to be seen and heard and affirmed in public spaces, social media, and in their civic engagement. Unique described her pride in being a Black woman and how she drew influence from other powerful Black women in her life:

I was just writing an essay the other day ... I said something like, I look at the Black women every day that surround me, and I be like, "Dang, I wish I could be one of them," but then I be forgetting that I am one of them.

While highlighting her pride in Black women, Unique also named the gendered challenges Black women face through her observations and identification with Angela Rye, an attorney and public advocate for social justice:

I really, really admire Angela Rye ... I feel like that's me in a nutshell. She is so blunt ... I'll watch everything she do ... she will tell you how she feel no matter – she's still gonna be herself .... And I feel like if that was me in a political setting, I would do the same thing. 'Cause it was one of these interviews she did, and ... I'm not sure if the man tried to ... cut her off or somethin', but she did something, and she put them in check .... And she continued politely ... with her message, and she was through. I feel like that's me. I would do something like that .... In the setting she is in, it's a majority white people and ... they kind of test her to see if they gon' ... bring that Angela out of her. And I feel like that's kind of me too. People try to test me, my intelligence and, just overall, my whole character to see if I'm gon' act up. So – cause I know a lot of people watching. I think they trying to test her to see if she gonna act up 'cause they know that a lot of people watching, and they gon' already automatically point the finger at the Black woman and be like, "She's mad. She's this. She's that." I feel like ... that's me. That's gon' be me.

In describing her admiration of Angela Rye, Unique also named the challenges that she and Angela share as Black women who are baited and goaded in public forums for being Black and a woman. Black girls and women are constantly subjected to having their intelligence questioned and their opinions minimized or silenced, particularly in white spaces and by white antagonists. Aligned with the experiences of Black youth in non-Black school spaces described in Chapter 3, Bree (age 15, she/her) attended a predominantly white and Hispanic/Latinx public high school (8% Black). She shared experiences of being ignored or invisible due to her race and gender and how such invisibility shaped her future behaviors:

I feel like males at my school, whether they're Black, doesn't really matter their race. I feel like they get more attention or, whether it's anything, like with sports or just – I don't even know. Random information. I feel like they get more attention or the word out more than females. So I feel like I have to work twice as hard not only because of my race but because I am a female and because we're not recognized or thought of first when it comes to information, so yeah.

This struggle for visibility and credibility often reinforces the efforts of Black girls to engage in changemaking to give back to Black communities and champion the causes of Black women. Through changemaking, Black girls and women disrupt narratives of Black women as threats, highlighting their power to manifest meaningful change. Further, Black girls demand space for their voices to be heard. For example, Camille (age 15, she/her) highlighted:

If you kind of just look at everything that's going on right now with the Black Lives Matter Movement on social media. A lot I see that, even amongst the Black community, people just don't take Black women serious … even with Breonna Taylor's case and a lot of other women who have been who've been killed in police brutality, they're just not taken seriously and not only by law enforcement and government but also just by people within our community. Because a lot of our experiences as Black women are invalidated by people just because they don't understand. So they just assume that we're lying or that it doesn't happen or that we're exaggerating. Because we face issues as women and then issues as Black people but then we also face issues that are unique to just specifically Black women. So I just feel like, as someone who knows what it's like to not have their voice heard, especially by members of their own community, I want to create a space or just a world for everybody to have their voice heard.

As Sara Vaughn discussed earlier, the lack of attention to issues affecting Black women made her work around Black women's health ***more*** important to her. Mea (age 16, she/her) also named the significance of Black women's voice and equality:

I think being a woman, a Black woman, is also very important. And then there's also that thing about sexism …. Being a Black woman, that also really sticks out to me, because women also should be able to have a voice too …. I feel like yeah, it definitely does, being a woman, that just triggers it more for me and it makes me feel like I also need to be participating. Because sometimes women might not get the same treatment as a man would and I feel like that's also really important to fight for.

Black girls' understanding of Black women's identity and changemaking was also generational, as these girls looked to their mothers, grandmothers, and aunts as role models. This connection is described in greater detail in Chapter 6. Success with Lex described it as follows:

Definitely my grandmother and my auntie. Just seeing them being civically engaged all the time, whether we're just going to the grocery store and seeing someone in need and give them money or food; whether we're participating in a big food bake event, they're just actively, civically engaged. And they're both strong Black women, so, yes, seeing that has really been significant for me … really they're just like, "You have to continue to stay strong and fight for what you want, and really just uphold the people that look like you around you." You gotta try to get what you want. And if someone's not supporting of it, move on and go find someone else that's supporting of it.

Historian Martha Lott (2017) described how previous social movements, such as the Civil Rights Movement, often did not center Black women's voices, beyond the invisible labor they engaged in to support the men of the movement. Black girls in our study are demanding visibility by emphasizing their perspectives as equally important as those of Black men. In continuing to lift their voices around women's issues and racial justice issues, Black girls push back against the legacy of invisibility experienced by Black women role models and draw strength from their examples of civic engagement. In doing so, they center the ways their identities as Black and women inform their participation in Black movements, naming how racism and sexism have impacted them.

Blackness across Geography and Social Class

Black identity also intersects with class and gentrification to shape change-making. Through both their educational and neighborhood experiences, several youth observed the divestment in majority Black communities and described their determination not to abandon the majority Black places that shaped them. In doing so, they challenged deficit narratives of Black existence and made space for Black futures.

Unique spoke to how the divestment in Black communities shows up in education, particularly through the pervasive stereotypes of Black people not caring about school:

Schools like mine that have majority color youth that are low income, achieve the economic gap, you could say so. It's like, we speak out on issues like that. And I'm really involved in that one. Because . . . I have so much passion for my school. I go to Crenshaw High School so a lot of people always try to judge us, be like "Oh, that's school's ghetto that school's this. Y'all don't go there, y'all just go there for the fights. . . ." They try to call us a fashion school. They try to call us a fashion show even though that's kind of true – those kids, they care about how they dress, but . . . that don't mean that we're not serious about our education.

The pride Unique felt about her school community is a direct challenge to negative stereotypes about Black intellectual worth that are embedded in political systems that impact Black educational investment. In these negative stereotypes, racist and classist narratives are intertwined. Unique further explained the racist and classist dynamic at play in school board decisions:

George McKenna, he's the person [school board member] for our district or whatever. Like he'll visit our school once a year and just say, "Oh, yeah, y'all don't need the money 'cause I don't think y'all know what to do with it." I'm like, sir . . . I go to the school every day. And . . . you can't really say what we need or what we don't need because you're not here experiencing what we experience every day.

As demonstrated by our young Black changemakers' experiences and aligned with our discussion in Chapter 2 of youth's civic purpose to redistribute resources for racial justice, youth take civic action to challenge disinvestment in Black educational spaces by exposing how those in power do not value or consider the needs of low-income Black communities. This type of changemaking addresses oppression that comes from both racism and classism.

Divestment in Black spaces is a personal and local issue, as Black youth value their neighborhoods and have seen their elders fight to stay rooted in their communities. Destiny described the generational fight for the Crenshaw community:

It was personal because I'm a Black person in America – Black woman in America, first off. Second off, I grew up in the area I protested in. And back in the day, when my mom was a kid, they were still protesting in that same area for different causes . . .. It was personal because, it's a family thing that everybody . . . from my grandma to now, everybody has to protest about something, and I wanna be a part of that.

Like Destiny, Black youth are fighting for their community because their investment in their community is personal and intergenerational; they are a part of a legacy of people who have fought to keep the community alive and thriving. These young Black changemakers see the threat of gentrification for their communities and a lack of resource investment in their schools, and they push back through changemaking. Their actions challenge deficit notions of Black people and also keep them connected to the communities they love. By negotiating the politics of place, Black youth understand their identities as critically connected to the spaces that they and generations of their families occupy, as Destiny highlighted:

Especially Crenshaw neighborhood, I see those in movies from back in the day . . . seeing how it used to be and how it is now and just seeing the – how do I explain it? Seeing our places, Black places being taken over by other races . . . is a part of my civic engagement too. Seeing people that are getting pushed outta their own communities and other races coming in and living there have been a big part of my civic engagement because we're fighting for that too. We fought for the Crenshaw Mall to stay our Crenshaw Mall. It's not getting taken over by a whole different race and change it to a whole different thing . . .. The places that some of our parents or grandparents grew up in LA is getting gentrified by other races. That's not ours anymore. Or things that once used to be ours, people are taking . . . How I say it? A lotta kids . . .. They wanna be Black when it's convenient, but they don't wanna be Black when stuff is happening.

Destiny's changemaking is motivated by both race and place, which is an experience shared by young Black changemakers who show pride in their community and its Black heritage. Youth are determined not to abandon the spaces that shaped them and are committed to preserving these Black-centered spaces. As we highlighted in Chapter 2, Black youth are bettering themselves educationally to return to infuse their gifts back into the community, modeling for others to do the same. Simultaneously, there is some tension between wanting to stay and engage in their home communities versus exploring opportunities beyond their neighborhood context, as Sara Vaughn described:

That's actually something that we've been debating a bit in my family. Like how much duty do we have to our community? And to our people? I don't know if you saw this, like a reference but there's this Blackish episode . . . they're raised in Sherman Oaks or something. And the grandpa was like, "You can't be afraid of your people." And my family has talked a lot about that. And, we're like, you know, we're one iteration out of poverty and both my parents went to law school and my mom has a doctorate degree. And both of my parents chose to come back to their communities. And I feel pretty torn in a way because . . . I feel drawn to like traveling and exploring the world. How much duty do I have to come back?

Like Sara Vaughn, some Black youth experienced tension between the success of "making it" out of the community and caring for a community that shaped them. The geographic spaces that these youth fight to change for the better are communities they intimately know. Youth like Destiny and Amir reject uninformed stereotypes of their communities. Amir (age 13, he/him) stated:

Compton isn't like what they make it seem in the movies and the news. They make it seem like this hood area in Bloods and Crips and gang activity. It's not really like that you don't really see gang activity at all. And if you do, they're just driving past on their ATVs [all-terrain vehicles] and I've never heard any gunshots before. And that's just, they make Compton seem like it's one of the worst areas in the world . . . . Everyone knows each other and if someone's gone, we will notice and the neighbors will notice. And so it's just one big community . . . it's basically like we're one big family.

As Amir highlighted, community is not defined through the deficit lens of the media, but through the lived experiences of those who are rooted in the community. Changemaking in these communities resists the negative narratives that dominate the cultural milieu and continues the intergenerational legacy of Black-centered spaces. In doing so, young Black changemakers demand that the world see the vibrance of Black communities as they create meaningful change within and beyond their local contexts.

FROM RACISM TO RACIAL JUSTICE

For almost all of the young Black changemakers in our study, changemaking resulted from personal experiences of being Black and firsthand exposure to racism. As youth's stories in Chapter 3 vividly highlighted, changemaking is a form of resistance against racism (Tuck & Yang, 2014) and a way to cope with racism (Hope & Spencer, 2017). We build on youth's stories of experiencing and resisting racism in non-Black school spaces by elaborating on how Black identity – via love, pride, and connection to Black communities – enables Black youth to respond to racism with changemaking.

The Power of Personal Narrative

When asked why Black youth become civically engaged, Success with Lex (age 18, she/her) responded "probably just from personal experience." She described how Black youth experience structural racism via incarceration and fatherlessness, concluding that experiencing these forms of structural racism "really motivates them [Black youth] and influences them to keep going because they know what it's like firsthand." Other young Black changemakers also articulated the power of this personal experience in advocating for change. For example, Quinn invoked the importance of personal narrative in changemaking, conveying that people cannot deny the problems that Black youth face, because young Black people are witnessing and sharing their experiences firsthand. Quinn shared:

Oh [being Black] definitely matters, cause it's like, I'm showing my point of view, you know, of a Black kid in this community. How we're affected, you know. That's one of our main arguments when we go up against somebody that, you know, that's in our way, that we're trying to, you know, change things . . ... We have firsthand experience. So you can't say it's not happening because we're right in your face.

Quinn articulated what critical race theorists Daniel Solórzano and Tara Yosso (2002) described as counter-storytelling – using narratives to challenge the dominant perspective on race. The dominant narrative tries to render racism as obsolete and, by extension, changemaking for racial justice as unnecessary. Counter-storytelling is a collective practice that facilitates identity development and exploration *and* can challenge injustice (Pender et al., 2022). In this tradition, Quinn emphasized that people cannot deny the problems that Black youth face, because young Black people are bearing witness to their and others' experiences that counter a dominant narrative. Harvey talked about the connection between experiencing racism and changemaking in a similar way and said, "Certain situations that other races don't go through, we do, like minor situations just because we're us. There's minor situations in everything that shouldn't be, but you know, they still are because of our race." She went on to say, "I think that when people hear from the person that it's actually happening to, it kind of makes them – I wouldn't say feel empathetic – but I feel like it gives us some sympathy but also knowledge on what's happening and how they can change it." Here Harvey spoke to the power that sharing experiences of oppression can have for the listener (in gaining valuable knowledge) and the storyteller (in helping to create change).

Mia (age 16, she/her) had a similar perspective about the power of personal experiences to effectively create positive changes for Black communities, such as ending policing in schools, saying:

I think Black youth have a lot to speak about when it comes to experience about not having access or knowing what it's like to be shut out for a fact they can't control . . .. I go to a primarily minority school. So what I mean by that is mostly Black and Hispanic students. I see a lot of really civically engaged students at my school being able to speak from personal experience, about the causes they advocate for, and I feel like it's Black youth – especially given the historical circumstances that have influenced so many of our lives and our families' lives – we have lots to speak of when it comes to whatever organization or cause we are passionate about. So I feel like as a Black youth, for example, who is advocating for the ending of police in schools . . ., a lot of Black youth are able to speak from personal experience of being policed in their schools, from a very young age for doing something that a white or other race peer . . . has not been policed for. So I feel like a lot of the personal and ancestral . . . experience that Black youth have been exposed to and accustomed to, is what really makes our civic engagement unique.

Young Black changemakers described how their identity – *who* they are – is directly connected to personal experiences of anti-Black racism. Instances of racism that are unique to Black experiences guide the types of change Black youth seek to make in their communities and beyond. They share their stories because being Black is important to them, Black people are important to them, and they want others to understand the gravity of racism and be motivated to join them in changemaking.

Nearly every young Black changemaker mentioned the influence of racism on their changemaking journey, although they differed in the types of changemaking they focused on, their own racial background, and the racial demographics of their neighborhoods and schools. Tsehai, a 14-year-old girl, who described herself as an Ethiopian adoptee raised by white parents, talked about the importance of the history of racism in the United States. She shared:

That sort of trauma, the trauma of being enslaved, is a part of being a Black person in America now. And I don't personally relate to the history . . . I came over from Africa. So it's a kind of bizarre dichotomy because it's not like I personally relate to having enslaved ancestors, but I do understand.

Even though her own ancestral lineage does not include victims of the transatlantic slave trade in the United States, that history of racism still resonated with Tsehai as an important reason for changemaking. While the history of anti-Black racism in the US is not a part of her personal narrative, this history contributes to how she experienced being Black and came to understand her own identity in relation to changemaking. She went on to say:

I face the lasting effects as a Black person, you know, and that massive shared history, I think has [an] immense effect on the people you are and the people you become, and how you relate to people . . . . And I think that's what is really important to being civically engaged, giving back to your community. How you relate to your community affects how you deal with your community and how you want to help in your community.

Similarly, Damian (age 18, he/him) who identified as both African American and Hispanic described how his grandmother's experiences with racism influenced his changemaking. He said:

Not only Black people, but Hispanic people, they also get racially profiled just for being Hispanic . . . . I find it unfair for my grandmother to go through the things that she goes through. Just because she doesn't have papers, she can't really get a job anywhere. Because she doesn't have papers. And she has a daughter too that she has to take care of and I just, I don't think it's fair. I want to change that, somehow.

Experiences of anti-Black racism drive the civic engagement of young Black changemakers. These young Black people described a sense of responsibility in being uniquely positioned to respond to racism through changemaking because of their Black identity. Being Black is an important part of their identity, and their connection to Black communities strengthened their resolve to be changemakers. These changemakers have a unique vantage point for social change because they live the reality of racism and experience the consequences of racial oppression. As Tom (age 17, he/him) described it:

... being Black, it's just we get to experience this stuff, you know, firsthand. So, if anybody is gonna enlighten anybody, you know, it's gonna be us 'cause nobody's gonna fight for us, you know. We gotta be the ones to, you know, spark the change. People can join us, but, you know, at the end of the day, it starts with us.

Resisting Stereotypes through Changemaking

Negative stereotypes and preconceived notions of Black people are core components of cultural racism, and a driving force for young Black change-making (Hope, Gugwor et al., 2019). Some youth described changemaking as a tool to challenge unidimensional and negative stereotypes of Black people and Black youth specifically. Similar to the "prove them wrong" mantra that Black youth use to challenge academic stereotypes portraying Black people as intellectually inferior (Howard, 2013), these young Black changemakers used civic action to directly contradict the negative beliefs about Black communities that permeate the US cultural zeitgeist. Changemaking in Black communities is a reclamation of the powerful and transforming collective identity of Black people in the United States. H.E.R. (age 13, she/her) described the collective power of challenging stereotypes:

I feel like society puts us in this box where we're either in a gang, we're poor, we're just in the very lower class or whatever. So I feel like Black people especially – or even in the people of color doing civic engagement, I feel like it showed them that we're not these people that society puts us in this little box. We are not these people.

H.E.R. called out the dominant cultural narratives that perpetuate negative stereotypes of Black people, and highlighted changemaking as a critical tool to resisting cultural racism. These negative stereotypes are especially prevalent in the media. Though there has been some shift in efforts to present more positive, robust, and nuanced images that represent Black communities, such as in films like Black Panther and Hidden Figures, the dominant narrative remains of Black people as societal delinquents, rather than positive contributors to American life. These negative images can have negative implications for Black youth's racial identity development. To protect and affirm their identities in the context of this cultural racism, Black youth seek out – and create – positive affirmations of Blackness (Adams & Stevenson, 2012;

Adams-Bass et al., 2014; Adams-Bass & Henrici, 2018). Damian underscored how dominant narratives of Black people are reinforced by news and social media, and named how changemaking forces a shift in dominant narratives by ensuring that Black people's positive contributions cannot be ignored or denied:

[Changemaking] sets a positive image on us. Because, you know, how the news, they portray us in a bad way. They don't show the good stuff we do in the community. And if there's a bunch of people doing good things, then they're gonna have to show that . . . we're creating a change over here.

As H.E.R. and Damian explained, changemaking demands public attention to the ways that Black people hold institutions accountable and lead positive change. Black changemaking exposes the hypocrisy of our most influential social institutions – such as media, government, and schools – that have explicit missions to serve all people, but ultimately fail to support the communities (such as people of color, sexual minorities, those experiencing poverty) for whom these institutions were not built. By continuously highlighting tensions between what is portrayed in media and dominant cultural rhetoric versus the reality of Black youth as social change agents, Black youth challenge the harmful narratives that threaten their identities and their humanity.

Coping with Racial Trauma through Changemaking

Changemaking is also a way that Black young people cope with racism. In my (Hope's) writing with Dr. Margaret Beale Spencer (Hope & Spencer, 2017), we described this type of changemaking as an adaptive coping strategy that young people use to reduce the negative effects of racism on their lives and well-being. Soleil, Layla, and Joe Cornell each spoke about engaging in changemaking to cope with the racism they witnessed and experienced. Soleil (age 13, she/her) said she is a changemaker, "Because it's [police violence against Black people] affected me personally. It's made me scared to walk down the streets or even go for a run by myself because we've been killed for doing simplest things like sleeping in our own bed, for holding a hairbrush or a toy gun, or skittles . . . . It's just affected me personally." The unchecked structural racism in the criminal legal system that results in the unjustified killings of Black adolescents and adults left Soleil in a state of fear. In response, she became a part of changing racist systems. Layla (age 16, she/her) shared a similar experience:

Watching the news, sometimes it can be very overwhelming just because of the stuff that's going on. But, I feel like it helps me learn more about the world we live in and how to navigate the world because obviously, we're still in this – it may not be slavery going on, but there's still a racial injustice going on. So – being a Black young girl, it helps me navigate the world. You know, don't do this, don't go to this place at a certain time. It keeps me informed on what I should be doing to make a change in the world.

Layla described feeling overwhelmed by racial injustice. She also leaned into her identity as a "Black young girl" to understand racial injustice and work toward dismantling it. Her racial (and gendered and age) identity strengthened her resolve, and perhaps even ability, to make changes in the world. Kevin (age 17, he/him) also described changemaking as a proactive coping response to racism, sharing:

I want to change the situation [of police brutality] that we are faced with and that suffering. I just want people to be safe where I come from and they not be scared. We not. My mission is . . . not to be part of the negative interactions that is going on the last couple of years. I really want for everybody just to be happy where we come from.

In these examples, as well as in the stories from Chapter 3, we see young Black changemakers acknowledge the fear, feelings of being overwhelmed, and negative emotional and psychological effects of racism in their lives. They also leverage changemaking, bolstered by their racial (and other) identities, to cope with the ways that racism affects them. In this way, changemaking is more than the outcomes from any one action or any one particular change in the community. Changemaking becomes a tool for coping with racism that strengthens how Black young people negotiate and concretize their commitment to Black communities in a culture where racism undermines their very existence.

COLLECTIVE IDENTITY AND THE LEGACY OF CHANGEMAKING

Black identity is both personal and collective. Youth interpret and define their Blackness from their personal experiences. They also recognize how being Black in the United States ties them to a larger collective community, experience, and history defined by resilience and community uplift in the aftermath of slavery. Black history is a tool for learning about oneself and building collective identity that also informs Black youth's changemaking to challenge racism. Given that Black history involves many social movements, learning about Black history can motivate changemaking as a continuation of the legacy initiated by one's Black ancestors (Chapman-Hilliard et al., 2022). Young Black changemakers learned about their history through their own participation in social movements, even more than what is taught in schools. What they learned inspired both racial pride and further fueled their changemaking. Quinn (age 16, she/her) conveyed her racial pride from learning about Black history:

Knowing more about the history kind of made me prouder to be Black because it's all this stuff. Where would the world be at right now, where would anybody be right now

[if] it wasn't for, you know, what my people have done? You know the inventions they made, everything they thought of, you know, everything. And it makes me proud but it also frustrates me because … it's ultimately a question I ask, everyone asks … . Why? Why was it [racism] always a problem?

Similarly, Martin (age 14, he/him) described being Black and changemaking in this way:

Well, I just feel like it's kinda been an uphill battle for us … . We have always had to, you know, stand up for our rights and ourselves … . It's been an ongoing fight, for, I don't know, the country I suppose. Trying to, you know, make our world … a better place for everyone, right? Our rights, our liberty, our equality. Always been a big thing. We have always been as people, you know, to a degree civically engaged. It's kind of been I guess a tradition that's been passed down.

For Quinn and Martin, changemaking – particularly for rights, liberty, and equality – is a legacy passed down by Black communities through generations. This is a legacy of resistance, as Dr. Nicole Webster (2021, p. 8) described, wherein from the late 1800s and early 1900s to today, "African American youth were always challenging systems of oppression with their critical thinking and forethought and sacrificing their bodies to confront systems of oppression." Indeed, when Black youth connect Black history to current struggles, they engage in racism analysis, a form of critical reflection that is instrumental for informing their sociopolitical development and deepening their changemaking (Bañales et al., 2023). Success with Lex also connected her involvement in the modern day Black rights movement to the Civil Rights Movements of the past. She said:

Definitely seeing that the Black Lives Matter Movement has grown bigger than that movement is crazy to me because the Civil Rights Movement just invoked so much change. The Martin Luther King era. The Malcom X era. All of that has invoked change. But seeing that in this day in time our movement is bigger than that, I feel like we're on to something, and this decade might just be the decade where we finally get to change that we've been fighting for.

This legacy, for Quinn, Martin, Success with Lex, and others, is the historical through-line of being Black and civically engaged in the United States. Changemaking is an inherited part of being Black and being a part of Black communities. Black collective identity is rooted in the past and future of Black people as active resistors of racism and oppression.

Destiny, a 16-year-old girl who was involved in mentoring, volunteering, and protesting, among other civic actions, also critically reflected on how being Black and engaging in changemaking is unique because of the history of Black people in the United States. She stated, "Seeing … things that happen to our ancestors or hearing stories about our ancestors or learning about other protests for Black lives back in the day or slavery, the Jim Crow era – all of that comes to now." When asked what was unique about civic engagement for Black youth, Destiny said, "[Civic engagement] being, basically, powerful. I feel like that's unique because in other races . . .. They have not been through a deep struggle, and it's unique seeing how people can come from being inferior [to] being the main people making the change right now."

Black youth's motivation and passion for changemaking today is derived in part from the legacy of changemaking of years passed. Contemporary literature on civic purpose suggests that civic motivation and purpose is "meaningful and committed intention to contribute to the world beyond the self" (Malin et al., 2015, p. 104). As we also highlighted in Chapter 2, young Black changemakers are deeply future oriented and committed to a better world for Black people, yet their stories challenge this definition of civic purpose as beyond the self. Instead, their civic purpose is rooted in the legacy of Black ancestors and community, which is a core part of their personal Black identity. In other words, Black youth's civic purposes are deeply personal and serve the broader collective. The goals of young Black changemakers of the past become part of the identities and civic purpose of today's young Black changemakers. They value the progress that has been made by changemakers who came before them and strive to continue that tradition. As Sara Vaughn stated, Black youth "can't let that ball drop now," but instead need to keep fighting for racial justice.

Collective identity, rooted in Black history, also inspires commitments to leaving a legacy for future generations of Black youth. A core part of being Black for these young Black changemakers was fighting for a better world for future generations. Layla said, "So I feel like it's our . . . duty to carry the torch and pass it on to future generations. And then also in the midst of carrying the torch, making more differences at the same time."

Young Black changemakers saw themselves as a part of a larger collective of Black people with shared goals, which helped them stay motivated to continue changemaking. Destiny talked about how being disconnected from one's racial history has consequences for how youth engage with and think about Black community organizing. She shared:

To be honest, a lotta my friends don't know a lot about that type of stuff. They were never taught it, or they're just seeing it on TV and brush it off their shoulders. And then, now, they're coming to the realization of the stuff that's happening, and they never knew this type of stuff happened in America. And at 16 years old, I feel like you should know – if you're a Black person in America, you should know this stuff.

Destiny articulated how being disconnected from Black history may contribute to Black youth being unmotivated or unable to be a part of modern social change work. The development of personal and collective Black identity is a process, and not all Black youth have the same experiences, knowledge, and personal connections to history. For example, Sean (age 16, he/him) said, "I don't really have an answer for that" and "I don't know" when asked what is unique about being Black and civically engaged or how Black identity connects to civic engagement. Not all Black youth have the same opportunities to learn and connect to their history and identity. Critical reflection and knowledge of the challenges Black people face is a central aspect of becoming engaged in the work of racial justice. Youth with a strong Black collective identity were motivated by Black changemakers who came before them and invested in leaving a legacy behind that future generations could not just be proud of, but thrive in Black joy and Black safety. Black youth's collective identities embody an Afrocentric worldview that emphasizes the value of community interdependence and intergenerational knowledge as key facets of building community cultural wealth (Belgrave & Allison, 2018).

THE TAKE AWAYS

Young Black changemakers take pride in their connection to Black communities of past and present. This strong and positive Black identity motivates their changemaking. Black identity intertwines with other identities – such as gender and social class positions – to inform experiences of oppression and changemaking in response. Commitment to and love for Black communities empowers young Black people to cope with and resist racism in ways that protect their personal identities from threat and draw on the strengths of their personal narratives. Young Black changemakers find civic purpose and power in the legacy of Black social justice leaders and lean into that history to honor their place in Black communities. The relationship between identity and changemaking is reciprocal. For these young people, pride and connection to being Black fed their desire to eradicate racism through changemaking. Engaging in changemaking for a better world for Black people also deepened their connections to Black people and Black communities.

Contributions to Research

Our study supports research showing that racial identity is linked to Black youth's civic engagement (Hope, Gugwor et al., 2019; Mathews et al., 2020), and expands thinking on *how* racial identity and changemaking are connected for Black youth. Racial pride is one experience that explains this connection. Our findings align with research which shows that racial pride is important for Black youth development broadly (Rivas-Drake et al., 2014) and civic development specifically (Bañales, Hoffman et al., 2020; Chapman-Hilliard et al., 2022; Hope, Cryer-Coupet et al., 2020). We add to existing research by showing how Black youth explicitly connect pride in being Black with pride in changemaking that empowers and improves Black communities. Further, racial pride is reinforced through changemaking. In a previous study, Mathews and colleagues (2022) found that racial identity exploration and civic engagement were reciprocally related for Black college students. Our study extends this research by offering evidence that racial pride is also reciprocally related to changemaking. Changemaking builds racial pride for Black youth, and Black youth with racial pride are motivated to engage in further changemaking.

Second, we showed how coping with and resisting racism connects Black identity and changemaking. Frequent and widespread experiences of racism – including interpersonal, institutional, and cultural racism – shaped Black youth's convictions to pursue changemaking. A positive Black identity gives youth strength as well as tools, such as personal narratives, to resist racism through changemaking. These young Black changemakers were especially driven to make changes that reduce the likelihood of experiencing racism and create spaces for Black young people to experience love, joy, and wholeness in their Blackness. Our findings align with Dr. Della Mosley and colleagues' (2021) critical consciousness of anti-Black racism model, wherein witnessing and experiencing anti-Black racism motivates racial justice activism, and this connection between experiences and action is facilitated by growth in racial and intersectional identity. Research on Black youth civic engagement is incomplete without considering the role of both identity and experiences with racism.

A third contribution of these findings is the role of legacy in the arc of racial identity and changemaking for young Black people. Racial identity is both personal and collective, and transcends time across past, present, and future. Young Black changemakers are deeply committed to honoring and continuing the civil rights fights of generations past and to advancing well-being for the generations that follow. The central importance of collective identity and the legacy of changemaking in Black communities has implications for two specific areas of the civic development literature: social responsibility and civic purpose. Social responsibility and civic purpose describe pursuits of civic action beyond the self (Malin et al., 2015; Wray-Lake & Syvertsen, 2011). Because of the roles of personal and collective racial identity, Black youth's civic purpose is deeply connected to their sense of self and rooted in their feelings of belonging and commitment to Black communities. This motivation is good for the collective, including oneself. Our study findings help expand the meaning of civic purpose beyond altruism to incorporate collective responsibility for Black youth.

A fourth contribution of these findings is recognizing the importance of intersectionality in understanding changemaking for Black youth. Youth shared experiences of being Black *and* women, and experiences being Black *and* from lower resourced communities. For these young Black change-makers, experiences at the nexus of racism and sexism and classism high-lighted the varying ways that Black people experience oppression. These experiences provided expanded context and purpose for the types of change-making youth pursued and envisioned. Young Black changemakers who understood their Black identity through an intersectional lens were inspired to be more inclusive in their pursuits of racial justice. Our findings align with research from Dr. Veronica Terriquez and colleagues (2018), who found that undocumented youth activists who understood their identities through a framework of intersectionality engaged in activism that was inclusive of queer undocumented youth. Future research can build on these findings to develop more comprehensive frameworks for youth civic development that context-ualize racism within the web of other co-conspiring systems of oppression like sexism, classism, and heterosexism. We did not cover every identity-based oppression Black youth experience, just the most salient ones for these youth; Black youth draw on other identities and experiences of oppression that inform their changemaking in important ways that research should further explore.

Together, these findings advance sociopolitical development theory by illustrating how personal and collective racial identity, and intersectional identities, are central to the processes of becoming a young Black change-maker. Racial and other social identities are starting to be more formally integrated into models of sociopolitical development (Mathews et al., 2020; Watts & Halkovic, 2022), and our findings highlight complex ways in which identity motivates changemaking, develops alongside changemaking, provides tools for resisting racism, and deepens critical reflection about Black history and legacies of changemaking.

Practical Insights

From these young Black changemakers, we learned that racial identity is a core part of how young people decide to participate in civic life. For practi-tioners who work with youth in civic spaces, supporting them in developing racial identity and deconstructing experiences of racism are central compon-ents of walking alongside young Black changemakers. Identity matters for changemaking. Cultivating a sense of belonging to and responsibility for Black people and Black communities is the foundation of changemaking for

Black youth. Pride in and connection to Black communities provides a stable point of departure for young Black changemakers to make sense of the racism they witness and experience and to chart pathways to racial justice through taking action in their schools and communities. Practitioners must not ignore the personal, and racialized, connections young Black changemakers have to their civic work.

Adults should consider the praxis of critical race consciousness in work with young Black changemakers, which involves critical reflection on racism, racial reflexivity, and anti-racist action (Aldana et al., 2019; Bañales et al., 2023; Watts & Halkovic, 2022). For Black young people, critical reflection includes thorough analysis and critique of white supremacy, including the history of racism nationally and locally, and knowledge of interlocking systems of oppression that feed off of racism. Racial reflexivity is the situational reflection of how race and racism are shaping one's thoughts, experiences, and responses to oppression. Reflexivity allows young people to grapple with contradictions in their own behavior and their goals for racial justice, process their emotional responses to racism and action, and imagine new futures for Black identity and community outside of white supremacy. Educators in schools, community organizations, and youth-serving programs can support changemaking by providing space and opportunity for young Black people to engage in critical reflection and racial reflexivity. These processes foreground Black identity development, which in turn, support and amplify Black young people's resolve to pursue racial justice. Organizations and leaders who seek racial justice should engage in their own critical race consciousness praxis to be best positioned to support young Black changemakers in their own journeys.

Up Next

This chapter demonstrates how personal and collective identity are signature strengths that develop alongside changemaking and motivate Black youth's changemaking to resist and cope with racism and create a better world for other Black people. Supporting a key tenet of sociopolitical development theory (Watts et al., 2003), Chapters 3 and 4 have shown that experiences of racism are catalysts for Black youth's changemaking. This chapter supports another key idea that Black identity is central to Black youth's development as changemakers. In the next two chapters, we elaborate on the role of early and formative life experiences for Black youth's development into changemakers, a third principle of sociopolitical development theory. In Chapter 5, we focus on the significant people and experiences who launch Black youth into changemaking.

Black Girl by Zoie Brogdon

5

Launching Points

LAURA WRAY-LAKE, SARA BLOOMDAHL WILF, &
MARIAH BONILLA

> It was a sixth grade video, like, I saw this dude . . .. He was inspirational. And
> he helps out the community and I said, 'I want to be just like him,' and that
> day, like, 'Imma better myself and help out the community.'
>
> Jaylen

Jaylen (he/him) was sitting in his sixth grade classroom watching the morning
news when inspiration struck. A story of a Black man helping his local
community appeared on screen, and Jaylen knew right then that he also
wanted to be engaged in his community, deciding that day, "Imma better
myself and help out the community." This man's story was especially inspirational for Jaylen because the man was Black like him, and because there is
"so much going on in the world about racism and stuff" so "you barely see
Black people help the community." Jaylen, like other youth we described in
Chapter 4, had a desire to see Black people challenge and upend negative
stereotypes about them, and he wanted to be part of that change. After
watching the news video in class, Jaylen started seeking opportunities to help
others and drew on other influences from his daily life. He was inspired by his
uncle, who gave him a talk that emphasized the message to "be yourself, be a
better person." He got involved in feeding the unhoused through his mother,
who not only encouraged him to volunteer, but "she did it with me." His
school counselor identified a beach cleanup opportunity and drove him there,
where he also felt encouraged by peers who are "supportive about me." As a
15-year-old tenth grader, four years after his memory of being inspired in
sixth grade, Jaylen was active in many forms of community helping, including
helping neighbors, mentoring younger children through a summer program,
and volunteering to help the environment and the unhoused. He also participated in an anti-bullying campaign through a school organization and spent
time posting about social issues including racial justice on social media.

As Jaylen's story shows, young Black changemakers evolve and grow in
their ways of being civically engaged. We have already shown how experiences with interpersonal, cultural, and institutional racism serve as key

launching points into changemaking and how Black identity and Black cultural values and legacies spark Black youth's changemaking and shape it over time. In this chapter, we look at other launching points for young Black changemakers – influential factors that get Black youth started on their journey to changemaking. Jaylen's launching points began with inspiration drawn from a news story of a Black man engaging in community helping, and also his mother, uncle, counselor, and peers who offered encouragement and access to opportunities. These influences set him on a course to becoming an active community helper working to fulfill his civic purpose of joining with other "Black teens and men to better their community" and "to better ourselves as a culture, all of us together."

We identified three launching points for young Black changemaking that go beyond the two launching points (racism and racial identity development) already discussed in Chapters 3 and 4; namely, influential people, fun experiences, and youth agency. These factors do not reflect the full gamut of people and experiences that plant the seeds of young Black changemaking, but they do help tell the story of how young Black changemakers get started. Describing these launching points highlights the strengths of Black youth, their families, and their communities. Early life experiences and relationships are foundational to Black youth's sociopolitical development, with most of the research emphasizing the role of families (Watts & Halkovic, 2022). Agency, or youth's feelings of power and capability to make change, is also understood by many to be a central ingredient of changemaking (Watts et al., 2011). By using Black youth's stories to map out these three launching points, we can better understand *how* these influences set Black youth on a path to changemaking and gain insights into how families, schools, and communities can make opportunities for changemaking more widely available and accessible for Black youth.

INFLUENTIAL PEOPLE

Jaylen and other young Black changemakers clearly recognized that other people influenced who they are today as young people and as changemakers. We learned both *who* is influential as well as *how* these people support Black youth's civic engagement. First, who are these influencers? Family members, especially mothers, are primary and powerful influences in Black youth's lives, and their influences take different forms. Thirteen-year-old Amir (he/him) summed it up perfectly by saying his mom was "my launching point." Influential people in youth's civic journeys extend beyond family and include counselors or teachers, peers, and Black leaders locally and well beyond. We highlight how early civic involvement with families, encouragement from multiple sources, and inspiration by Black leaders influence youth to become changemakers.

Early Civic Involvement with Family

For many young Black changemakers, helping begins in the family. In fact, families were such an important influence for young Black changemakers that we devote the entire next chapter to understanding the role of families in supporting young Black changemaking. Here, we briefly name how families act as launching points, and we go into detail in Chapter 6.

Often, youth's earliest experiences of civic engagement happened in childhood. Some youth's journeys of civic engagement began with helping members of their family, including younger siblings, older relatives, and family members with health or mobility needs with everyday tasks. These experiences taught youth how to care for others. As we further describe in Chapter 6, helping family is an important form of changemaking for Black youth. This care and compassion grew to extend outside of the family and into the broader community.

Some youth recalled family members bringing them along to civic activities with family since early childhood. These youth participated from such an early age with their parents, and particularly their mothers, that civic activities were ingrained in their lives. In these activities, youth witnessed and learned from the civic engagement of their own parents, who often expected them to participate. Youth did not always immediately see a deeper meaning in these activities, but later came to reflect on how foundational these early experiences were for becoming changemakers. For example, Muffin (age 16, she/her) explained how when she was younger, she "didn't really pay attention to this stuff" and was just "there because my mom was there and I had to come." But later, Muffin came to "appreciate it more" and more deeply enjoy and find meaning in these civic activities. Additionally, in the context of voter registration, Muffin recognized her past experiences had developed her skills and she "already knew what to do." Research around the world shows that parents act as role models for children through their own civic engagement (Schulz et al., 2010), and that "parents are the first and best civics teachers" (Gould et al., 2011, p. 8). Yet, not enough research has studied Black families as influencers of their children's changemaking, and we say much more on this in Chapter 6.

Encouragement and Recruitment from Multiple Sources

Many youth are initially drawn into changemaking by others around them. Family members and others – such as peers and school staff – can play this role, as Jaylen's story showed. Tom's story also illustrates the power of being asked and encouraged to participate for sparking long-term civic commitments. Tom (age 17, he/him) initiated several civic activities due to encouragement from others, and later became more deeply invested in these activities for his own reasons. For example, he first started volunteering at a shelter for unhoused people to meet his school's community service hours requirement. Across the country, many schools require community service as part of their curriculum. According to the Education Commission of the States (2022), Maryland and Washington, DC have state-wide community service requirements for graduation, and 27 other states have policies that allow community service hours to count toward one's high school degree or allow school districts to craft such policies. These policies become mandated "encouragement" for youth to get involved in their communities. Required service has numerous civic, health, and academic benefits for youth, especially when youth see the service as meaningful and have opportunities to reflect on the root causes of social problems (Van Goethem et al., 2014). Tom's experience clearly reflects this larger pattern. He volunteered at the shelter for the unhoused as a requirement, but his experience ended up being a major influence on his desire to stay engaged, his identity as a changemaker, and his efforts to use his talents toward a larger purpose. Reflecting on a time when he helped an unhoused woman find a winter jacket, Tom connected the experience to his personal development and growth, including finding a purpose:

Like that [experience] made me realize ... it's not that hard at all to change somebody's life, you know, because for us that was just an old coat, but for her that's, you know, something that was really important .... I feel like as a 17-year-old, you kind of always just try to find what your purpose is, especially ... at this time in your life .... You're growing up and you're starting to because your path is starting to become more confined ... this is kind of what you're doing now and this is who you're becoming. So I feel like when I do stuff like that [helping], it makes me feel like I'm doing something. I'm using my talents, using my abilities and my position in life, to, you know, help others.

In another instance, Tom was a mentee in a mentoring program for Black young men based on his mom's encouragement. In addition to volunteering with his mom since childhood, Tom described his mom as "always finding programs for Black people" and enrolling him in these activities. In this particular program, his mentor inspired him to realize his power to make a difference through civic engagement. Tom also got involved in debate club because a friend asked him to join, but then became passionate about showing the white youth in the club other sides of political issues and presenting his opinions, which he called "a voice of reason." He stated:

My girlfriend's friend was running the political club, and nobody was really going to it. So she was like, "Oh, we should go sign up just to show our support." ... And so, when we signed up, we showed up to the first meeting. And it was really interesting to see because if I'm gonna be honest with you, it's ran by kids who aren't like me, it's a lot of conservative white kids .... And they say, you know, the goal was trying to create a safe space for all political views, so they could come in and debate. But I quickly noticed that it wasn't like that at all ... immediately when I saw that, I was like, "Oh this is where I gotta be, you know, I gotta stay, because if I leave, then you know, there's gonna be no voice of reason." . . . So staying in this club kind of gave me . . . more perspective on what's really going on. And gave me the ability to form my own opinion, you know?

Clearly multiple external sources recruited Tom into civic engagement, yet his story also illustrates his agency in taking full advantage of these various opportunities. Classic models of volunteering and political participation extol the value of being asked: Simply being asked to participate is a major factor that gets people of any age involved in civic life (Nesbit, 2013; Verba et al., 1995). This launching point may get a young person's "foot in the door," but that is just the beginning. Other people may have sparked his initial engagement, but Tom maximized his potential and embraced opportunities to help, to learn, and to grow as a changemaker.

Other youth, including Jaylen, shared how school counselors encouraged their entry into civic action. Counselors helped launch them into changemaking by connecting youth to opportunities, but counselors were also impactful by conveying to Black youth that they matter. Quinn (age 16, she/her) said her teachers and counselors introduced her to multiple civic opportunities because "they saw something in me and saw that I could really help other people" and it "felt good" to be seen in this positive light. Similarly, a school counselor saw that Damian (age 18, he/him), was "vocal" and doing well in school and "she wanted me to just be a part of the program to hopefully be a voice in our community." Through his counselor, Damian got involved in a community organization for boys and young men of color, where he got connected to people, resources, and ways to make a difference in his community. This role of school counselors in creating launching points for young people struck us as notable because school counselors are under-recognized for their efforts in developing changemakers. We wondered if counselors were more likely to encourage changemaking at particular types of schools, but we could not determine this with the information we had available. Given that counselors may play important roles in linking youth to opportunities and recognizing their potential as changemakers, it is important to do more research on counselors as facilitators of changemaking.

Inspiration from Black Leaders

In launching into changemaking, Black youth drew inspiration from Black leaders, including contemporary Black leaders in the arts or civic life, like Nipsey Hussle, Ava DuVernay, and Michelle Obama, historical Black leaders of the Civil Rights Movement, and inspirational Black leaders in their own family and community. Across the board, Black youth were inspired by other Black people due to their strength to withstand and cope with racism and to stand up for themselves in the face of this oppression. The words "strong" and "powerful" arose again and again as youth shared how other Black people inspire them to be changemakers. Phea (age 17, she/her) was inspired by her mom who is a "strong Black woman," which Phea defined as being determined to "keep going" in the face of obstacles and also as being sensitive to others' needs. Success with Lex (age 18, she/her) also used the term "strong Black women" to refer to her grandmother and aunt. Her aunt was a Black Panther, and the civic engagement of her aunt and grandmother inspired her to continue this family legacy by supporting other Black people and fighting for racial justice. They advised her to "continue to stay strong and fight for what you want, and really just uphold the people that look like you around you." Thus, Black youth, and especially Black girls, invoked the image of Strong Black Women to describe inspiring figures who resist racial oppression and fight for the humanity of themselves, their families, and the Black community.

Here, we pause to offer a short aside about the more complex ways in which scholars discuss the Strong Black Woman Schema – an archetype or common image of Black womanhood in society. Black feminist scholars like Drs. Patricia Hill Collins (2000) and bell hooks (1981) called out the deeply problematic roots of society's stereotypes of Black women, including using strength as a narrative to control and marginalize Black girls and women. Indeed, societal expectations to always be strong can harm Black girls' and women's health and well-being, and at the same time, many Black women find strength, power, and inspiration in this identity for civic engagement and for everyday living (Jefferies, 2022). Dr. Martinique Jones and colleagues (2021) interviewed Black female college students and found that Black girls and young women today are redefining what it means to be a strong Black woman in ways that resist society's negative stereotypes.

For Black girls and all young Black changemakers, Black leaders in civic spaces and beyond are powerful inspirations for Black youth because they see people like them in leadership roles. Representation matters. For example, research shows that teachers of color are important for improving well-being and achievement among students of color (Egalite et al., 2015). Representation of one's own racial or ethnic group on TV shows and movies can also be important for positive racial and ethnic identity development (Ellithorpe & Bleakley, 2016). In our study, Black representation in civic life inspired Black youth to become changemakers. Layla (age 16, she/her) was initially drawn to participate in dance based on inspiration from Misty Copeland, who made history as the first African American Principal Dancer in the American Ballet Theater. Layla followed Copeland's career and attended her intensive training courses. She shared that Copeland's performances "showed me I can do the same thing as being a Black girl who may not look the same as everybody in my dance studio . . .. So that's kinda what sparked my passion." Layla's passion was mentoring children to help them develop a love of dance, and she wanted to start a non-profit focused on performing arts to give other youth, especially Black youth, the opportunity to dance.

When Black youth draw inspiration from Black leaders, they often identify connections to their own qualities and capabilities. As we shared in Chapter 4, Unique (age 17, she/her) admired Angela Rye, a Black female Democratic political commentator for various news outlets including CNN. Unique admired her style, strength, and character in political conversations and disagreements, and wanted to embody those qualities, saying "That's me. That's gon' be me." Unique also saw herself reflected in the inspiring Black women of present day and historical times. "I look at the Black women every day that surround me, and I be like, 'Dang, I wish I could be one of them,' but then I be forgetting that I am one of them. I feel like Black . . . history . . . made me really just kind of find myself and be like, 'Dang, you really are one of these people,' and like, 'Dang, you really are. . .You should feel honored.'"

For some youth, particularly boys from predominantly Black neighborhoods in Compton and Inglewood, male rappers like Nipsey Hussle and Chance the Rapper were inspirational figures. Youth were inspired by these musicians due to the music itself and because these musicians came from these youth's neighborhoods and returned to support the community. Nipsey Hussle was shot and killed in his LA neighborhood on March 31, 2019, a year before we began this study. He was a well-known rapper and advocated to end gun violence, donated to numerous community causes with an emphasis on Black youth and education, and spearheaded neighborhood revitalization projects (Blay, 2019). Kobe (age 17, he/him) explained his close connection to Nipsey:

Nipsey Hussle . . . he's a real role model. I like Nipsey, he from our neighborhood, I grew up on [location], right down the street from the 66th, so . . . to see everybody want to be him, you know, to see him make it out the hood and to do all them big things, like that, and still come [back to the neighborhood], you know, because it's this respect thing, you feel me.

CJ (age 18, they/them) also looked to rappers for inspiration around civic engagement, explaining that rap could motivate youth "to have confidence in yourself, and don't be afraid, can't let no one stop you." Both CJ and JD (age 13, he/him) described rap as helping them process and heal from trauma, such as the death of a friend or gun violence. JD described a transformation in his changemaking from helping family to supporting his broader community, and he attributed this turning point in part to Nipsey Hussle's example: "Nipsey says he wanted . . . Black people in his community to get justice and have rights to do things that they need and want. So, I wanted to lead and get started with that at a young age." Similarly, hearing about Chance the

Rapper's changemaking in Chicago inspired Cory (age 15, he/him), who envisioned his own mark on the world. Cory said:

I want to be able to become a positive influence in the world. I want to be able to talk about an issue and people will listen, they will change stuff. I feel like that would be the greatest thing ever, becoming something big and then being able to use a platform and change something. I know there's a rapper, I don't really listen to him, but I like him. His name is Chance the Rapper and a lot of times we'll talk about things in this community, like in Chicago, and how he wants to change it, things like that. I think things like that are really cool. And I would love to do something like that in the future.

These youth's experiences align with Dr. Nkemka Anyiwo's research highlighting the role of hip-hop culture and rap music in Black youth's sociopolitical development (Anyiwo et al., 2022). Anyiwo and colleagues surveyed nearly 500 Black adolescents and found that Black youth who consumed more hip-hop media (including music and music videos) had higher agency to address racism and took more civic actions to advance racial justice. Moreover, when Black youth reported hearing empowering messages from rap music, they also reported greater awareness of racial inequalities in the US and more agency to address racism. Thus, our work and the work of others show the potential of Black rap music and musicians to inspire Black youth to become changemakers.

Summing Up: Influential People Who Spark Young Black Changemaking

Black youth launch their changemaking journeys with the help of various influential people. Some they know and see every day; others provide inspiration from afar. Influences from families, peers, school counselors, and mentors in community-based civic organizations demonstrate how everyday interactions can be a spark that launches youth on a journey of changemaking. Notably, the most inspiring figures in their lives were Black. Drawing inspiration from other Black people was personal and powerful for Unique, Layla, Phea, Jayden, CJ, and many others who see themselves and their possible futures when they look up to other Black leaders, many of whom were the same gender as the young person. As discussed in Chapter 4, Black youth's racial and gender identities shape how they engage in changemaking, and their identities also relate to where they find inspiration. And as Chapter 3 showed, having Black teachers and administrators was a critical resource for navigating anti-Black racism in schools. Overall, the importance of Black representation in any space cannot be overstated. Black civic leaders are inspirational for young Black changemakers. Although society often relegates celebrating Black changemaking to February (Black History Month), there is no shortage of historical and contemporary examples of Black changemakers, and examples are evident in youth's own homes, family legacies, and community spaces.

FUN EXPERIENCES

One reason Black youth initially got involved in changemaking was to have fun with others. This launching point conveys two simple and perhaps obvious truths that may be easy for adults to forget: Teenagers are social beings who like to have fun and seek belonging in groups (Baumeister, 2012), and civic engagement can be fun. Youth referred to "having fun" while changemaking in a variety of contexts ranging from registering voters, to handing out flyers at community block parties, to forming long-lasting friendships through civic activities. Similarly, Dr. Parissa Ballard and colleagues (2015) found that the desire for fun is one of many motivations that bring youth from diverse racial and ethnic backgrounds into civic activities. Building social relationships is closely intertwined with having fun for adolescents, and for youth in our study; having fun often included positive interactions with peers. Black youth's stories about joining for fun remind us that their civic engagement is not always or only about struggling against oppression, but also includes positive, uplifting, and joyful experiences.

Even before she drew inspiration from everyday and national Black leaders, having fun with friends was a launching point for Unique's changemaking. Unique was highly involved in a community-based organization, through which she focused on community organizing and building student power through leading civic actions at her school. In exploring how Unique first became engaged in this organization, she shared that although her grandmother had also been involved in the same organization, she was recruited by a peer. Unique explained that initially, going to this organization for the food was "the main goal," and that on her first visit, she decided she wanted to spend more time with people in that space:

It's really a pretty building, I swear to you, it's real pretty ... inside out. So when I walked in there, I'm like, "Oh, wait, I kind of want to be here a little bit more. I want to eat. I want to talk, I want to be with y'all. I want to really be here." So that's kind of why I stayed, and then yeah, when they start telling us about ways that we can help ourselves in school. I'm like, "Oh, wait so y'all aren't only feeding us, y'all are teaching us." This is really upgraded school. But better.

Thus, for Unique, the welcoming environment, the chance to talk and spend time with friends, and the food were key ingredients for fun that hooked her into this space. She deepened her changemaking over time and took advantage of many opportunities the organization offered, a growth process of youth in organizations we elaborate on in Chapter 7. Importantly, in describing why she was involved in the organization, Unique also shared:

I would say that it's really important to kind of invest in where you come from because literally what's happening. If you don't invest in your own community, it's kind of like having somebody else tell your own story .... If they not living it, then they can't really tell it.

Thus, it was not just any organization that drew Unique in; she was also drawn to the fun and welcoming space because it was embedded in her neighborhood, about which she cares deeply. She was drawn to being part of an organization where other youth of color gathered and that reflected the South Los Angeles neighborhood where she was raised.

Tsehai (age 14, she/her) also explained how her changemaking activities were instigated by a desire to have fun with friends. Tsehai said that her friends would tell her about opportunities, such as, "Oh, do you want to be on Model United Nations, this is a really fun, you know, program," and that's how "a lot of stuff just sort of popped onto my schedule. And I sort of found how much I cared and how much I liked it from the people around me doing it." In this way, joining to be with friends is closely tied to being encouraged or recruited to participate by peers. When Tsehai described engaging in a volunteer activity, we could feel the fun and adventure she experienced and sense the enjoyment she gained from giving to and interacting with others. She shared:

One time [volunteering] I went out with a friend of mine, and we hopped . . . into one of the trucks with my friend's dad and her brother . . .. I was sitting in the front seat and they're sitting in the back of the truck, with no seats or anything. And it was a super, just a fun experience. And these are all people that I look up to, like my friend, I really look up to her and I look up to her dad and stuff. And I went out. And we handed food to these people, and they really needed it, you know, and having conversations with these people, and seeing how much this just . . . I think the bag . . . was worth about $70 to $80 you know, this $80 of stuff was gonna make this person's you know . . . holiday season because there was things like blankets that they needed . . .. Cultivating a positive environment doing this work, you know, makes it also easier to keep going . . .. And the just joy and appreciation from those people that got these things.

For Tsehai, one fun part of changemaking was being in community with others she respected and another was feeling joy from helping others. Unique and Tsehai, along with others, initially engaged in changemaking to have fun, often with friends, and then stayed because they enjoyed and valued change-making and the community they were building. Similarly, Kevin's experience showed how having fun and building community are closely intertwined. Kevin (age 17, he/him) shared that he participated in "a protest, a block party, where people can have fun and just be around other people, and show community that we share engagement, and just be powerful who they are." These experiences were important to Kevin because "it encouraged me to engage. I don't know how to say it but to me, engaging and being powerful in who you is means that you have to be [open] and stuff like that I guess." Like Unique's story, part of Kevin's experience of fun and connection with others was being with other Black people from his neighborhood. Kevin shared that part of his motivation to be civically engaged was "being proud of the community you come from."

Importantly, fun may be a launching point, but fun alone is not enough to sustain changemaking. Youth explained that changemaking spaces needed to continue providing opportunities beyond initial fun experiences. Sa'Myah (age 18, she/her) noted that some changemaking experiences were "fun," yet she lamented that ultimately "nothing really lasts," when describing her shorter stints with certain changemaking activities. If organizations are not proactive at engaging youth beyond their initial experiences, young people may choose to drop out of specific activities or organizations. Even the highly civically engaged youth we talked to would leave settings that were not enjoyable or valuable to them. Everyday racism, as we described in Chapter 3, makes some spaces unwelcoming and untenable for Black youth. In Chapter 7, we delve more into the kinds of opportunities and experiences within organizations that help Black youth sustain their changemaking over time.

YOUTH AGENCY AS A DRIVER OF CHANGEMAKING

Not all launching points stem from outside influences: Youth are also active agents of their own civic development and chart their own changemaking journeys. Agency can be simply defined as a person's feelings of control over their own actions and future. In relation to civic action, agency is the perceived capacity and motivation to challenge oppression and create positive change in community and society. Agency has been studied extensively and called by other names, including efficacy and empowerment (Christens, 2019; Hope, 2016). Compelling research has shown that youth with political interest seek out people, opportunities, and discussions that support their political actions over time (Stattin & Russo, 2022). These findings suggest that youth are agentic in intentionally seeking influential people and opportunities to support civic action. Youth agency is a powerful force in the civic journeys of Black youth specifically. As Dr. David C. Turner III (2021, p. 423) stated in his work on Black Transformative Agency, agency is a tool Black youth can use to "transform their relationships with their peers and social institutions around them." Aligned with sociopolitical development theory, which was developed based on Black youth's experiences (Watts et al., 2011), youth agency can set off a cycle where youth propel themselves toward changemaking, and through taking action, build more agency through seeing the power and impact of their actions. It is important to recognize and document the power of youth agency at the beginning of one's changemaking journey as well as when it is in full bloom. Here, we highlight how youth agency operates as a launching point for change-making through youth's pursuit of passions and personal transformations.

Pursuit of Passions

Young people's interest in a particular topic can lead them to seeking out civic activities that align with these interests. Although many young Black changemakers launch into this work due to their passion about an issue or cause, Mia's (age 16, she/her) story stands out. When asked how she became initially engaged in a health equity club at school, she explained her journey of finding a civic opportunity that matches her passion:

In the ninth grade, I was struggling to find, kind of a passion, not really a passion project, but something at my school that I was really passionate about getting involved in. So, I had a few extracurriculars here and there like the Black Student Union, and the volunteer organization. But neither of those causes were active enough for me at that time. So, when I found [a health equity club], I was really interested in the mission about empowering women and other menstruators and making sure that people have access to what they needed to stay clean and healthy. I'm actually a person who has had my menstrual cycle for a very long time and have faced struggles with access at school. So, the whole objective and the mission of the club is something that I was actually pretty passionate about. So, when I went to my first meeting, and I saw how passionate that the President was about what she was advocating for, it really drew me in. So, I've actually been a member of the [club] since the ninth grade. And through my . . . two and a half years in the club, I have become the Vice President and the advertising coordinator. So I been really involved with the hands-on stuff that we do, and just the initial mission and how valid and how pressing that it was, really got me involved. And it's something that I'm very passionate about.

It took a few tries for Mia to find an organization that aligned with her interests and enabled her to act on her passions. Furthermore, for Mia, like many other Black youth, passions and interests are rooted in personal experiences and intersecting identities, as we described in Chapter 4. In Mia's case, she had some family economic hardships and faced school inequities, which included struggles to access menstrual products. Her own experience with inequity fueled this passionate pursuit of gender-based health equity. Mia's story also reinforces the idea that agency can intertwine with or lead to influential people, as she was inspired by her peer's leadership once she found her way to this civic space. Youth can have more than one important launching point on their journey.

Personal Transformations

Several young people described moments of personal reflection in which they launched their own journey into changemaking. In these moments, youth realized they wanted to make a transformational change in their lives and that change included civic engagement. This launching point was not very common in our study, but it shows the personal power youth have to create their own civic starting points and life transformations. These experiences are a powerful display of youth agency, as youth decide themselves to change the course of their lives, often against a backdrop of economic inequality and white supremacy that seeks to deter and harm their development. The story of Quinn's entry into changemaking illustrates how personal transformations came about and launched changemaking.

Quinn was an eleventh grader in South Central LA deeply engaged in community organizing and focused on challenging inequities faced by students, especially students of color, in the Los Angeles Unified School District. She was also active in the Black Lives Matter Movement. When reflecting on how she came to be so civically engaged, Quinn shared, "I wasn't always like this . . . I was kind of a bad kid low key." Quinn realized she wanted to make a change that would set her on a different life path. She shared:

I realized that I don't want to be . . . stuck, you know, in the same neighborhood not doing nothing, not being able to pay my bills and stuff because I didn't get an education. So, seeing my future and how it's going. It just made me want to change and join our community. All these . . . groups to help other people who realize their future, realize they need to, you know, get on it.

Quinn's story was similar to several other youth who went from unengaged to actively changemaking based on a realization that they personally wanted to grow and change for the better. Sa'Myah described how she was "negatively engaged" in skipping school, and she decided to get her credits to finish school and graduate, with the help of a mentor. This experience changed her beliefs about herself. Sa'Myah shared:

Yeah, six classes then 12 online. It was so stressful and emotional depressed, stressing, everything, anxiety, just overwhelmed. But then I overcame and I was like, "Dang, this is the start. This is who . . . you really are, you can do whatever you want." And from there on, I just been manifesting everything I want.

Sa'Myah was actively engaged in her local community, and this helping was part of her shift to "manifesting everything" she wants out of life. The youth who spoke about having personal transformations also described growing up in communities marked by economic disadvantage or exposure to community violence. Black, Latinx, and Indigenous populations disproportionately experience poverty in the US as a direct result of structural racism. As Dr. Nia Heard-Garris and colleagues (2021, p. S108) explained, "white supremacy and American capitalism drive structural racism and shape the racial distribution of resources and power where children and adolescents *live, learn,* and *play.*" When Black youth living in contexts of economic disadvantage start to recognize these racial and economic inequities, especially when these realities are experienced firsthand, powerful transformations can occur in agency and civic action (Ginwright, 2010b; Kirshner, 2015; Watts et al., 2011). These young Black changemakers were harnessing their own personal power to chart a positive course for themselves that included changemaking to correct racial and economic injustices.

Young Black changemakers identified many factors and influences that sparked their journeys into changemaking. In this chapter, we emphasized three salient launching points: influential people, fun experiences, and youth agency. First, influential people across many contexts and who ranged from personally known to nationally recognized serve as models, encouragers, recruiters, and inspirations for young Black changemakers. Second, the promise of fun and social interactions get young people in the door for civic activities, where they build deeper connections and have a cascade of meaningful experiences. Third, youth's own agency leads them to chart their own trajectories by deciding to become changemakers and seeking out changemaking opportunities that allow them to pursue their passions. Our description of these three launching points builds on our prior discussions of experiencing racism and developing Black identity in Chapters 3 and 4, which are experiences that also launch changemaking.

Contributions to Research

By identifying multiple launching points for Black youth's changemaking, our work contributes to knowledge about how Black youth's civic development begins. Prior research has documented many factors that relate to higher youth civic engagement (Wray-Lake & Ballard, 2023), yet has not often clarified what factors *initiate* youth civic engagement. Political scientists and developmental scholars have long been interested in the questions of "Why do people participate in civic life?" and "How do we get more people to participate?" (Flanagan et al., 2009; Uslaner & Conley, 2003; Verba et al., 1995; Youniss & Yates, 1999). Through Black youth's narrations of their own civic journeys, we pinpointed salient factors that lead youth to initiate civic actions, shedding light on the developmental sequence of civic engagement. Influential people, fun experiences, and youth's own agency are certainly not the only launching points that matter for Black youth, but this work sets the stage for research to further investigate multiple factors that propel Black youth to start their journeys into changemaking. Some youth's civic journeys started in childhood, and research needs to better recognize and study how the seeds of civic engagement are planted and grow during childhood (Astuto & Ruck, 2017; Karras et al., 2020; White & Mistry, 2016). Some launching points also play a role in sustaining Black youth's changemaking over time, as factors that initiate and continue to motivate youth's civic engagement are not necessarily distinct.

Importantly, this study advances knowledge of specific launching points that operate for Black youth. Black youth's lived experiences shaped the nature of each launching point we identified. Regarding influential people, other research corroborates that influential people can inspire and motivate civic engagement for youth across backgrounds (for a review, see Wray-Lake & Ballard, 2023). Yet, Black leaders were particularly inspiring to young Black changemakers, and some Black youth especially resonated with Black leaders who shared their neighborhood background or gender. Regarding fun experiences, prior research has shown that youth in general join civic activities for fun and social reasons (Ballard et al., 2015). Yet, some Black youth in our study were drawn to social spaces where people shared their racial identity and came from their local neighborhoods. They wanted fun experiences that also built community in spaces where they were welcomed and valued. The value of connecting with other Black people is a thread that runs throughout this book.

This set of launching points for young Black changemakers provides some contrast to other research on youth's reasons for joining civic and community-based programs. For example, Dr. Reed Larson and colleagues have mapped youth's motivations to join community organizations. They identified youth who start with external reasons for joining like community service hours, to be with friends, or parent pressure, and then document how youth become more intrinsically motivated over time, pursing the action for its own sake or its larger purpose (Dawes & Larson, 2011; Pearce & Larson, 2006). Our study departs from this typical pattern in two ways: First, young Black changemakers often started with larger goals and purposes in mind, illustrated by the launching point of agency and also discussed in Chapter 2. Certainly, agency can and is developed over time as young people continue to be civically engaged, but many young Black changemakers have agency and use it to chart their own course of development into changemakers. Second, Black youth's reasons for joining civic activities may not be easily separated into extrinsic versus intrinsic categories. When parents, friends, or others encouraged them to engage, Black youth often saw this encouragement as an opportunity to be in community with others, for example, by engaging in civic actions alongside family or friends. We did not find a dominant pattern in youth feeling pressured or mandated to engage. Black youth acted in response to influential people they had close relationships with or felt inspired by. They sought community connections as part of fun experiences they hoped to gain. They used their own agency to drive their decisions to act. Thus, for Black youth, their initial launching points already hold personal meaning, and their civic actions further deepen in meaning and purpose over time.

Practical Insights

In continuing to dispel narrow perceptions of Black youth and their change-making, these findings show us that no single event or experience launches young Black changemaking. Instead, Black youth have a lot of different starting points in their journeys, some of which begin early in life, and take many different paths into changemaking. They exhibit significant agency in determining their own pathways to changemaking, which should be recognized and celebrated. They also rely on inspiration and encouragement that can come from many different sources, such as family, school, peers, and community organizations. The public and adults who work with youth can benefit from understanding the diversity in Black youth's changemaking journeys. Naming these launching points honor Black youth's lived experiences and honors the strengths of Black communities that support Black youth in making and leading change efforts to create a better world.

Identifying this set of powerful launching points, which are uniquely experienced by Black youth, should be informative for anyone interested in having more young Black changemakers in the world. Community-based organizations, educators, and social movement leaders can benefit from knowing how to gain more Black youth voices and presence in their spaces, and these launching points offer insight into strengthening recruitment pathways into changemaking for Black youth. For example, inspirational adults can draw Black youth into changemaking work. Civic opportunities need to be fun and have space for community building and social connection, particularly with other Black people. Organizers and civic leaders must respect youth agency, recognizing that youth have their own interests and passions that drive their engagement. Black youth voice and leadership in civic engagement work should be prioritized. Additionally, building on findings from prior chapters, it is important for anyone working with young Black changemakers to try to eradicate racism in civic spaces and create opportunities for individual and collective healing alongside changemaking (Ginwright, 2010b).

School counselors can play a role in supporting young Black changemaking, which is a role not often named for school staff who hold this position. The instrumental role of school counselors in implementing school-wide civic initiatives is starting to be documented in research (Voight & King-White, 2021). So, we call out to all school counselors and affirm your potential and power to encourage changemaking. Communicate to young people about their potential as changemakers, as having an adult who believes in them goes a long way. Connecting Black youth to opportunities can be the start of their journey into impactful changemaking.

Up Next

This chapter demonstrated multiple ways that people and opportunities can influence Black youth to become changemakers and showed how Black youth themselves act on their agency to forge their own path to changemaking. Naming these launching points expand sociopolitical development theory and the influential role of early experiences in this developmental process. From our findings on launching points, it is undeniable that families are a central node of influence for young Black changemaking and key players in the early influences that lead to Black youth's sociopolitical development. Their influence and encouragement play out in different ways, and we turn to youth's stories of their families' role in Chapter 6.

The Embrace by Meazi Light-Orr

6

Families and Young Black Changemaking

DOMINIQUE MIKELL MONTGOMERY, DOMONIQUE KIANNA
HENDERSON, VICTORIA MILLET, ELAN C. HOPE, &
LAURA WRAY-LAKE

A big inspiration in my life are my siblings . . . they motivate me to do very
important stuff . . .. Seeing them speak out about everything makes me want
to speak out.

Zia

Zia (age 14, she/her), a Black and Filipina girl, is a high performing student, a
frequent community service volunteer, and an advocate for racial justice via
protests and online interpersonal actions to support the Black Lives Matter
Movement. Zia repeatedly noted that her family was a central source of
encouragement and inspiration for her civic engagement. "I'd say [how
I first got engaged] was the help of my mom. 'Cause I know that my sisters –
I'd say my stepsisters and my sister before me, they were Girl Scouts as well."
Zia had been actively involved in Girl Scouts since kindergarten, continuing a
legacy of participating that her older sisters started. Her mother was a primary
source of encouragement to participate in Girl Scouts: "Since my mom came
to the United States and was just learning all about this, and she learned about
the Girl Scouts. She thought it'd be best to put me in too 'cause it's helped [my
older sisters] out, and it should help me out too." In addition to her mother,
Zia's siblings have greatly shaped her trajectory, setting an example for
advocacy by "speak[ing] out about everything" and teaching Zia to do the
same. Zia did speak out, using her voice on social media to express her
passion for racial justice because "you see so many situations where my fellow
members of the Black community are harassed or being put down . . . [it's]
just very upsetting to me." Zia was encouraged to stay civically engaged by the
values her family conveys, including respect for others, awareness that "some
people have different perspectives," and that "it's most important that I speak
out . . . [about] everything that's right." Zia's family played a foundational role
in helping her remain devoted to the goal that "nobody should be treated
differently because of their ethnicity or how they think or how they feel."

This chapter focuses on family influences on young Black changemakers.
Like Zia, other young Black changemakers in our study described how family

members greatly shaped their own views on, and participation in, change-making. Given the importance of family as a launching point as described in Chapter 5, here we more deeply explore how families shape changemaking. These insights came from posing open questions to youth about what influenced their civic journeys. We did not explicitly prompt youth to share about their families; rather, the salience of family became apparent as we spoke to young people and provided them space to share their stories. In this chapter, we describe five main ways that Black youth's families have shaped young Black changemaking. Two types of family influences emphasize family members' roles in encouraging Black youth's changemaking; we show how: (1) family members – especially mothers – connect youth to changemaking; and how (2) family communication shapes youth's changemaking values. Three types of family influences showcase Black youth's agency in pursuing civic actions that center their families, and we highlight how: (3) Black youth take civic actions to directly help family; (4) Black youth take civic actions to protect their families from racism; and (5) Black youth honor their family legacy through changemaking.

We are certainly not the first to recognize that family influences on young Black changemaking run deep. A rich existing body of knowledge shows us that Black changemaking is rooted in the bonds, traditions, and civic legacies of families. Strong kinship bonds and commitments to family are signature strengths that have enabled Black people in the United States to survive and thrive in the face of centuries of racial oppression (Anderson & Stevenson, 2019; Hill, 1999; Murry et al., 2018). Through racial socialization, families help Black youth navigate racial oppression via conversations and messages that prepare youth to face biases and instill cultural traditions, values, and strengths; these exchanges happen with parents and also with siblings and extended family members (Bell et al., 2000; Collins, 1990; Hughes et al., 2006; Jones et al., 2021). Resistance has long been a cornerstone and strength of Black families and communities. From rebellions of enslaved Africans, to outcries over lynchings, the Civil Rights Movement, Million Man March, the Black Lives Matter Movement, and countless other less acknowledged movements, deep-rooted traditions of collective action form a legacy within Black families that the future can be better and that, together, Black people have power to create a world where Black families can safely lead full lives beyond the reach of white supremacy (Allen, 1995; Kelly, 2009; Pope & Flanigan, 2013; Wells-Barnett, 1997). Black families engage in many forms of civic engagement that Black youth also described in Chapter 2, including community-building initiatives, political campaigns and movements, Black service and advocacy organizations centered in Black culture, educational programs, and religious organizations (Gasman et al., 2015). Black families have undoubtedly played a major role in fueling and sustaining Black people's long struggle for civil rights in the US. We build on this knowledge with words from today's young Black changemakers about how their families continue to play this role.

In their stories, youth named the family members who influenced their entry into changemaking, often by connecting them to opportunities. Mothers and fathers were primary sources of connection to changemaking, along with extended family members and elders. By focusing on the family members who connected youth to changemaking and how they have done so, we illustrate the breadth and diversity of Black youth's family networks and the individual and collective role family members play in cultivating young Black changemaking. We start with fathers and extended family members, and then move to Black youth's most frequently mentioned source of entry into civic engagement: their mothers.

Martin (age 14, he/him) attributed his entry into civic engagement to his father. According to Martin, "every year, on Martin Luther King Day, [a service organization] does this thing where they beautify the schools . . . . I do that every year with my dad." Martin has been doing community service like this event and others with his dad "for as long as I can remember." Martin's dad also introduced him to political engagement, such as by taking him to the annual "Pride March – it was just always me, my dad, my brother, my sister." Martin's dad was his source for learning about politics and the world. He said:

My dad's kind of really been the more politically active one, introducing us to these political things . . .. He always explains these things. Tells us about what's going on in the world. I actually don't follow the news that much. He's kind of my source of news . . . about politics and stuff – he's where I get all my news from. So, he explains what's going on in the world, why it's significant. Like on a weekly basis every time we see him.

Martin's father has ensured that volunteer days, marches that celebrate lesbian, gay, transgender, queer, and questioning (LGBTQ+) identities, and discussions of current events are civic activities ingrained in Martin's regular routine. Other youth described how their fathers served as connectors to the broader community. Cory's (age 15, he/him) father facilitated opportunities for his civic engagement. "I participate in religious programs and services . . .. My dad, he's a deacon in the church. So, a lot of times, we'll help get the stuff that we need [for the] church program." Like Martin, Cory and his father participated in community helping together.

Elder family members such as grandmothers, aunts, and uncles also influenced youth's civic engagement journeys. Creative's (age 18, she/her) uncle played a role in connecting her to civic opportunities. She stated, "I do participate in religious programs and services. So, my uncle owns a church and since I'm a dancer, he's asked me to be lead dancer of his group. So . . . whenever we have shows about dance and stuff, I lead and choreograph, and I teach everyone the moves." Nicole (age 18, she/her) was connected early in her life to civic opportunities through her grandmother. She shared, "My grandma is in [community service organization] and basically, they do volunteering. So, when I was little, I would help out with that." In explaining how she got started in following the news, Unique (age 17, she/her), like Nicole, pointed to the role of her grandmother:

My grandma makes sure I'm in there with her every morning . . . . Mainly, if there's something about anything with politics . . ., she tend to make sure that I know . . . . Also at school, we had this one teacher . . . he has this . . . daily warmup. And . . . it'd be political related. So, I kind of appreciate her for the news in the morning because it be helping me in the class.

Unique's grandmother started a tradition of morning news watching with her, and this daily tradition benefited Unique academically as well. Multiple family members play active roles in connecting Black youth to opportunities for civic action, but perhaps none so powerfully as mothers. Consistently and without prompting, many young people in this study detailed the ways their mothers acted as a primary connector to civic action opportunities, returning to the impact of their mothers multiple times during their interviews.

As an example, Tom's description of his own civic journey demonstrates the powerful influence of mothers on young Black changemaking. A 17-year-old attending an elite public charter school, Tom (he/him) was highly engaged in school-based organizations such as debate club, service work supporting the unhoused, and community-based organizations focused on developing and supporting Black men. Tom's parents have master's degrees, and he reported they are well off financially. His family placed a priority on helping those with fewer financial resources. When asked how he initially became engaged in his current array of civic actions, Tom named that his mom brought him along to participate in her civic work with an organization focused on connecting mothers of color to civic opportunities and emphasized what he gained from the experience. He said:

They [organization] do feeding the homeless, like every Tuesday. And so, I started to go to that. And I remember I started doing that when I was pretty young . . . . But then also, during the wintertime, they would give away coats. And I remember this one homeless lady she came in, and my sister, you know, before we went, everyone in my family would give us stuff, you know, that you don't need any more, like coats, and then we would go and . . . give it away. And I remember seeing this homeless lady wearing my sister's jacket. And she was so happy. And . . . that made me feel really good.

Tom's story demonstrates the power mothers play in shaping youth's civic journeys through connecting them with civic opportunities early in life. These experiences are not single, isolated events, but rather repeated opportunities that offer a host of experiences that support youth's long-term civic actions. By bringing Tom to volunteer with her regularly since he was young, Tom's mother normalized civic action and made it into a habit that also reflected a family priority. This is what political scientists and psychologists describe as civic modeling – a form of civic socialization where children learn civic values and knowledge through witnessing their parents or other family members engage in civic and political action (McIntosh et al., 2007). Tom was inspired by his mom, and through her learned from the wisdom of Black history and experience as well. His mom had "been here when the Rodney King stuff was happening and thus had more experience than me." Tom's mom shared her past experiences of protesting with him, accompanied him to some protests, and taught him "never to succumb to authority . . . just because they're in this position." Tom witnessed and learned from the civic engagement of his mother *and* his mother invited him to participate as a young changemaker. Martin's dad, Cory's dad, and Unique's grandmother were also examples of what it looks like to engage in civic modeling.

Tom was not alone in pointing to his mother as a primary connector to civic opportunities that jump started his civic journey. Soleil (age 13, she/her) noted that "my mom got me into [an all-Black Girl Scout troop] four years ago," which became one of her main civic activities. Similar to Tom, Soleil's mother planted the seeds for long-term civic engagement by connecting her to meaningful civic opportunities early in life. As we presented in the opening story, Zia had the same experience as Soleil of starting Girl Scouts early due to her mom's encouragement. Amir (age 13, he/him) shared a similar story of his mom as a bridge to civic opportunities, stating, "when I was about eight years old, me and my mom started volunteering. And so, after I got to [a city within Los Angeles], I was about 12 years old . . . my mom said that she wants me to start going to the 100 Black Men meetings." Amir's mom demonstrated a developmentally informed understanding of how to cultivate civic engagement; she started early by co-engaging with Amir in service and, as he entered adolescence, identified a civic opportunity that aligned with his autonomy needs (something he could do without her) and identity needs (that would support his development into a young Black man).

Indeed, mothers of Black youth are not selecting and encouraging civic opportunities haphazardly or out of mere convenience, but based on recognition of what their Black child needs to grow and thrive. Psychologists find that for Black families, racial socialization (communication about race) and civic socialization (communication about civic engagement) are intertwined and together support the civic and identity development of Black youth (Bañales, Hope et al., 2021). For the young people in this study, many mothers focused on connecting their children to Black-centered organizations and opportunities, some of which were also gender-specific. This goal of mothers comes through in the connector stories we already described: for example, Soleil's mom sought out an all-Black girl scout troop for her daughter, and Amir's mom encouraged him to join 100 Black Men of America, a national African American-led mentoring organization that emphasizes health and wellness, education, economic empowerment, and civic leadership (100blackmen.org).

Other youth's stories demonstrate the ways in which families who are already connected to Black organizations use those ties to enrich their children's civic experiences. KJ (age 16, she/her) began her civic engagement through her mother's long-term connection to a Black sorority. "When I was very, very young ... my mom is ... part of Delta Sigma Theta. And so, in their chapter and everything, they always, always volunteer. And so, I would go with her to some of the volunteer opportunities." Delta Sigma Theta is a Black sorority with over a century-long history of changemaking (Delta Sigma Theta Sorority, Inc., 2022). KJ's mother joined Delta Sigma Theta before having children, and this organizational resource helped her connect her daughter to civic opportunities. By connecting their children to Black civic spaces, mothers set a powerful chain of events in motion: These spaces encourage Black identity development, education on Black history, and connections to Black community and culture, which help Black youth sustain their changemaking. We discuss youth's experiences in Black-centered organizations in Chapter 7.

For the young Black changemakers in our study, mothers were undoubtedly the most salient connectors of civic engagement in their lives, who play a uniquely pivotal role in Black youth civic engagement. These mothers exemplify what Dr. Patricia Hill Collins (2000) called motherwork, where Black motherhood, by necessity, includes challenging systems of oppression, preparing children to experience racism, and empowering them to navigate societal systems. Through motherwork, Black mothers recognize that forward progression within their own family unit – such as through encouraging their Black children to help the Black community, participate in Black organizations, and challenge racism – advances the Black community as a whole (Naples, 1992; Rodriguez, 2016). As journalist and Black mother Dani McClain (2019, p. 208) stated, this generations-long practice "recognizes that individual survival, empowerment, and identity require group survival, empowerment, and identity."

Across youth's descriptions and accounts of different family members' influences, a clear set of strategies was evident that families used to introduce Black youth to civic engagement. These strategies included seeking out and identifying specific opportunities for young people; encouraging young people to participate; participating in civic action alongside young people; and establishing family habits or traditions of regular engagement together. Young Black changemakers shared insights into how these family strategies can have a dual goal of encouraging civic engagement and building opportunities for racial socialization and Black identity development.

FAMILY COMMUNICATION SHAPES BLACK YOUTH'S
CHANGEMAKING VALUES

Young Black changemakers shared how they are influenced by family communication about values. This finding aligns with decades of research in psychology and human development showing that family communication is important for young people's development (Lee et al., 2013; Pearson et al., 2010; Shehata, 2016). Specific to changemaking, research has documented how family discussions about social and political issues influence whether and how a young person is civically engaged (Bañales, Hope et al., 2021; Barnes & Hope, 2017; Verba et al., 2003; White & Mistry, 2016). Yet, we have a lot more to learn about what family communication around changemaking looks like in Black families. Black youth's own perceptions of how these conversations shape their trajectories offer a valuable lens on how families influence young Black changemaking. Young Black changemakers benefited from explicit conversations about the value of changemaking with parents and from broader conversations that encouraged them to chart their own courses of changemaking and supported them along the way.

Family Conversations about the Value of Changemaking

For some youth, discussions with family members about changemaking were a key influence on their journeys toward civic engagement. Families placed high value on changemaking and conveyed this to young people. Sara Vaughn (age 15, she/her) summarized this idea plainly, saying, "I mean, for a lot of my friends that are really engaged, it's also a value thing. Like a family value that's been passed on." Some family conversations define specific ways of engaging as a family priority. Jen (age 15, she/her) was highly engaged in a family-based service organization and in her school's Black Student Union, and her mother conveyed the importance of supporting communities of color. Jen's mother "wants me and my brothers to be involved in as much as we can, like, mainly stuff for people of color, so that we could make a change." Jen has embraced this vision for her own changemaking, describing her civic purpose "as being the change … because I have yet to see a Black person or a young, Black female to make a change in this community." Ashley (age 16, she/her) also shared how her parents communicate their visions for changemaking and fighting for the rights of all people, especially Black people. Ashley said:

My parents are always talking to us to fight for us, fight for others, it doesn't matter who you are. Fight for others and definitely for your own people. Help others in need because if you can give them something that's always going to be helpful. Always uplift your own people. Don't ever tear them down just to make yourself feel better. That's not helping.

Ashley had internalized these messages from her parents, as helping her community and fighting for others through protesting racial injustice defined her current changemaking. These messages from parents also echoed in her own visions for her future changemaking and career, where she wanted to uplift and invest in Black communities through her own medical practice. She said:

I want to go to medical school and . . . have my own practice. I'm thinking of just having all African American workers and then donating some of my profit [to] different organizations, Black organizations, because I just know that, we need this. It's important to uplift your own people.

Martin's father also communicated the value of being civically engaged. When describing the origins of his civic actions, Martin said, "[My father] he's like an inspiration to do these things. It's more like he says 'Okay, so here's what's going on in the world. Here's what we can do . . ., we're gonna go on the Pride parade thing.' He explains it and then we kinda just do it." Through his communication about "what we're gonna do," Martin's father conveyed the type of changemaking he wanted his children to embrace. In his interview, Martin acknowledged he was still determining whether or how he would sustain civic action over the long term, yet he gave his father credit for pushing him to consider civic action as a future option for himself.

Although families convey specific values and priorities about changemaking, Black youth ultimately exercise agency to decide whether to embrace these values and priorities for themselves. For example, A.G. (age 15, she/her) explained that when she was nervous about going to volunteer with an organization serving people who were unhoused, her mother reminded her of the value of helping others. A.G. shared, "I was just nervous for some reason, and she [mother] was like, 'You get to help these people and their families and the children. Think about it,' so then after, I was like, 'You know, I should do it. It's the right thing to do.'" A.G. decided to engage in this act of helping, which snowballed into many other civic activities for her thereafter, and her mother's reminder of their family value of helping was instrumental in this changemaking journey.

Jen, Martin, and A.G.'s stories are examples of how racialized civic socialization happens in Black families. Family members helped Black youth establish a deep value and priority for civic engagement, and families conveyed social justice values of supporting people of color and advocating for the rights of disenfranchised people. In Black families, communicating about civic engagement often goes hand in hand with communicating about race and racism (Bañales, Hope et al., 2021): Parents of Black youth communicate the importance of civic engagement and often connect those experiences to the realities of being a Black person in the United States. Jen shared that one reason her mother valued civic engagement pertained to defying negative stereotypes of Black youth, which is another example of Black motherwork (Collins, 2000). By communicating the importance of civic engagement, Jen's mother "wants us to be different, she doesn't want us to be stuck in the stereotype of a Black person. So, she tries her best to get us away from that." We described in Chapter 4 how some Black youth engage in changemaking to defy negative stereotypes, and here we see that some families have this motivation for encouraging their Black children to be changemakers, as well. In Black families, the value of changemaking is often closely aligned with Black culture and identity.

Family Discussions Encourage Reflection and Autonomy on Changemaking

In addition to family conversations aimed at conveying an explicit value or type of changemaking, open conversations in families can support Black youth's civic actions, reinforce the values youth already assign to civic engagement, and encourage young people to decide for themselves what kind of changemaking values to pursue. As Mea's story shows, her impressions of the meaning and purpose of her changemaking deepened over time, in part due to ongoing open-ended discussions with her parents.

Mea (age 16, she/her) was primarily engaged with a family organization that she describes as "basically where Black families come together and do community service." Initially, Mea valued her civic actions because she had fun and made social connections, a valuable launching point for civic engagement described in Chapter 5. In middle school, Mea had an awakening where she started to "really understand a lot of stuff that's going on in the world," noting her new understanding of racism and the importance of Black people fighting for justice. Some scholars would describe Mea's experience as the precritical stage of sociopolitical development, where young people gain new and more complex analysis of social justice and oppression that can support critical actions to challenge oppressions (Watts et al., 2003). At this point, Mea's actions took on new meaning because she became committed to contributing to the thriving of the Black community. Importantly, ongoing conversations with her parents sustained her actions and beliefs about the value of civic engagement for society and the importance of being engaged across the lifespan: "We always have talks. And they always tell me it's important that you really get involved and stay focused and stay awake of what is going on, and that really helps me stay focused." Mea's parents were emphasizing the value of being civically engaged, similar to Jen or Martin above, but they also kept the conversations open and did not force any specific views on her. She noted, "I don't know what their goals would be. I know of course they have goals, they want to see change and everything too." Mea was not simply adopting her parents' civic purpose, but rather was encouraged more broadly by these family conversations to embrace the idea that civic action is meaningful and impactful. Through Mea's story, we learn that parents can communicate the value of being civically engaged while also leaving room for agency and autonomy as young people develop their civic identity. The core family values of "making a change" and "staying involved" are important foundations for changemaking. However, parents can still give youth space to discover for themselves what kind of changemaking they aspire to.

Families also offered youth encouragement for their self-defined change-making values, which helped them to sustain their long-term civic efforts and commitment to those values. JD (age 13, he/him), who engaged in various self-initiated activities to support the Black community in South Central LA, described receiving this type of encouragement. When asked what keeps him engaged, JD remarked, "What keeps me going is the family that loves me . . .. They tell me to keep doing what you do, because it's helping the community out, even though it's not helping them a lot. It's making little moves to help them to get to where they need to go. And the encouragement helps me to do better and be better." JD did not describe his family members as civically engaged, actively connecting him to opportunities, or discussing civic issues per se; rather, their encouragement of his interests gave JD the support he needed to sustain his commitment to changemaking. Similarly, James (age 16, he/him) told us how his parents supported him in following his passion for changemaking. When asked what helps him stay so deeply involved in community helping, James responded, "My parents. My parents are always allowing me to do what kind of, I don't want to say what I please but, if it's something I'm passionate about, they'll try to make space and make time for me to do it."

Like JD, Jaylen (age 15, he/him), who was engaged in many types of changemaking, from mentoring youth to participating in meaningful art, credited family for helping him sustain his values. Jaylen described feeling like a moral person, saying, "I'm a good, I'm a nice person"; bettering himself and making others happy were central to Jaylen's personal values. In his efforts, Jaylen was motivated by "my uncle. He's also inspirational too. My uncle always gives me a talk." Jaylen's uncle encouraged him "to be [my]self, be a better person." In this way, Jaylen's uncle encouraged Jaylen to continue his civic engagement through affirming and uplifting him but did not pre-scribe a particular trajectory. Nicole shared a similar story about conversa-tions with her grandmother, who posed questions to Nicole about what mattered to her, supporting her decisions and challenging her to grow, without expectations or demands. Nicole said:

Well, she [grandmother] supports me by, first of all, asking questions like, "Is this something you sure you want to do?" And supporting me in the decisions I make and guiding me in the right direction . . .. If I'm in the wrong, she'll tell me I'm in the wrong and without expectation and tell me what I could do to improve myself.

For JD, James, Jaylen, Nicole, and others, family conversations kept them committed to their changemaking values. For these young people, the role of family was not prescriptive – the family messages did not outline a specific set of expectations, actions, or beliefs. Instead, these young people were on their changemaking journeys, and family members encouraged these relatively independent youth to continue pursuing their goals.

BLACK YOUTH TAKE CIVIC ACTIONS TO DIRECTLY HELP FAMILY

The next three big ideas in this chapter focus on how Black youth take civic actions that center their families. First, Black youth take civic actions that center their families by directly assuming responsibilities to ensure the physical and emotional well-being of family members who need this support, such as elderly family members and younger siblings. In these examples, families are both the influence of and the target of Black youth's changemaking. Black youth are showing agency to care for their own families, which in turn supports and strengthens their larger community.

Ray (age 17, she/her) spent considerable time taking care of her grandmother who recently moved in with her family after her life partner passed away. "She [grandmother] has seizures and stuff, so she was living up there with [her partner] for years, and then he passed away, so she had to move back down here because, you know, she really can't take care of herself . . . . I just help her do a lot of the stuff that she [needs] help to do." Ray used her time and energy to take care of her grandmother and considered this an important form of civic engagement. CJ (age 18, they/them), like Ray, primarily focused their civic action on ensuring their family's well-being, and for CJ, the family member was their father:

My dad – he has MS [multiple sclerosis]. He's been having it for almost 25 years. So, by getting around and stuff . . . I try to help. A lot of stuff around the house . . . . Washing clothes, mopping the floor, cleaning the bathroom, all that stuff, I do the household stuff . . . I'm basically being his legs for him.

CJ considered this family role their first, core experience of civic engagement. Previous research with Black youth and other youth of color has acknowledged that helping family members is a vital form of youth civic engagement (White-Johnson, 2012; Wray-Lake & Abrams, 2020). Stories like these from Ray, CJ, and others bring continued attention to legitimizing helping family members as a civic action. Some scholars explicitly exclude helping family from definitions of civic engagement, assuming that civic engagement must be done outside of the household to be legitimate. Yet, according to Black youth, family helping is a central part of their civic engagement.

Kobe (age 17, he/him) expressed passion about protecting his sister from community stressors like poverty and violence: "I don't want her to see, you know, that's why I be trying to shield her from real life stuff, but trying to give her real life stuff, information." Further defining his civic purpose, Kobe stated, "I mentor her, tryna, you know, put her on the right path." Kobe felt like he was exposed to the negative aspects of life at too young an age and did not want that for his younger sister. He explained:

Every day, I do [mentor] because I always talk to my sister. Now I'm learning, because as a kid, I was always hardheaded. So, my sister, she a young woman, she got them young woman tendencies, so she hardheaded. But you got to keep working with her, that's how I put it. I can't just give up on her, be like okay. Cause what would that make me? That will make me weak in a way ... I just know what I'm supposed to do, it's just like, "Okay. Just be that, you know, person in her life that just gonna guide her to the right things, you know, that's gonna have her back regardless, like the shoulder she gonna cry on." And that's what big brothers here for.

In this example, Kobe described engaging in community helping, and particularly mentoring, to protect his younger sister from a world that, based on his lived experience, could do her harm. In his efforts to mentor and support his sister, Kobe again illustrates that for young Black changemakers, civic action is not limited to the outside community or general public, but also includes purposeful engagement within the family.

Damian (age 18, he/him) was engaged in an organization focused on youth of color's development from a social justice lens and was passionate about beginning a trend of success in his family. Similar to Kobe, Damian expressed a desire to shield his brother from negative influences and used active mentorship to serve that purpose. He stated, "I want to be ... a role model for my little brother. So, he can, not necessarily go with the path that I'm going, but just be successful and the people after him." He actively shielded his brother because "he watches me a lot. So, I always just try to just be a good role model for him, like never doing anything bad so he won't see me, he won't get influenced into that type of life to go down a bad road." In this way, Damian protected his brother from negative influences by acting as a strong mentor and setting a good example by civic modeling in a similar fashion to the parents and elder family members of other changemakers in the study.

Like Kobe and Damian, part of A.G.'s civic actions included mentoring her sibling. A.G.'s understanding of the precarity of Black life greatly impacted her civic purpose, which included wanting to ensure her younger sister similarly understood the impact of racism. She reflected, "It saddens me to see others treated terribly because of their race, and I know it can happen to me, and it happens to other people, kids who are Black." In this context, A.G. mentored her younger sister, saying: "I want her to understand how I do because I don't think she sees ... how racism is as bad as a thing like I do – so I wanna encourage her, for her to recognize that type of thing." A.G. wanted to ensure her sister was well-informed, particularly on the impact of racism on the lives of Black people; thus, she mentored her sister with an aim of providing both racial and civic socialization.

Youth including Mea, Ray, Kobe, Damian, and A.G. took various civic actions to help and support their family members. These demonstrations of commitment to family are also part of pursuing the civic purpose of creating a better world for Black people.

BLACK YOUTH TAKE CIVIC ACTIONS TO PROTECT FAMILY FROM RACISM

Black youth navigate a systematically racist context that includes police brutality, discrimination, and invalidation targeting the Black community (Witherspoon et al., 2022). As we highlighted in Chapters 3 and 4, we echo other scholars (Hope et al., 2023) in finding that experiences of anti-Black racism guide civic engagement for Black youth. Some young Black change-makers described the connection between racism and changemaking by centering their own families. Because families are nested within communities, and the Black community is an extension of their family unit for many, young Black changemakers centered their family's well-being when envisioning community or societal change. Their experiences of anti-Black racism are deeply personal because anti-Black racism affects their family members. In this way, changemaking in response to racism is guided in part by the civic purpose of protecting family well-being.

Black youth take civic actions to protect parents, younger siblings, and others from racialized violence by problem-solving or advocating on their behalf. Mea shared her feelings about deadly police violence targeting Black people and why she planned to advocate for racial justice:

Having a Black dad, having Black brothers, I think that also really triggers me . . . .. On the news you see, it's Black men that are being targeted. So that . . . kind of puts fear in my heart. And I feel like as kids, we shouldn't even be having to have fear in our heart [s] right now. We should be wanting to have fun, just live life, like we're in high school. But you know, we see all this stuff going on. And then this makes me want to protect my family and do the best that I can 'cause I don't want to see them get hurt.

Mea was highly engaged in community service with a Black-centered organization, and in response to the egregious and highly publicized police violence against Black people in 2020, Mea planned to expand her changemaking to protect her family's well-being by "go[ing] to protests I mean and just participat[ing]." Mea felt frustrated that her family was at risk and that she must carry that burden daily, yet she viewed civic actions as a tangible way to protect her family. As described in Chapter 4, some Black youth use civic actions as an adaptive coping strategy to respond to the inherent risks of racism, and civic actions also support racial identity development and well-being throughout adolescence and into adulthood (Hope & Spencer, 2017).

Collective actions to challenge racism and preserve the safety of loved ones are vital to Black survival and well-being, especially in communities where police and others frequently do harm to Black people (Garza, 2020).

Just as Black youth take civic actions to protect their families, their families also strive to protect them from racism and racial violence that is ever-present in society. This mutual desire for protection, when combined with the precarity of Black life in the US, can, at times, create complex family dynamics, as represented by the reflections of Quinn.

Quinn (age 16, she/her) was highly engaged in community organizing and activism, particularly around educational and racial equity for the low-income Black and Brown community in which she lives. Quinn described her civic purpose as creating more equity and ensuring people in her community are "having the same opportunities" as others. She was motivated to create opportunities for Black people so society can "have more Black presidents . . . more Black people all around." Quinn continued her activism in the summer of 2020, as the goals of the protest movement deeply aligned with Quinn's pursuit of racial equity and her lived experiences of police brutality. However, Quinn's family grew concerned about her safety. She recalled the complexity of navigating civic actions to protect her family and community from systemic racism, while they worried about her protesting in the height of summer 2020 when police violence against protesters escalated. Quinn stated:

[Protesting] was a big thing with my family because they were kind of scared for me. When it came to the protests and stuff, because you know, a lot of stuff is going on . . . . I think it was [on] Washington or something like that, whole shut down, and you couldn't get in contact with anybody, you know, everything that was happening they were worried about it . . . I didn't tell nobody that I was going to that protest. So, when they found out they were really upset they were kind of yelling at me. They're really just trying to make sure I was okay. It was kind of upsetting, you know? I was like, "I'm trying to fight for you and your children and stuff, and you want me to stop?"

Through protesting, Quinn was fighting for her family and future generations to be free from racism, yet Quinn's family wanted to protect her from anti-Blackness in the present moment as well. Black youth and their families resolve these conflicts in different ways. As we highlight further in Chapter 8, some youth focused on online civic actions against racism during the summer of 2020 because their parents did not want them to attend in-person protests. Regardless of how these tensions are resolved, Black youth and their families endeavor to protect each other and their larger community from racism.

BLACK YOUTH TAKE CIVIC ACTIONS TO HONOR FAMILY LEGACY

Black youth honor their family legacies in different ways through their changemaking. Some youth build on existing family legacies of powerful contributions to communities and success by engaging in civic action. Other youth devote their energy to civic actions that cultivate new legacies, honoring their families by generating new reasons for family to be proud and creating pathways to changemaking for future generations. Black youth seeking to honor their family legacy through changemaking are demonstrating feelings of responsibility and duty to pay it forward and continue this mission to seek liberation from social oppression (Taylor, 1998). JD exemplified this idea of honoring family legacy, sharing that his civic actions matter "because my great grandma['s] parents, my ancestors used to be slave members and they couldn't read or write . . .. And if they tried to, they would get . . . they leg off, so it would make me push even more, push more Black people to . . . wake up." The resilience his ancestors displayed pushed JD to strive to create change by mobilizing the Black community for racial justice.

Success with Lex (age 18, she/her) was highly engaged in volunteering at food banks and reaching out to public officials to advocate for investment in low-income communities like her own. She was inspired to become civically engaged from seeing "strong Black women" like her grandmother and aunt engage in the community. Success with Lex named their influences as "really significant for me," and then expanded on this multigenerational legacy of changemaking:

My aunt was a Black Panther and my grandmother, she's basically dang near one. She's actively wrote to local government officials. She's very active in trying to better Black communities and Latino communities, so growing up around her and seeing what she did, I feel [they] really inspired me to do the same thing.

Success with Lex embraced her role in continuing this legacy, as problems "are still not solved. I feel like I have to keep pushing until they get solved." Whether through helping or activism, youth seek to build upon legacies of changemaking in ways that honor their families. Changemaking legacies give strength to Black youth's individual and collective identities (Chapter 4) and, as we highlight in Chapter 8, also feed into Black youth's actions and visions of social movements that continue this work.

Other youth sought to cultivate new legacies through changemaking. Damian wanted to start a new cycle of success in his family, stating:

I always didn't want to be part of stats of people going to jail . . .. I wanted to start a cycle of my family, of success. Instead of going to jail and all this bad stuff . . .. In my family, the highest anybody has gone was Community College, and I said, "but I'm striving for more than that." I want to start a trend in my family to go further.

Damian wanted to begin a new tradition for his family of going to college and being "impactful in his community" and have that become his family's legacy. Like Damian, JD exemplified how the absence of familial civic legacies can drive changemaking that cultivates new legacies. The absence of JD's father motivated him to create new family traditions of changemaking. JD explained, "the role [of] my father is that he's not here. When he's not here, it's helping me more, because he's the one that's losing … because I'm making the right steps in life to not be him and it's making me grind more, dedicate myself, even though he's not here."

Family legacies of changemaking are also closely tied to learning about Black history, because you have to know your history to honor it. For example, Tom explained how his changemaking is intimately tied to Black history, a knowledge that was part of his identity and emphasized by his mother since childhood. He shared:

A lotta people watch CNN for three days and then think they're Black activists. And I'm just kinda like, no [laughs] …… My mom has been … showin' me documentaries and making sure that I'm educated on my history and how we got here and, you know, how systems are set up just so when stuff like this happens, I feel like I can help other people because I know what I'm talkin' about. So, yeah, it felt personal because this is who I am. I was raised on this, you know?

Tom's approach to changemaking was rooted in the impactful historical teachings from his mother. In making the connection between historic and modern racism, Tom was demonstrating critical race consciousness (Bañales et al., 2023). This knowledge and analysis, which guided his changemaking, was an integral part of his family's legacy of Black changemaking.

Like Tom, other youth we interviewed saw honoring family as intertwined with honoring the Black community in taking civic action. Soleil articulated this connection when explaining how changemaking is unique for Black youth, starting with the idea of negative perceptions of Black people as the "rules of our life." Soleil stated:

I mean, it's part of the way, rules of our life, how we're perceived in the world. We have to step in on these issues and try and change it because it's not right. It's … been happening for too long and … I think it's time with the uprising of technology and social media, and now … things are getting filmed and it's everywhere. The unique thing about it is that it brings people together. It builds a community between people who are struggling with the same issues and just have a hard time with it, and people just gathering around and then saying, "Hey, I relate to you in that way and we can go through this together." So, community and family is something that I've always found really special about fighting about these issues.

As Soleil conveyed, family and community are at the center of changemaking for Black youth. Black youth are working together with family and community to challenge racism and create better futures for other Black people. Black youth are brought together by a shared vision, often part of their family's history, values, and future.

THE TAKE-AWAYS

For young Black changemakers, families are a keystone of their civic engagement. Mothers, fathers, siblings, and extended family members connect youth to opportunities for changemaking and engage with them, which provides foundational launching points for youth's deeper journeys into changemaking. Through conversations, families discuss the value of changemaking and also make space for supporting youth's own chosen changemaking paths. These conversations help youth sustain their civic action and support youth's attempts to create change in the world around them. Yet, families' influences on Black youth are not only adult driven. Young Black changemakers demonstrate agency in pursuing civic actions that center their families. For some Black youth who are engaged in helping their family members, civic engagement quite literally begins at home. Young Black changemakers are also driven to challenge racism in part to protect their own families, and they seek to honor their families' legacies by working to make the world better for their families and other Black people.

Contributions to Research

Our findings show how civic socialization in Black families is often intertwined with racial socialization. This builds on recent research from Dr. Josefina Bañales and colleagues (2021), who found that, in Black families, the aims and practices of communicating messages about race and racism to Black children often overlap and co-occur with messages about civic engagement. For the young Black changemakers in our study, families encouraged participation in Black-centered organizations and they connected what it means to be Black with being civically engaged in family discussions. These family interactions emphasize Black families' values of helping, of advancing liberation for the Black community, and of supporting the civic engagement of their children. The dual emphasis in Black families on racial socialization and changemaking is foundational to Black youth's changemaking journeys.

Our work aligns with the thinking of Black feminist scholars and others that Black mothers are often agents of social change that synthesize resistance to racial oppression into the fabric of everyday family practices (Bucholtz, 2014; Collins, 1990). Black mothers often share a collective understanding that any forward progression through personal success or changemaking for their children or family unit advances the liberation and thriving of the Black community as a whole (Naples, 1992; Rodriguez, 2016). As influential agents of social change, Black mothers educate their children about the benefits of civic engagement, teach cultural practices that align with helping and collective action, and contribute to initiatives that better the Black community. With overlapping systems of oppression interfering with Black people's access to opportunities, mothers aid in resisting these injustices by involving their children in civic activities (Collins, 1990). This multigenerational practice of motherwork is important to continue studying because through everyday mothering, Black mothers are pursuing the survival and thriving of their own children alongside the survival and thriving of the Black community (McClain, 2019). Black mothers are not the only ones doing this work; research could benefit from further exploring how fathers and other family members support changemaking, as youth in our study highlighted their meaningful roles.

Black youth see helping, protecting, and honoring family as core goals of their changemaking. Black youth do not just learn to be civically engaged from their families; they also actively choose to take civic actions that center their families. Black youth play a socializing role themselves, such as through mentoring siblings and creating new legacies of changemaking to pass on to their families. Given the rampant anti-Blackness that pervades the US, many Black youth fight for their families' (and especially siblings') well-being as they advocate for racial equity more broadly. Pursuing racial justice is not just an important value for Black youth; it is necessary for the survival and thriving of themselves, their family members, and future generations of Black people. We need to better recognize how deeply personal and necessary changemaking is for Black youth. Their civic engagement pushes back against anti-Black racism and is rooted in honoring family legacies, fostering the wellness of family and community, and forging new paths to Black liberation. Young Black changemakers are inspired by the changemaking work of their families and ancestors. Future research should do more to showcase the meaning and value of family legacies for sustaining youth's changemaking.

Practical Insights

Young Black changemakers rarely act alone, and Black youth's families can serve as support and motivation for changemaking, and can be collaborators with a shared civic purpose. Black changemaking is a family affair, and family-focused civic organizations may offer valuable spaces in which Black youth and their families practice changemaking. Civic organizations that work with youth should recognize the powerful role Black families can play in Black youth's changemaking and create opportunities for Black family members to engage with and support the civic work of Black youth.

It is essential for community-based organizations, schools, and other entities to supplement family efforts to encourage civic engagement. Black families should not have the sole responsibility of upholding the value of civic engagement and leading or guiding their children to advance racial and social justice. Black youth need to feel supported in their changemaking outside the home, as we described regarding schools (Chapter 3) and organizations (Chapter 7). Civic spaces could offer opportunities for healing for Black youth, who are often shouldering heavy burdens of protecting their own families and the wider world from racism. Black youth should not have to bear this alone. Supporting young Black changemakers can help advance

Black youth's goals to protect and honor the legacy of their families by creating spaces where they feel safe to voice their opinions and advocate for change on behalf of their community without feeling silenced or undervalued.

Up Next

This chapter has illustrated a central take-away from this book: Black families encourage changemaking in multiple ways. Building on sociopolitical development theory, families are a major early life influence on young Black changemakers' journeys, along with other launching points we described in Chapter 5. Another key aspect of Black youth's sociopolitical development is access to opportunity structures for civic engagement outside of family contexts. Families alone should not be tasked with supporting young Black changemakers in their journeys, and as shown in Chapter 3, schools may be sites of Black youth's resistance, but do not always offer supportive contexts for Black youth's civic engagement. Supportive spaces for Black youth and their changemaking are found in some community-based civic organizations. Chapter 7 focuses on how civic organizations are hubs for opportunities that foster Black youth's agency and help sustain changemaking over time.

7

Organizations and Black Youth Agency

LAURA WRAY-LAKE, SARA BLOOMDAHL WILF,
MARIAH BONILLA, & ELENA MAKER CASTRO

I like how my [organization] ... how encouraging they are .... I feel like
spaces like that – they really get kids to be civically engaged .... Having an
adult really cheerin' me on and hypin' me up. Stuff like that really wants me to
work hard and do stuff like that. If we have more spaces like that, you know,
more kids my age would be doin' it.

Cory

Cory (he/him), a 15-year-old first-generation Nigerian American, started his
interview by detailing 16 different civic actions. His actions were deeply
embedded within two civic organizations that were central to his changemaking journey. In one organization, Cory organized around racial injustice in
schools, sharing: "I campaigned with my organization ... about ... stopping
willful defiance in school. You can't suspend a student for not listening in
school because it's not gonna help them. They're just gonna miss out on
lessons and [it will] just negatively affect them." With another organization, a
school-based Youth Participatory Action Research (YPAR) class, Cory
described working to improve his community through education efforts and
action research, saying, "A lot of times we'll go and we'll do surveys and then
we'll take the information and then we'll educate people in our community."
Through these organizations, Cory described growing as a person and becoming empowered as a changemaker, explaining, "I get educated in things that
are affecting my community, I find out ways I can change it. And I can take
the information and I can teach it to somebody else, and then they can teach it
to somebody else. And that way, it just spreads."

We return to Cory's story – and the stories of other young Black
changemakers – throughout the chapter to illustrate the role of organizations
in helping youth sustain their changemaking over time. More specifically, this
chapter is about how civic organizations help build youth's agency. As defined
in Chapter 1, agency refers to youth's feelings about their ability and power to
create change in their community or society (Watts et al., 2011). Agency is a
main driver of civic action (Diemer & Rapa, 2016; Hope, 2016) and youth also

strengthen their agency through civic action (Christens et al., 2011; Levy, 2018). Developing agency is key to understanding how Black youth sustain their changemaking over time, especially in the context of anti-Black racism that youth and their families face (see Chapters 3, 4, and 6). Youth develop their agency from many different sources, but interestingly, despite how important agency is for changemaking, research is still lacking information on where agency comes from and how it develops. Cory's description of his YPAR experience offers a snapshot of his agency. He shared:

> I was paired up with a younger student, so he didn't know how to do. He wasn't able to ... come up and talk to people. So, I would lead him and I'd tell him to do it this way, and not say certain things. And I feel like ... I want to do it again. I feel like it was fun, because I feel like doing things like this really helps.

Cory's agency was reflected in his ability to organize and teach others these skills ("I would lead him and I'd tell him to do it this way"); in his desire to continue acting ("I want to do it again"); and in his personal power in noting that his work "really helps" to make a difference.

This chapter demonstrates how youth-focused civic organizations support Black youth's agency. We present five key ways that civic organizations build youth's agency from young Black changemakers' perspectives. Namely, these organizations help Black youth to: (1) see the impacts of their civic actions; (2) take ownership of their civic work; (3) gain critical knowledge; (4) feel encouraged by adults; and (5) be in community with other Black people. These experiences overlap and accumulate to help Black youth develop agency and, as a result, sustain young Black changemaking. Before we delve into how civic organizations build agency, we first describe a few distinguishing features of civic organizations represented in this study.

FEATURES OF CIVIC ORGANIZATIONS

A comprehensive study of civic organizations would require collecting data on the organizations' missions, practices, and staff in addition to youth perspectives. This undertaking was not part of our study. Nonetheless, through interviews with Black youth across Los Angeles, we learned that young Black changemaking happens in a wide variety of civic organizations. Broadly defined, civic organizations are clubs or groups to which people voluntarily belong and work together to meet community needs and interests or to benefit group members. A subset of civic organizations focus on youth. Examples of youth-focused civic organizations include community-based or national non-profits; school-based civic groups, clubs, or classes; and religious institutions. Some organizations in this study entailed school–community collaborations. For example, one community-based organization trained youth in organizing and then youth led equity campaigns in their schools.

Unique (age 17, she/her) described this structure, adding "we basically build student power." Another non-profit organization taught a class during school hours and offered community-based action experiences. Cory saw this organization as centrally focused on "educating," compared to another community-based organization he engaged in that emphasized "advocating" by offering opportunities for collective action among Black boys and young men.

In our study, 25% of youth described active involvement in a church or religious group. Some youth emphasized helping activities in churches, and others described political education and collective action. Ashley's (age 16, she/her) church had a movie night where they showed clips of Black Civil Rights Movements in history, and then later went to protest together. Ashley shared why this activity was meaningful for her: "I love going to church. I was brought up going to church. So that was a no brainer and then me just being a Black girl in this world, that was just a no brainer going to protests, and then going with my pastor made it even better for me." Although church is not a central site of changemaking for all Black youth, for some, this involvement builds on a legacy of collective civic action to uplift the Black community and advocate for civil rights (Calhoun-Brown, 2000; Haggler, 2018).

Civic organizations are a key place where young Black changemaking happens, and young Black changemakers experienced opportunities for building civic agency across all these settings. Besides their institutional locations, civic organizations differed in other ways. We identified two distinguishing features of civic organizations that matter for Black youth's experiences of changemaking: the organization's philosophy of changemaking and whether or not they centered experiences of Black youth.

Organizations' Changemaking Philosophies

Civic organizations in our study can be distinguished by their central focus on service or activism and organizing. Service organizations had a main goal of helping others in need. For example, NA (age 13, she/her) described a service organization for Black youth:

[it's] basically where Black families come together and do community service and stuff like that. So, most of these [civic actions] actually come from that. We do organize a lot of programs and stuff to give back to the community. We make little bags I would say, like toiletries and everything for the homeless people, or families that are just poor or lower income that need help.

Other organizations focused on activism and organizing to change laws and policies in their schools or communities. We call these advocacy organizations. For example, Unique was involved in a community-based advocacy organization that trains organizers and activists to challenge inequities in their predominantly Black and Brown communities and schools. She shared a story of advocating for educational equity with the school board:

George McKenna [school board member], he'll visit our school once a year and just say, "Oh, yeah, y'all don't need the money 'cause I don't think y'all know what to do with it." I'm like, "Sir, I go to the school every day. And it's not like you can't really say what we need or what we don't need because you're not here experiencing what we experience every day." So that's something that I really like, I'm really, really into at [the organization].

As evident from these examples, civic organizations emphasize different philosophies of changemaking that shape the kinds of civic opportunities offered to youth. We return to this distinction between service and advocacy organizations at times in the chapter to show how these organizations build youth agency in similar and different ways.

Organizations' Centering of Racial Identity

Some civic organizations predominantly serve or center Black youth, and others do not have this focus. This difference can shape Black youth's civic experiences in an organization. Just like the non-Black school spaces we described in Chapter 3, when a young person is the only Black person in the room or one of a few, organizational spaces can feel unwelcoming. Sa'Myah (age 18, she/her) left one civic organization because she was the "only dark-skinned person" there and felt unwelcomed saying, "sometimes it did mess up the way I was trying to engage in things." Mia (age 16, she/her) also had the experience of being "the only Black face in the room" at a school club, but this experience motivated her to represent an image of Black leadership. She wanted "to be that one that other Black kids or even people of other races look up to" with peers seeing her as "the only one in here who is Black, but she is the leader."

Other Black youth participated in civic organizations specifically designed for them. Linda (age 13, she/her) explained why she chose to participate in a service organization for Black women, saying: "They really thrive on making young Black women greater people and opening their eyes to the problems of the world." That mission was important to her "because I want this world to be a better place . . . when my child walks into this world." Black-centered organizations are sites for identity development, civic education, and community building (Ginwright, 2010a). Black youth gain value from spaces where they feel particularly welcomed and valued for their race and culture – ideas we also presented in Chapters 3 and 4. NA shared how her Black-centered service organization supported her Black identity development:

It's a bunch of young, Black kids and teens who, we all come together, and it's a lot of leadership and civic engagement. We do a lot of volunteer work, and we also have a lot of discussions about the struggles and the things that come with being a young Black, young ... African American in today's society.

Black communities have a history of civic organizations that have served as crucial nexus points for Black changemaking. For example, Civil Rights Movement successes were due in large part to efforts of the Black Panthers and the Student Non-Violent Coordinating Committee; Black-led organizations that featured many youth as leaders (Brown, 2009). When we refer to Black organizations, some are designed for and by Black people, and others are Black-centered, meaning that these spaces may include non-Black youth who have shared liberation goals to address racial inequities faced by Black people and uplift Black people's humanity.

With these features of civic organizations as a backdrop, we turn to how civic organizations benefit young Black changemakers. Organizations build Black youth's civic agency in five main ways, through offering youth opportunities to: (1) see impact from their civic actions; (2) take ownership of their civic work; (3) gain critical knowledge; (4) feel encouraged by adults; and (5) be in community with other Black people.

OPPORTUNITIES TO SEE IMPACT FROM CIVIC ACTIONS

When youth see the impact of their civic actions, they see themselves as capable of making a difference again and are motivated to keep trying. Both service and advocacy organizations offer opportunities for Black youth to see the impact of their actions, yet Black youth's experiences differed in these two types of organizations.

Seeing an Impact through Service

When volunteering with service organizations, young Black changemakers often named the tangible and immediate impact of their work. For example, Tsehai (age 14, she/her), whose civic activities ranged from philanthropic work to building a school in Africa to organizing with her Black Student Union at school, described her work with an environmental conservation program as most memorable because of its tangible impact:

That one felt ... very tangible, you could see the effect of the work, you know .... And then doing the work was really fun. I think there's a lot of pride in doing the work after it was completed. One of the trails we worked on unfortunately kept flooding anyway because they just needed to build a bridge over that section. So that was a little disappointing because despite doing eight hours of trail clearing, it still flooded anyway. But that was really satisfying. And we spent ... a whole day planting trees, little saplings. And I think we planted somewhere near 260 trees or something on this riverbed. And it was super fun.

Tsehai felt competent and took pride in completing the hard work of clearing trails and planting trees because she saw the direct results of this work, despite the setback of the trail's re-flooding. For O.A. (age 15, she/her), the most meaningful changemaking experience was volunteering with a food bank: "It just made me feel better as a person because . . . we get to make little boxes for the homeless, and the hungry, and who need food, and so I feel like I was a good assistance there." Seeing immediate, tangible results of helping gave youth a sense of agency that they were making a difference.

Youth also experienced the direct impact of helping through the emotional responses they felt and perceived in these interactions. While Damian (age 18, he/him) did not quite know how to name this feeling, he stated, "I don't really know how to explain it as much, but it's just a good feelin' helpin' other people out." The feelings of people receiving the help also indicated to youth that their service had a tangible impact. Muffin (age 16, she/her), who volunteered to help meet basic needs of unhoused people, shared, "I really like feeding the homeless because, you know, I just got to see the smiles on their faces, like once we gave them hygiene bags . . . it just made me happy to see them happy." Ashley explained that through her efforts to provide Christmas boxes to youth with incarcerated family members, her impact was spreading joy to recipients: "We try to make them have a Christmas type of feeling, you know, because not everyone gets to have that feeling."

Youth's positive feelings about helping can grow into deeper feelings of agency. Quinn's (age 16, she/her) first experience of helping gave her positive feelings, leading her to continue seeking that experience. She explained: "It was like one time I helped somebody, I just kind of always just like the feeling that I, you know, helped them, so I just kept going back doing even more." She went on to say, "Just kind of feels like I'm whole or something like that." The positive cycle of helping and seeing and feeling positive results from these actions accumulated agency, propelling Quinn to adopt an identity as a helpful person who felt complete when doing this work. O.A. liked the immediate and tangible experience of helping someone in need, but when asked how the experience made her feel, she connected this experience to a deeper sense of agency as a changemaker, saying:

The things I did – how it made me feel better as a person because . . . with who I am as a person, I feel like we need to advocate and change the world and to have positive values. And I feel that participating like we still do – because we get one step closer to where I want to be in life.

Thus, youth like Unique and O.A. took action to help others through opportunities offered by service organizations. In the process, they further developed their sense of agency to make a difference in small or bigger ways.

Seeing Impact through Advocacy

In contrast to community service, the impacts of organizing and activism are not always immediate. Successes such as a campaign win or a policy change are usually hard fought over a long period of time, and such successes are powerful agency-building experiences. Unique experienced success in getting a large group of people to attend a protest at Los Angeles Unified School District headquarters to advocate for equitable school funding. She said:

I felt empowered. I felt like I could move the world. Because we actually got it to happen, that's the crazy part. It's one thing when you want something to happen, and then you just speaking on it, but when you really acting on it, that's something different. So when that happened, I was like, "Oh, we can really do this, like we're really out here." So yeah, I feel empowered. I felt unstoppable, I was like, "Okay, Unique, you better go girl."

Sara Vaughn (age 15, she/her) built agency through her advocacy work for Black women's health, where she was able to reach a large number of people. As part of a Black advocacy organization focused on women's health and wellness, she started a podcast that became very popular during the COVID-19 pandemic. She shared:

So, I have a podcast with [a Black advocacy organization] . . . on sexual health and . . . Black teenage girls. And I talk about issues of health and wellness, like STIs [sexually transmitted infections] and also just connecting with people and talking about things that we aren't otherwise able to. And yeah, so that's gotten a lot of traction that I didn't really expect it to.

When asked what made this podcast experience really meaningful for her, Sara Vaughn elaborated by putting the experience in the context of the COVID-19 pandemic and also recognized the impact of her work:

Just getting to connect with people in this way, especially when we're disconnected right now with quarantine and self-isolation. Just realizing that there's so many other ways to connect with people and realizing that I have ability to make a change in that way. There are so many, through this and through work at [organization], I have found so many gaps in the resources we are afforded, the education that we get. Just feeling like I can play a part in filling those gaps.

Unique and Sara Vaughn recognized their power as changemakers for racial and economic justice. Their stories illustrate the potent role of successes in organizing and activism in helping youth see their impact and thus, grow their agency.

For other youth, feelings of agency grew more gradually through continued advocacy work. Damian illustrated this gradual growth in capacity for changemaking when he said, "I've been a part of the [Black-centered advocacy organization] since I was in ninth grade. And . . . I just developed an interest about the stuff around me and how I could help make a change." When we asked Kevin (age 17, he/him) what made a YPAR activity memorable for him;

he said he shared his YPAR experience "to show that I'm capable of doing these activities to care for [the] community I was raised in and to be part of programs that helped me do that." As youth like Damian and Kevin stay engaged in advocacy organizations over time, they are developing agency through understanding and seeing their role in making change in their communities.

In organizing spaces, speaking out builds youth agency, even when the desired change is not achieved. Quinn provided a good example of this when she went with her organization to advocate for equity at a school board meeting: "Our group went and gave our speeches and talked to ... the whole board about the way they spend their money .... The new rule they're trying to put out would take money from schools in not as good communities and give it to, you know, the wealthier schools." Although the group was not successful that day in achieving their objectives, as the school board member "kind of took us as a joke," Quinn and other youth were impacted by having their voice heard more broadly – they were featured on the news – and were seen as concerned community members and not just students: "I felt like we got our voice out to the community, to everyone else. So, they know that we actually care. And that we're not just trying to go to school." Quinn clearly saw the impact of her and her peers' voices, which was an agency-building experience, even though she also endured negative pushback from school board members. Destiny (age 16, she/her) attended a community-led protest against gentrification, saying: "It was very powerful, us walking to the [location] and speaking up there and just speaking up – speaking in our community that's being gentrified ... speak our minds in that community, still, before we're ... moved outta there, basically." Quinn and Destiny's stories show how through collective action, advocacy organizations support the development of youth agency, even in the face of setbacks. Speaking out against racial and economic injustices helped youth to realize their power and gave them the motivation to continue changemaking.

We observed a key difference between service and advocacy organizations. When Black youth saw their impact through service, the impact tended to be immediate and tangible, such as meeting someone's needs in the moment. In contrast, seeing impacts through organizing and activism required effort over a longer period of time, and success was not guaranteed, yet these experiences can build agency over time regardless of the outcomes of youth's efforts. The organization's focus on Black identity did not appear to play a distinguishing role in these experiences. Black youth's descriptions of seeing an impact through organizing and activism tended to explicitly focus on racial justice and occur in Black-centered organizations, but service opportunities occurred in Black-centered organizations, as well.

OPPORTUNITIES TO TAKE OWNERSHIP OF CIVIC WORK

Civic organizations build youth agency by providing youth opportunities to take ownership over civic activities. Leading civic activities helps youth recognize their skills and their power to effect change. As KJ's (age 16, she/her) story illustrates, youth often do not step into civic leadership overnight, and feelings of ownership gradually grow from being involved in an organization over a period of time. KJ described her civic purpose as making a difference in the lives of others, saying "my passion is probably helping others. Really, really helping others." KJ predominantly engaged in changemaking through a Black service organization and her school's Black Student Union. We shared KJ's experience with her Black Student Union in Chapter 3. In both organizations, she took on leadership roles over time. KJ started volunteering when she was "very, very young" with her mother, and recalled joining the organization and thinking "Wow, we're doing volunteer opportunities like every month!'" Through these opportunities, her expertise grew and she became a leader. KJ shared:

And so, we started to do that [volunteer with the organization], and then once I became in the teen group and whatnot, I was like, "Okay. I really like this," and not necessarily I wanted for everybody to do what I like to do, but it's sort of like, "well, I have my own stuff that I want people to do that I feel like people would really like to do." I was like, "Well, I can't just go around telling people, 'Oh, go do this.'" So, I was like, "Maybe I should try running for a position that would allow for me to be a leader and people can engage in the opportunity." That's really what happened.

KJ wanted to take ownership and decide the direction of activities, and that led her to seek out a formal leadership opportunity in the organization. When we interviewed KJ, she was beginning this role as a regional leader of her organization, representing over 25 chapters and more than 600 youth volunteers. She was organizing a large summer conference, and as a leader, was able to infuse her interests in racial justice by planning a panel discussion between Black youth and police officers to create dialogue in the aftermath of George Floyd's murder. Echoing key launching points from Chapter 5, KJ, under the guidance of her mother, joined the organization in childhood to find community with other Black youth and to help others. As an adolescent, she had developed agency and had expertise to motivate other Black youth and create opportunities for changemaking on a larger scale. KJ's Black service organization offered meaningful opportunities within the organizational structure for Black youth to increase their responsibilities, take leadership, and leave their own mark on the organization.

Organizations also allowed youth to take ownership as changemakers by making day-to-day decisions. Zia (age 14, she/her) explained that girls in her Girl Scout troop could earn badges "based on different topics that we feel is very important." She took the opportunity to give a presentation to the troop about Juneteenth, and at other times, she initiated conversations about police violence against Black communities and the Black Lives Matter Movement. The presentations and discussions allowed Zia to take ownership in her own growth as a changemaker. Zia reflected, "I get to learn and grow as a person. And it helps me in education." Not all Girl Scout troops – or organizations in general – are equally open to taking cues from youth and letting youth choose directions for their activities. Zia shared that her current troop is a "very supportive network" that is "respectful and better at listening" compared to previous troops Zia was part of that "haven't necessarily been very respectful towards me speaking." After "being ignored for too long" in one troop, Zia transitioned to a Black-centered troop that gave her space to express her voice in ways that support her own and others' growth as young Black changemakers.

Through a Black service organization, Camille (age 15, she/her) developed the capability to use her voice over time as she assumed more decision-making power in the organization. She shared:

As I've gotten older in [organization], I've really gotten more of an appreciation for doing civic engagement and stuff and organizing it myself based on what I care about. Because when I'm younger, it's just like, "Oh, let's make lunches for homeless people." But now that I'm older, it's a lot more in my hands ... I've taken that experience into a lot more areas of my life ... I've learned how to advocate for not only myself, but people who don't have voices, in terms of, like, stand up for everybody.

Being able to organize civic actions herself was key to Camille's transition from a helper to someone who used her voice to stand up for herself and others. This transition illustrates growth in agency. Camille's agency extended well beyond the borders of the organization into other areas of life. We saw her agency at work in advocating for racial justice through her Black Student Union in Chapter 3. Camille and KJ's stories show that leadership in Black-centered service organizations can provide agency that some Black youth use to launch into advocacy for racial justice.

In Black-centered advocacy organizations, activities were often youth led. Adult leaders coordinated opportunities for youth to speak to local government or community members about racial and economic inequities, and then handed them the mic to let them shine. In Quinn's example above, she advocated for educational equity to her school board. In getting her voice out to the community, Quinn was putting her agency into action. In reflecting on why she has stayed connected to the organization over time, Quinn reiterated the value of youth ownership in the organization: "It's really run by the students. So, it's like we get to pick what's going on. So, it's like, really, you can't get bored from it. You know, we're more engaged. Yeah. And everyone else is because students are running it."

Organizations support young Black changemaking by giving youth opportunities to take on leadership roles and have their voices heard.

Service organizations tended to provide these opportunities within the organization, and advocacy organizations tended to create opportunities to amplify youth voices on a larger community stage. These experiences remind us of the power of youth-led civic actions and the importance of structuring spaces and activities in ways that prioritize youth voice and decision-making. Research emphasizes the value of youth decision-making in afterschool program decisions (Akiva et al., 2014), youth-adult partnerships in community organizations (Zeldin et al., 2017), youth participation in local governance (Augsberger et al., 2018), and youth-led research that creates community change (Ballonoff Suleiman et al., 2021). Youth ownership and voice, scaffolded over time by adults, are opportunities that grow youth agency. On the flip side, civic organizations that lack authentic opportunities for youth voice and ownership may not offer as meaningful experiences for youth. Sometimes, adults in civic organizations tokenize youth participation, hijack youth goals by inserting their own, or devalue or diminish youth voice in other ways (Clay & Turner III, 2021; Conner et al., 2016; Gordon, 2007).

Black-centered organizations appeared to be spaces in particular where Black youth felt ownership. As Black youth took more ownership and used their voices in service or advocacy spaces, they brought attention to racism and racial justice. As part of their attention to Black youth's identity, Black-centered organizations may be more apt to recognize and encourage Black youth's desire for voice and leadership (Ginwright, 2010a). Like Zia, Black youth may feel more comfortable and encouraged to share views about race and racism in Black-centered organizations.

OPPORTUNITIES TO GAIN CRITICAL KNOWLEDGE

Some organizations offered Black youth a chance to gain critical knowledge that went beyond what they learned in school. Critical knowledge entails understanding racial, economic, and social inequalities and their roots in systems of oppression (Hope & Bañales, 2019; Watts et al., 2003). As illustrated in Chapter 4, critical knowledge helps Black youth learn more deeply about what it is like to be a Black person in the United States and connect their experiences to Black history and legacies across generations. Youth discussed opportunities for gaining critical knowledge exclusively in Black-centered organizations. Gaining critical knowledge built Black youth's agency to resist racial oppression while also supporting Black youth's racial identity development.

Black organizations provided an important space to learn about Black history in ways that gave Black youth agency to continue a broader change-making legacy. In describing what he gained from participating in a Black mentoring organization for boys and young men, Amir (age 13, he/him) explained that "they taught me a lot of things about who I am and what I can do . . .. It was mostly hearing the stories of all of them knowing that about the Black Panthers, and them teaching the history about it. It was . . . things I didn't learn in school. They taught us and . . . it was very informational." Amir's story underscores that Black organizations are one of few spaces where Black youth can learn about these histories in community with other Black youth. Organizations offered these teachings in various ways, including speakers sharing personal experiences, lectures, and videos, followed by group discussion. Damian explained how a Black-centered YPAR-focused organization opened his eyes to Malcolm X's personal history and experience in prison, and these learning opportunities gave him "resources and a pathway" to make his community a safer and more equitable place and "more information on how to do it." Through building critical knowledge in Black-centered organizations, Damian and others gained more competence as changemakers and a stronger connection to a legacy of Black changemaking.

Experiential learning was one way organizations helped youth to connect their lived experiences to structural oppression. Cory explained how this type of critical knowledge building worked in a Black YPAR-focused organization:

> They'll teach us about Black history, they'll teach us about different things in our community, and all types of stuff . . .. Okay, so first semester we'll learn about . . . history and different topics. And then, second semester, we'll come back and we'll start with our YPAR, which is like a research project. So last year, me and my class, we did a project about how our area was a food desert, or a food swamp; how we had more fast-food restaurants, more liquor stores. But if we go to the more affluent communities, they'll have a Trader Joe's or Ralphs, or more healthy options, and how we have more options that are life ending and more options that are bad for your health than our white counterparts.

Cory's critical education from the organization strengthened his knowledge of the history of structural oppression against Black people in the United States and how it was still operating in current times:

> Think of slavery as a small domino. It still ripples to today, like police officers, they weren't made to protect and serve. At first, they were just slave catchers trying to catch slaves. And it still affects us today . . . I feel like what's unique [about young Black changemakers] is the fact that we are changing something in the system that wasn't made for us to do good.

Critical knowledge of anti-Black racism as well as celebration of legacies of Black changemaking helped Black youth understand who they were and how they could contribute to positive community change. In effect, they developed civic agency alongside Black identity. To reiterate a quote we shared earlier, Cory explained how critical knowledge building empowered him to make change:

> I get educated in things that are affecting my community, I find out ways I can change it. And I can take the information and I can teach it to somebody else, and then they can teach it to somebody else. And that way, it just spreads. And then I feel like if everyone knows about something, it could change like that.

Often, youth talked about these learning opportunities in Black-centered advocacy organizations, although Black-centered service and mentoring organizations also sometimes offered critical knowledge-building opportunities. For Muffin, a Black service organization provided opportunities to learn about Black culture to promote identity development. She shared:

I guess my identity, you know, I struggle with that sometimes. Especially in [the organization]. We do have a regional conference. And that's where all the teens gather from the far West region. And we come together, and . . . we present on this one issue. And last year's was the theft of our identity. So yeah, I like . . . doing this . . . and me, you know, being a part of my culture and stuff like that, you know, it helps me. But at the same time, I crave more. I want to know more.

In naming Black identity theft, Muffin was referring to the fact that many Black Americans do not know their specific ancestry or African tribe of origin because the African slave trade erased connections to this history and denied many Black individuals a connection to their heritage (Cox & Tamir, 2022). Black-centered organizations gave Muffin and others the chance to learn about and reclaim their Black identity, and critical knowledge building about anti-Black racism and Black history is key to this process.

Young Black changemakers often felt more equipped to make change after gaining this knowledge. As Amir indicated in describing what he "didn't learn in school," some civic organizations fill the gap left by formal education by offering critical knowledge-building opportunities to Black youth. Although these opportunities can be offered in any organizational space, Black-centered civic organizations – especially those focused on advocacy but also service – were most likely to play this role. The few youth in our study involved in YPAR emphasized this approach as a potent tool for critical knowledge building, which aligns with research showing that YPAR builds youth agency (Anyon et al., 2018) and racial identity (Davis, 2020). Black youth would benefit from more opportunities to engage in YPAR.

OPPORTUNITIES TO BE ENCOURAGED BY ADULTS

As highlighted above, youth develop more agency when they have opportunities to lead. But, as Black youth engage in changemaking, many still very much want adults there with them. They do not want just any adult: they want to engage in changemaking with adults who encourage and champion youth agency. For NA, who participated in a Black service organization, a supportive community kept her engaged, including adult organization leaders who worked alongside her and believed in her. She reflected:

Oh, what keeps me going? . . . knowing that I am supported because a lotta times, it wouldn't just be me there. It would be my classmates and a few of my teachers would also be there with me . . . people being by my side through the whole thing and believing that, you know, we could really help these people and help them to survive. So yeah, those two things really helped me to keep going and stay passionate about it.

NA's sentiment of having others join her in "believing we could really help these people" reflects her sense that she and others together can make change. Tom (age 17, he/him) also expressed the meaning and value of having an adult who believed youth were capable of making a difference, sharing that his mentor in a Black service organization "knew that I could make a change and he saw stuff in me that he saw in himself." When adults believe youth are capable and tell them so, youth are more likely to believe themselves as capable. This is one way adults can build youth agency.

As illustrated in Cory's quote that opened this chapter, adults in organizations can be youth's champions, cheering them on as they do important changemaking work. When Cory went with his Black-centered advocacy organization to speak about racial inequity to the school board, being supported by the adult leaders was one the most memorable parts of his experience. He emphasized this detail more than any feelings he may have gotten from being in the spotlight of news reporters, recalling how "they [staff] were really encouraging." He went on to say that "having an adult really cheerin' me on and hypin' me up. Stuff like that really wants me to work hard and do stuff like that." Cory and others viewed encouraging adults as key ingredients to their agency and to sustaining their changemaking over time.

Adults in organizations seemed especially impactful when they developed close bonds with youth. Kevin powerfully stated that a Black-centered advocacy organization "changed my life." One life-changing factor for Kevin was the "big mentor" who served as a "role model." Adult program leaders treated him "like I was one of their sons and stuff." He elaborated: "I don't know how to explain it, but it was basically like they helped me to be better." From youth's stories, it was clear that developing these bonds often involved adults spending significant amounts of time with youth, getting to know them, and sharing their own personal stories.

Youth tended to value having adult leaders who came from a similar community and shared a similar background to their own. We again return to Cory. By learning the details of an adult leader's personal changemaking journey, Cory recognized the leader was giving him "positive examples to look at in my life." The adult Black changemaker's story gave Cory insights that influenced his drive to continue changemaking. He shared:

He just gave us personal insight on how he used to be like one of those kids, that was just like not caring about school, drifting by. And then when he got the chance to go to school and how he really changed and became such a hard worker. I feel like seeing those positive examples influenced me too.

We shared in Chapters 5 and 6 how families and other adults inspire young Black changemakers, and here we emphasize the influence of adults in civic organizations. Through a Black-centered advocacy organization, Cory was continually inspired and supported by adults, especially because he could relate to them. Describing another adult organizer, Cory shared what made the leader so impactful:

The way he's able to relate to us. He went to . . . high school in Inglewood. It wasn't like he went some far place. He was just right down the road from a lot of us. And I like how he's completely honest with us and he can relate with us. I feel like those characteristics really help . . .. 'Cause I feel like, if you're able to connect with the adult, it's not a . . . teacher. It's more of a relationship than . . . a teacher over student . . . kind of thing. It's more one-on-one. And you can express yourself more. And you can just feel more comfortable.

As Cory explained, these relationships with adults go deeper than a typical student–teacher relationship, as adults "come to us with love and teach us." Cory's story also illustrates synergies among different opportunities for building agency in describing how adult support allows youth to take ownership by "express[ing] yourself more." Other youth in Cory's specific organization shared similar stories, which speaks to the power of a program model that fosters connections to program leaders. Adults can provide this support to young Black changemakers in any type of organization. Having mentors with shared identities and experiences is critical for Black youth to have a safe space to build their agency (Brooms & Davis, 2017; Lindsay-Dennis et al., 2011).

OPPORTUNITIES TO BE IN COMMUNITY WITH OTHER BLACK PEOPLE

In Black-centered spaces, Black youth felt welcomed and safe and were able to be seen and appreciated fully as Black youth. Quinn described her Black-centered advocacy organization as feeling like a "second home" and "nice hangout place." Other youth shared this sentiment that their organizational spaces felt like home and the members like family, such as Cory who shared, "What keeps me involved, I feel like, is just having a relationship with all those people" and that people in his Black-centered advocacy organization "really uplift you. It just felt like a family." Kevin described the experience of being drawn into a Black-centered organization by people and relationships, and it is these relationships that continue to draw youth deeper into changemaking, supporting their agency to continue the work. He shared this about his journey:

I'd say by meeting people . . . starting to make friends that been with me since like today, you know, your freshman year, I didn't exactly know too much people, you know, so, but then I started getting wrong and hanging out with other people. And . . . ever since then, they shown me a brotherly love, you know. And then, as I became part of the program, I see more, more and more of my peers going . . . to events, actually a lot going to do projects.

Part of the power of being in predominantly Black spaces is being shown love and acceptance, such as the "brotherly love" Kevin spoke about. In Black-centered organizations, Black youth and adults may be more able to fully be themselves. Kevin illustrated this point as he described his experience with a "protest, a block party" that he helped organize with a Black-centered advocacy organization. This event was in part designed to build community, and as Kevin shared, the event offered a space "where people can have fun and just be around the other people and show community that we share engagement and just be powerful who they are." For Kevin, block parties where people could connect and have fun were important for developing agency. He noted that "It [the block parties] encouraged me to engage. I don't know how to say it, but to me, engaging and being powerful in who you [are] means that you have – you will be open and stuff like that." As others have documented (Ginwright, 2010a, 2015) and as we highlight across the book, Black organizing spaces are important sites for experiencing shared identity around being Black and proud, shared purpose in pursuit of liberation, and joy in community with others.

Similar to Kevin's experiences with block parties, Quinn described how her Black-centered advocacy organization created spaces for joy and community alongside organizing against racial justice, saying, "We're still gonna make it into something joyful, 'cause it is always, like no matter really what we're talking about … the meetings always end in a joyful like prayer-type mode." Having informal and formal spaces for shared joy and community with other Black people "no matter what's going on" can be important for healing (Ginwright, 2015) and for building solidarity and collective agency that sustains social movements (Sullivan, 1997). Through collective youth-focused practices, Black-centered advocacy organizations can build Black youth's agency to navigate and transform systems of oppression. Black scholar and organizer Dr. David C. Turner III (2021, p. 430) emphasized the collective power of Black communities. In addressing Black youth organizers, he said: "We organize together, we can accomplish things collectively that we cannot accomplish individually, so organizing each other and developing an agenda is central to the well-being of your communities."

Youth emphasized similar experiences of Black community in Black service organizations. Muffin, who has been part of her Black service organization for years, shared how connected she felt to the organization: "I felt good about it because the people that were in the group – I've been knowing since I was little. So … it wasn't a new environment for me." She further explained how, now that she had gotten older, she was "hanging out with them more … volunteering more and stuff like that, you know." Similarly, A.G. (age 15, she/her), also part of a Black service organization, recalled realizing that everyone in the organization was Black and thinking "'Oh, everyone's like me.' Because at my school, everyone's mostly white, so it was just different to see everyone like me. It was kinda cool . . .. So, yeah, that's when I started engaging in that . . . I'm proud that I got to help other people and less fortunate people . . . I want to continue doing that now."

For Zia, a deep community connection with other Black people was a main driver of her changemaking. As part of a Black-centered Girl Scout troop, Zia shared that "I've grown a greater bond with the community" by being involved over time, and that "being part of the community is what motivates me." For Zia, being in community with other Black people was intertwined with her identity as a Black person ("I'd say that I'm proud to be Black, and it shouldn't be a problem with anybody else") and motivated her agency to pursue her civic purpose, which included "that nobody should be treated differently because of their ethnicity or how they think or how they feel." Thus, Black-centered organizations – whether focused on service or advocacy – can provide opportunities for Black youth to share space with other Black youth, and in turn, build agency to engage further.

Black-centered organizations can also offer safe spaces to process difficult experiences with others who understand and can show support. For example, T (age 17, he/him) was part of a Black-centered arts-based program for system-involved youth, where he found a safe space with other youth to process difficult life experiences, such as living in a group home. He said:

They got spirit awakening here, when we talk to the people, express our feelings and stuff like that. And being a . . . youth going through the stuff that I'm going through – because right now I'm in a group home – it's good to have these releases. So that's why I really participate.

Soleil (age 13, she/her) explained that her all Black Girl Scout troop was a place where she could "vent" about her problems, and said that it was a safe space to process negative experiences like racism:

And it's our safe space. We talk about any other, you know, white men commenting or just saying their piece. And we just talk about how we feel and our experiences which most of the time is relatable for us which – it's nice. It's refreshing to have that.

Feeling part of a Black community – and the safety, support, and solidarity Black youth derive from this community – can help Black youth develop agency.

Black-centered civic organizations offer Black youth opportunities to build community with other Black people. In these spaces, Black youth feel safe to be themselves and process personal experiences, they experience joy and solidarity in their civic work alongside other Black people, and they further develop their Black identity. These community connections give Black youth motivation to keep coming back to the organization and drive to continue changemaking. In light of how systemic racism operates to fragment, isolate, and emotionally burden Black communities, building Black organizational infrastructure is a vital part of the solution to support

Black youth and communities' collective efforts to restore community well-being, resist racial oppression, and reclaim voice and vision for Black collective futures (Ginwright, 2015).

THE TAKE-AWAYS

This chapter shared Black youth's perspectives on how civic organizations help develop their agency and sustain their changemaking over time. Civic organizations supported youth in developing agency through: (1) seeing impact from their civic actions; (2) taking ownership of their civic work; (3) gaining critical knowledge; (4) feeling encouraged by adults; and (5) being in community with other Black people. Any civic organization that works with youth has the potential to create these opportunities for Black youth, but Black-centered organizations play an especially valuable role in offering safe spaces for Black youth to use their voices, opportunities for gaining critical knowledge about Black history, and opportunities for building community with other Black people. Service organizations offered opportunities to see immediate tangible impacts through helping others and providing opportunities to take ownership within organizational structures. In contrast, advocacy organizations offered opportunities to see impact over a longer-term effort and amplified youth voice to community audiences. Despite these distinctions, youth experienced opportunities to build agency across both service and advocacy organizations.

Contributions to Research

The findings offer new insights into what agency looks like for young Black changemakers. Agency is widely considered to be critical for young people's development as civic actors (Lerner et al., 2015; Watts et al., 2011), yet surprisingly few robust, multidimensional models or measures fully capture civic agency. In our study, Black youth's agency included feelings of competence, realization of one's personal or collective power, and the desire and drive to make change. Black youth's civic agency appears to be multidimensional, consisting of several distinct components. Future research could use our findings and others' work to develop more complete models of civic agency, and several promising conceptualizations can guide this endeavor. For example, Dr. Brian Christens (2012) argued for a multidimensional model of empowerment (a sister term to agency) that includes cognitive, emotional, and relational dimensions. Based on work with Black boys and young men, Dr. David C. Turner III (2021) put forward a framework of Black transformative agency to describe various ways Black youth develop and exert agency in combating oppression that differ based on the type of changemaking and whether agency is individual or collective. The stories we shared of young Black changemakers contribute to knowledge of what agency looks like and how it is experienced by Black youth.

Our study is a strong reminder that civic organizations are sites for Black youth's civic development. Civic organizations are influential settings for developing agency that may complement opportunities in other contexts like families and schools or fill gaps in youth's opportunities when they are lacking elsewhere. Black youth highlighted specific experiences in organizations that are levers of change for growing their agency and that should be further studied in applied research to strengthen organizational programming for Black youth. Youth did not become civic leaders overnight, but rather, they developed this expertise in a process that unfolded over time. Often, youth had been involved in an organization for years, which is significant given their young ages. To better recognize that community organizations are contexts for long-term civic development (Dawes & Larson, 2011; Terriquez, 2015), future research should consider longer-term studies that follow Black youth in organizations. Past research has examined young people's civic action and agency within a specific organizational setting (Christens & Kirshner, 2011; Ginwright, 2010a; Shiller, 2013; Terriquez, 2015), and others have looked across organizations (Richards-Schuster & Dobbie, 2011). Our findings highlight the importance of gaining greater clarity about how different features of organizations lead to different experiences and opportunities for Black youth's sociopolitical development.

Importantly, not all Black youth have access to high-quality civic organizations. Youth in our study were highly civically engaged, and they were all active participants in at least one civic organization. This organizational participation had great value for their sociopolitical development. Black youth can absolutely be civically engaged outside of a formal organization (Wray-Lake & Abrams, 2020), and as illustrated in Chapter 3, Black youth sometimes create their own organizational spaces. Nonetheless, lack of access to high-quality civic organizations, resulting in part from systems of economic and racial inequalities, is a barrier to civic engagement for some Black youth. We must work to identify and remedy inequitable access to civic organizations for Black youth and reimagine civic opportunities that are not inclusive spaces for Black youth.

Practical Insights

Our findings offer tangible recommendations for civic organizations who aim to support Black youth's changemaking. The five opportunities to build agency, identified by young Black changemakers, translate into a useful tool for critical inquiry to help organizations enhance the ways they support Black youth agency. We present this tool in Table 7.1, which offers a set of questions

TABLE 7.1 Assessing opportunities for Black youth agency: A tool for civic organizations

To develop civic agency, Black youth need to:	Three phases of assessing organizational settings		
	Assessing current practice	Determining strategies to enhance practice	Evaluating organization's capacity
See impact of civic actions	How do civic activities offered by the organization allow Black youth to see impact? What impacts do youth see?	How can the organization increase visibility of Black youth's impact or the frequency of opportunities for impact?	What training, expertise, time, and human and financial resources does the organization need to enhance Black youth's sense of impact?
Take ownership of civic work	What opportunities does the organization offer for Black youth to take ownership of their civic engagement? What does taking ownership look like within and beyond the organization?	How can the organization increase opportunities for Black youth voice, choice, decision-making, and/or leadership within and beyond the organization? What are the barriers to youth taking ownership?	What training, expertise, time, and human and financial resources does the organization need to increase opportunities for Black youth to take ownership within and beyond the organization?
Gain critical knowledge	In what ways does the organization offer opportunities for Black youth to learn and reflect on Black history, culture, structural racism, and resistance? What norms or practices in the organization are barriers to offering critical knowledge-building opportunities?	How can the organization add new opportunities or strengthen existing opportunities for critical knowledge building for Black youth? How can the organization ensure these opportunities occur in spaces where Black youth feel safe?	What training, expertise, time, and human and financial resources does the organization need to offer more opportunities for critical knowledge building?

Have adult support & encouragement	How do adult leaders encourage and support Black youth agency before, during, and after civic actions? What norms or practices in the organization are barriers to this kind of adult support?	What practices can the organization implement to strengthen Black youth's supportive relationships with adult leaders? How can the organization better support adults in their efforts to foster Black youth agency?	What training, expertise, time, and human and financial resources does the organization need to enhance adult support of Black youth?
Be in community with other Black people	In what ways does the organization offer opportunities for Black youth to build community with other Black people? When and where does Black youth community building happen in the organization?	How can the organization increase or enhance opportunities for Black youth to build community in ways that support agency and Black identity?	What training, expertise, time, and human and financial resources does the organization need to increase opportunities for Black community building?

to help organizations consider how they currently support Black youth agency and how they can enhance this capacity. We frame this as a tool for civic organizations, but schools or other youth-focused settings interested in building Black youth's agency could also use it.

Applying these findings to an organizational setting could occur in three main phases. First, civic organizations can assess their current practices to determine the extent to which they offer the five opportunities to build Black youth agency. Assessing current practices may include consulting the organization's mission and theory of change, examining implementation of programming, and importantly, hearing Black youth's perspectives of the organization and its agency-building opportunities.

In a second phase, an organization can develop strategies to strengthen opportunities in some or all the five areas. This visioning and planning step would ideally include voices and perspectives from across the organization, especially Black youth. Strategies could be drawn from research on Black youth agency and from learning from other organizations who have established strong program models for Black youth agency development. Third, an organization must evaluate its capacity for enhancing agency-building opportunities. Not all organizations are Black-centered and not all organizations have appropriate staff or training to offer some of these opportunities, such as conveying critical knowledge of Black history, creating Black community spaces, or being supported by adults who share a similar community or racial or ethnic background. In many organizations, creating or enhancing these opportunities would require considerable investments in staff and training. Other civic organizations are already Black-centered and are already richly offering all five opportunities to Black youth. They can be exemplars for other organizations and may also benefit from expanding their resources to sustain this important work.

These five opportunities to build Black youth agency in civic organizations are not the only ways to support the development of Black youth's agency. Practitioners, researchers, and young Black changemakers could augment this tool by adding other agency-building opportunities for Black youth. In interrogating an organization's practices, we reiterate how important it is to involve Black youth and center their experiences in these conversations. As shown in Chapter 5, Black youth often come to civic organizations with agency and should be key actors in determining opportunities to further their own sociopolitical development.

A Brief Note on Methodology

As a research team, we decided not to name specific organizations youth were involved in, because at the outset of the study, we promised to protect youth's confidentiality, and naming their specific experiences within these organizations may violate that agreement. Leaving organizations unnamed was part of our ethical agreement to our study participants. Other researchers take different stances on this (Schelbe et al., 2015), and we recognized during the writing process that our decision may, in some ways, have diminished the value of our work for these specific organizations: Many of these organizations that youth featured deserve to be uplifted and celebrated, and their work amplified. We want these organizations to know that we deeply value the work they do, and we hope that this chapter does some justice to the important role they are playing in the lives of young Black changemakers.

Up Next

This chapter laid out ways in which civic organizations can help Black youth grow and sustain their changemaking over time through building agency. Aligned with sociopolitical development theory, we found that civic organizations are key opportunity structures that support Black youth's changemaking (Kirshner & Ginwright, 2012). Agency, in turn, represents how Black youth chart their own courses in changemaking and build competency and power in the process (Christens, 2012; Hope, Smith et al., 2020; Turner III, 2021; Watts et al., 2011). Black youth's development in the context of organizations unfolds over a substantial period of time. In contrast, grave racial injustices that capture national attention and launch social movements can transform Black youth's changemaking more rapidly. In Chapter 8, we discuss how the murder of George Floyd and the racial justice protests in response to that murder influenced the lives of young Black changemakers.

8

Summer 2020

LAURA S. ABRAMS, JASON ANTHONY PLUMMER, &
LAURA WRAY-LAKE

I feel like this is definitely the beginning of something very big, but at the same time, this is kind of what our whole life has been leading up to. I grew up hearing about Trayvon Martin and Mike Brown, and all these people who were killed by police and all these injustices. And that was how I grew up, that was the world that I was raised into. So, I feel like this is kind of like, the breaking point, this is what everything in my life has been leading up to. So, it feels like . . . this is finally the moment where we're going to be heard, we're going to make a change. We're not just gonna sit back anymore. So, it's kind of exciting . . ..
Because I know . . . this is the beginning of something really big.

Camille

Since age 5, Camille (she/her), now age 15, has been involved in community service, such as helping people who are unhoused through a Black service organization. At age 12, Camille realized, "If I actually want to make change, you can't always just rely on other people, you have to kind of step up and do things for yourself." She became active on social media to spread awareness of social justice issues and "educate my peers and people who have no understanding of the experiences of Black people." In pursuing her civic purpose to help Black people be seen and valued, she led an initiative to start a Black Student Union at her school. In summer 2020, a period of time referred to as a "racial reckoning," "racial unrest," and "racial awakening," Camille felt the momentum for change toward racial justice when she said "this is finally the moment where we're going to be heard, we're going to make a change," and "this is the beginning of something really big."

The racial reckoning of summer 2020 encompassed local, national, and international initiatives seeking to redress historical racial injustices, find remedies for state sanctioned racial violence, and prevent such injustices from occurring in the future (Taylor, 2016). Research on the Black Lives Matter (BLM) Movement of summer 2020 found that younger people (under 30) and Black, Brown, and other people of color were most likely to attend the protests and support the platform of the BLM Movement (Barroso & Minkin, 2020). Yet, the BLM Movement obviously predates the events of summer 2020. It is little wonder that Camille expressed that her life, like those of her Black peers, had been leading up to this current moment, given what Black youth her age had experienced in their lifetimes. When Camille was about seven years old, Trayvon Martin was murdered. When she was nine, Michael Brown was murdered. On May 25, 2020, when Camille was 15, Derek Chauvin, a Minneapolis police officer murdered George Floyd by kneeling on his neck for nine minutes and 29 seconds while three other officers stood by and allowed him to die. In pleading for his life, George Floyd said, "I can't breathe"; Eric Garner uttered similar words when he died by police force in 2014, when Camille was nine. In 2020, Camille felt this moment as a breaking point, where "we're not just gonna sit back anymore." She was not alone in this sentiment. She and other young Black changemakers experienced summer 2020 as a pivotal moment in their lives.

This chapter is about how the young Black changemakers understood and participated in the racial reckoning of 2020. Our interviews with Black youth captured their experiences of the movement and reflections on society's recognition of systemic racism and state sanctioned violence against Black people leading up to and during this time frame. The history of racial justice is often presented as a story of progress, punctuated by major civil rights successes like Emancipation, the Civil Rights Movement, and the election of President Barack Obama. Our young Black changemakers recognize racial justice as paradoxical, with moments of progress and setbacks over the long road to Black liberation. As described in Chapter 1, Los Angeles is a city that holds these paradoxes, given its history of anti-Black police violence and its rich culture of community organizing for racial justice (Felker-Kantor, 2018). The Los Angeles-based young Black changemakers in our study felt seen and inspired by the movement, and took pride and joy in Black resistance, but also expressed sadness and frustration in reflecting on how far we have to go and what it will take to do better. They described shifts in their civic action, agency, and reflection in response to the racial reckoning, and they strengthened their civic purpose to create a better world for future generations of Black people.

FEELING SEEN, CONNECTED, AND INSPIRED

For the young Black changemakers, summer 2020 signified a powerful moment that reverberated throughout the world and woke many people up from their complacency about the existence of anti-Black racism. People across the world cared about the murder George Floyd, and by association, the plight of Black people in the United States, and many were actively protesting racist institutions and policies. These realizations were highly significant to Black youth. Lee (age 18, he/him) reflected that the large-scale racial justice protest movement "means everything to me. To see that it's people willing to put their life on the line for me. It's a great change from seeing people want to kill me. I do appreciate that."

Black youth felt that people cared, which catalyzed them to act. When asked "what this current moment means to you," Mea (age 16, she/her) replied: "It's really inspiring. I think it's because of the fact that this went global. You see people that protest all around the nation . . . . It proves to me that if we really fight for what we want and use our voice, that we can make a change." As Mea reflected, the global reach of BLM protests translated into optimism about social change (i.e., "we can make a change"), as most of the young Black changemakers we interviewed viewed the worldwide protest movement as inspiring and offering hope for a better future for Black people.

Like Mea, NA (age 13, she/her) felt inspired by the visibility of the movement and support of protests and diverse protesters around the world. She shared:

Well, what keeps me going really is when I see things in the news like people protesting, or I see people on social media spreading awareness about issues that I am also passionate about. That really keeps me going because I know that other people are out there supporting the same thing I am, and it gives me hope, and it gives me strength knowing that I'm not alone and that there are other people fighting for the same causes that I am and that are passionate about the same things I'm passionate about, and even though I might be young and just a kid, and I might not be able to do all the things that other people can do, I know that I still have a voice, and that's what really keeps me inspired and keeps me passionate about being civically engaged 'cause I know that eventually . . . I'll be able to make a change.

Wrapped up in this powerful statement are several key points about the significance of summer 2020 that illustrate how Black youth feel seen, connected, and inspired. In witnessing collective action via protests and on social media, NA felt connected to a community of like-minded people, which caused her to feel like "I'm not alone" and "there are people fighting for the same causes." From this larger community of supporters, NA drew strength and motivation to continue her own efforts, as seeing others take action "really keeps me going" and "gives me strength." Along with this inspiration to continue, NA expressed agency that, as a young person of 13, she could "be able to make a change." The ways the movement spread and the shared passions people expressed inspired a sense of agency that NA's voice mattered.

Black youth felt seen in part because of how many non-Black people responded to summer 2020. In Ralph Ellison's 1952 novel *Invisible Man*, the protagonist muses that he must be invisible because white people do not seem to see him. This was not the case for George Floyd. He was seen when his life was taken. Young Black changemakers noticed how non-Black people newly understood the connection between deadly police violence and structural racism, yet Black people have long understood and experienced structural racism. Tsehai (age 14, she/her) referred to summer 2020 as "a moment of recognition for the stuff that [Black youth] deal with on the daily." She continued:

It is probably frustrating for others, because I know it's really annoying to see that people are finally recognizing the fact that these things happen every single day to people like us. But I think it's first and foremost for me and probably a lot of others. It's nice to see that people will care, you know, to see the people that do care and demonstrate that they care.

Tsehai was expressing some of the complex feelings that other young Black changemakers shared: feeling seen and cared for by others, yet frustrated that it took so long for people to recognize racism. We elaborate on these complex feelings later in the chapter.

Young Black changemakers recognized the power of social media to facilitate the movement and to connect with a large virtual community of Black people and non-Black allies. Soleil (age 13, she/her) reflected on the power of video and social media in building the current movement, stating:

I think it's time with the uprising of technology and social media, and now things are getting filmed. And it's everywhere. The unique thing about it is that it brings people together. It builds a community between people who are struggling with the same issues and . . . people just gathering around and then saying, "Hey, I relate to you in that way and we can go through this together."

For Soleil and other youth, social media offered a community space for connecting and processing the police violence and racism of the current time. She went on to share, "We've really embraced each other with social media, and that's one of the upsides of it, is the community it builds with all these sorts of different people with different backgrounds, and ethnicities, fighting for the same cause – all ages." Here Soleil indicated, similar to NA, that the power of building an online community of people with shared struggles and "getting through this together" provided inspiration to persist in challenging racial injustices.

Tom (age 17, he/him) also reflected on the power of social media to create impact and advance the BLM and racial justice movements, emphasizing that anyone – including young people – could share in making this impact. He said:

So, yeah, social media, I mean, I think that's another thing why this movement was so different from anything in the past. Because, I mean, everybody could communicate with anybody and share their opinion at any time, so – and spread awareness at any time. I mean, really, you could post something and impact a large amount of people.

As Tom indicated, social media substantially reduces barriers for youth to participate in social movements. Wilf and Wray-Lake (2021) documented how social media operates as "a new type of civic space, like a city hall or public square" (p. 2), where young people find and create new ways of challenging oppressive systems, and they build community with others in ways that sustain their civic actions. Success with Lex (age 18, she/her) had a community of like-minded and civically active friends on social media. She said, "every time I go on social media, my friends have posted petitions. The accounts I follow are posting petitions to sign, so it's definitely kept me on my feet, and knowing that I kinda have that help and support from more people on social media, is definitely a relief." Here, Success with Lex echoed what NA also shared about not feeling alone. Social media was a platform where youth were able to garner awareness, support, and allyship from people of different backgrounds, ages, and ethnicities from all over the world. This connectivity, facilitated through technology, made Black youth feel seen; their struggles were viewed, shared, and validated by others.

In feeling seen, Black youth described how their struggles, their causes, and their fight for racial justice was embraced and supported – not just by the Black community – but by others locally, nationally, and globally. Feeling seen on a larger platform fueled Black youth's agency to continue change-making, as youth saw themselves as part of a widespread struggle for Black liberation that was facilitated and amplified through social media. This collective support made tangible the feeling that Black lives do indeed matter. Mattering is the feeling that one is valued and significant to a larger group, community, or society. Dr. Roderick Carey has written about mattering for Black youth, documenting how society and schools convey that they partially or marginally matter. He advanced a vision of mattering for Black boys and young men, saying, "comprehensive mattering of Black boys and young men begins when others view them as essential and significant, not a hindrance, to achieving a more just world" (Carey, 2019, p. 384). The attention to, interest in, and significance placed on Black youth's experiences during summer 2020 helped many Black youth feel that they mattered on a larger scale.

TAKING PRIDE AND JOY IN BLACK RESISTANCE

Young Black changemakers took pride in the 2020 movement, which was intertwined with recognizing the long history of Black resistance. For example, Success with Lex stated: "I feel like we're on to something, and this decade might just be the decade where we finally get to change that. We've been fighting for it for 201 years." She connected this moment with the Civil Rights era by noting:

The Black Lives Matter Movement has grown bigger than that movement. It's crazy to me because the Civil Rights Movement just invoked so much change. The Martin Luther King era. The Malcom X era. All of that has invoked change but seeing that in this day in time, our movement is bigger than that.

Other youth also described this moment as "big" or "huge" and were amazed that BLM was becoming a multiracial global movement. From May 26 to August 22, 2020, over 7,750 protests linked to the BLM protest movement were recorded in the US alone, in over 2,440 locations across all 50 states (Kishi et al., 2021). BLM protests took place in over 60 countries across all seven continents (Wikipedia, 2022).

Young Black changemakers viewed these protests as the precipice of major change; they sensed that something had "snapped" in this moment. As Camille articulated in the opening quote of this chapter, "this is the beginning of something really big." For Camille and others, summer 2020 was about building on past movements; including historical attempts to address racial injustice on a deep, systemic level. Sara Vaughn (age 15, she/her) was "thinking a lot about how the struggles that my grandparents fought have carried over into now." Cory (age 15, he/him) reflected on how today's movement can be both inspired by the past and also achieve new levels of success:

I look at things like the Civil Right Movement. And I look at how people back then were able to make history in a time where things weren't even connected and recorded and all of these things .... Makes me think because, if they can make such an impact back then with the little resources that they had, it makes me think, how big of an impact can we make now.

As these quotes relay, knowledge of the past struggles of Black people for civil and human rights was central to understanding why this time was a watershed moment – a breaking point. This breaking point was about continuing the legacy of fighting for racial justice set by their ancestors, but also pushing racial justice to a new level using new strategies and technologies. This critical knowledge of Black history and reflection on long-standing systemic inequalities is a core part of sociopolitical development (Watts et al., 2003). We have described in previous chapters how this critical knowledge can develop in the contexts of families and organizations. Here, we see that Black youth with this critical knowledge are poised to understand movements for racial justice as they unfold.

Seeing oneself as part of Black history and the legacy of civil rights struggles led to feeling proud to be Black. As summer 2020 raised awareness about systemic racism, it also shone light on the positive aspects of Black history, role models, and legacies of resistance. Building on the ideas of honoring family legacies from Chapter 6 and developing Black collective identity from Chapter 4, youth took pride in being part of this larger lineage of Black resistance in summer 2020. Feeling pride in being Black included an appreciation of how Black people resist racial oppression and maintain space for joy. Quinn's story illustrates this idea. Quinn (age 16, she/her) was a community organizer who was already actively challenging racial and economic injustices in her community and more broadly. She felt that summer 2020 "definitely gave us a platform to kinda speak" and that her organizing efforts had benefited from greater attention to Black youth's voices. When asked how being Black mattered for her civic engagement in the current political moment, she said:

Maybe it made me feel more proud to be Black .... No matter what's going on, we're still going to make it into something joyful, 'cause it is always, like, no matter what we're talking about … the meetings always end in a joyful like prayer-type mode. They'll have somebody come in and sing something about what you're talking about, or at home or somebody will play music, even at the protest. They had people singing, doing dances and stuff. It's always just, you know, some type of enjoyment no matter how sad or serious something is.

In this quote, Quinn described pride in her community and the joy that was fostered in the community during this experience of collective resistance. We shared this same quote in Chapter 4 to illustrate how collective civic actions can foster pride in being Black, a core aspect of Black identity. Quinn's experience included Black community traditions such as spirituality, singing, and dancing (Boykin et al., 2020). Black joy encompasses love of community, recognition, Black traditions, and the feelings associated with being Black and free (Tichavakunda, 2021). Whether through song, poetry, or any other form, Black joy serves as a reminder that Black people are more than their struggles (Williams, 2022). Black pride and joy are important parts of activism and movement building, and they are core to Black identity. The pride and joy young Black changemakers felt was rooted in critical knowledge of the past, their identities as Black youth, and recognition of summer 2020 as a transformative moment.

Young Black changemakers in our study were proud of the resistance to racism they saw in 2020. Some progress was made to redress racism and promote racial equity due to efforts led by Black youth and communities. For example, unlike past cases of police shootings of unarmed Black men, all four officers involved in the murder of George Floyd were charged with a criminal offense. Officer Derick Chauvin was subsequently convicted of second-degree murder and civil rights violations, and sentenced to 22.5 years in prison (Chapel, 2021). In response to the uprisings, many city councils pledged to make police reforms to curb racial profiling and to form alternative responses for mental health crises. Across the nation, confederate monuments were taken down and buildings on major college campuses that held the names of confederate leaders or slave owners were renamed. The federal government recognized Juneteenth as a national holiday, and numerous corporations released statements in support of Black lives and vowed to embrace more equitable policies. And, in a notable local victory from a year-long campaign led by Black youth organizers in Los Angeles from 2020 to 2021, the Los Angeles Unified School District voted to divest $25 million of funds from the school district's police force and to redirect around $11.5 million of those funds to supporting Black student achievement in the district (Gomez, 2021).

Unfortunately, some of these successes were short-lived, as not all companies, cities, and schools have lived up to promises made in the name of racial equity or to remedy past or present racial injustices (Roberts & Grayson, 2021). A telling example comes from Minneapolis, where George

Floyd was murdered. Despite the City Council's promise to "end policing as we know it," the City Council retreated from this pledge (Herndon, 2020), and voters rejected a measure that would structurally change policing in the city (Kaste, 2021). Also, white backlash to racial progress has been evident in many different forms, from policy to public perceptions, where white people substantially decreased their support for the BLM Movement from June 2020 to September 2020 (Thomas & Horowitz, 2020). Kali Holloway (2021), writer for *The Nation*, summarized the backlash as follows:

> ... instead of addressing this country's pervasive racism and anti-Blackness, white Americans locate the problem somewhere within Black people themselves. We're in yet another of those moments, as last summer's promised "racial reckoning" turns out to be a white lie. Black demands for full citizenship and equality are being treated as entitlement, calls for white racial accountability redefined as white persecution, and anti-racism falsely construed as anti-whiteness. To reestablish unchallenged white dominance, a movement of white resistance, or anti-anti-racism, is working tirelessly to blot out what it sees as a problematic presence – purging Black folks from democracy by stripping voting rights, erasing Black struggle from history by banning the teaching of slavery and its legacy, and prohibiting protest that threatens the white supremacist status quo (par 1–2).

In this context, it is unsurprising that some young Black changemakers expressed sadness and doubt about the movement and its power to make long-lasting change in a white dominated society as well as frustration that society has taken this long to recognize that Black lives matter.

EXPRESSING SADNESS AND FRUSTRATION

The young Black changemakers expressed a multitude of emotions – sometimes all at once – about summer 2020, including feeling joyful, inspired, as well as sad, angry, and disappointed. Some youth also felt exhausted and overwhelmed, and others expressed heightened fear of police violence. Soleil described her feelings of being overwhelmed about this moment coupled with the necessity of taking action:

> It's really overwhelming that even at such a young age, we have to get involved. But, if we want to see a change, and we want to make it happen, then it's something that we have to do. And life is never easy. We have to do these things in order to make sure that generations that come after us have a better experience than we do.

Her thoughts on the necessity of resistance and its emotional burden underscore the challenges faced by Black youth in summer 2020 and Black youth navigating a racist society at any point in time. Black people are exhausted from the extreme, daily stress of racism and racism-related vigilance. As Dr. C. Maylik Boykin and 13 other Black scholars (2020) stated, "The exhaustion deepens with each new death of a Black person at the hands of police," and "is amplified by well-intentioned non-Black people" (pp. 776–777). As we highlighted in Chapter 3, in times of greater attention to racism, but also more generally, Black youth are often burdened with educating others, explaining racism and its harms, and managing the denial, emotionality, and defensive responses of non-Black people.

Black youth experienced racial trauma during summer 2020. Soleil, in addition to feeling exhausted, shared that the barrage of media attention and videos of Black people being killed by the police made her feel a deep despair. She shared:

Honestly, it's unacceptable. It's affected me deeply to a point where sometimes it hurts so much to move. So I've been taking a break recently ... it's seeing all these dead Black bodies on the internet, sometimes gets ... [short pause]. So, I don't know how long I'll be taking. I said a week but probably longer because it just stays with you even if you try to get it to go away. It's ... saddening really.

Having to witness the repeated, graphic violence of the murder of George Floyd and other Black people was deeply upsetting and traumatizing. For these youth, the ebb and flow of the cycle of violence, murder, and then public response and news spin was painful, making youth like Soleil "hurt so much to move." For Amir (age 13, he/him), his sadness was rooted in thinking about the effort Black people have to exert in order to receive justice, stating: "And it's really sad, how we have to do this just to get justice for people."

As part of racial trauma, youth expressed fears of being part of protests, particularly due to racialized police violence. Joe Cornell (age 17, he/him) called the arrests and violence against Black people at protests "hard to watch." He described one scene "seeing, on the front lines, protesters with their hands up and still getting beaten with batons and knocked to their knees and tear gas and just all this really graphic stuff." This police violence made some Black youth think twice about in person protests. Bree (age 15, she/her) said "when people are protesting, all they do is get shot at or with rubber bullets or gas, so I think maybe the media is definitely putting fear into the community. So, it's getting us [students in the Black Student Union] to stop protesting, which I don't want to happen, but I feel like because of everything that we see, it's putting a fear into us." A.G. (age 15, she/her) expressed how she and her family had to overcome fear in order to go out to protest, stating: "So we were protesting for Black Lives Matter and me and my family made a bunch of different signs, and we went to this protest. At the beginning ..., honestly, me and my sister were really scared, but then after – at the end of it, we were really proud of ourselves, and we were happy that we did that."

These youth's stories map onto a larger pattern found in research: Drs. Ashley Maxie-Moreman and Brendesha Tynes (2022) documented the effects of witnessing traumatic events online for Black college students, with traumatic events online defined as seeing images or videos of a Black person being beaten, arrested, or shot by police. Black youth who were more exposed to these traumatic events had higher levels of symptoms such as hypervigilance, emotional distress, anxiety, fear for safety of self and family members, and social isolation. Responses to racial trauma can be varied and can look different from post-traumatic stress disorder symptoms (Williams, 2018).

Some youth connected their distress in response to police violence in summer 2020 to personal losses and losses to incarceration, death, and the plight of their Black family members. Ray (age 17, she/her) had a deep personal reaction to George Floyd's murder, connecting her own experience with her father dying in a car accident at age seven to George Floyd's young daughter, stating:

I feel really connected to George Floyd's daughter because it was like that was me at a point in time . . .. I want the killings to really stop from the police, and just everybody in general because I feel like . . . you don't know who you're killing. At the end of the day, you don't know if you're killing somebody's mom, dad, sister, brother, uncle, aunt. You don't know that.

Other youth described directly experiencing police violence or witnessing police violence with their friends, neighbors, and family members as victims. Lee described being once held at gunpoint by a police officer, saying the officer "pointed a gun at me because she thought I was a suspect. But the other officer quickly realized that the dogs weren't attacking me; they were attacking the bush where the man was. Yeah, he had told her to put her gun down." Destiny (age 16, she/her) had the experience of police "pulling a gun on me and my cousin and friend . . . we were just walking, going to school in the summer." Through the repeated broadcasting of the murder of George Floyd and the ongoing cycle of state sanctioned killings of numerous unarmed Black people throughout history, some Black youth experience emotional pain due to having to relive these personal experiences of police violence.

The fear that these young Black changemakers felt and faced in the protest movement of summer 2020 is not new or unfamiliar. Quinn pointed out that historically, free Black people had to worry about being enslaved. Black people who escaped slavery had to worry about being captured. During the Civil Rights era, Black people engaged in resistance had to worry about lynching. Today, police violence against protesters may serve a similar purpose to stoke fear of resistance among Black people.

Several young Black changemakers expressed disappointment that it took such a graphic display of police racism and brutality for white people to "wake up" and acknowledge racism. Linda (age 13, she/her) expressed this sentiment, saying, "I feel like this political action should have been taken a long time ago." That state sanctioned violence was still a reality in 2020 evoked anger and disappointment, alongside a host of complex emotions. For example, Tsehai (age 14, she/her) explained:

I'm happy to see the world starting to take a look and slow down to recognize and try to help. But it's making me very disappointed in the country that I live in. And there's a lot that I'm proud of America for. And there's a lot that I know America has done [for] other countries. But it has made me very disappointed in the country. And in the people in the country.

This is an excellent example of the juxtaposed positive and negative emotions youth felt: on one hand, youth felt happy to see growing attention to racism, but on the other, a frustration about the slow pace of change and continued realities of anti-Black racism.

Moreover, several Black youth expressed concerns about performative allyship, which is defined as someone from a non-marginalized group expressing support for a marginalized group that is not helpful and some-times harmful (Wellman, 2022). Phea (age 17, she/her) described a TV network's effort to highlight Black films during the current political moment as "irritating." KJ (age 16, she/her) shared her frustration with "Blackout Tuesday" in the context of attending a predominantly white school, stating:

People didn't even say anything at my school. They went for at least two or three weeks without saying anything at all and posting pictures of them at the beach. And they know what was happening, because my Instagram explorer page is full of it, so I know theirs is. And then, when the whole Blackout Tuesday happened, they posted a picture of a black screen and a black fist and think that it's cool.

KJ further noted that what made her mad was that the blacking out of their profile picture was the sum of their engagement in responding to the current political moment. Specifically, "if you click their profile page and you view their story, it's stuff of them out having fun with their friends – hint – while we're in the middle of a pandemic." The idea of taking the "easy road" or posting a "black square" was seen as performative and lacking the substance needed to effect real change. Reflecting KJ's feelings, Dr. Mariah Wellman (2022) studied the impact of #BlackOutTuesday, the day that so many social media influencers and users posted black squares on social media to show solidarity with the BLM Movement. She concluded that:

The posting of black squares was performative allyship utilized strategically to build and maintain credibility with followers. Influencers were unable to genuinely merge their existing brand image with the Black Lives Matter Movement long-term, resulting in the memeification of social justice activism and no substantial progress toward diversity, equity, and inclusion within the wellness creator industry on Instagram. (p. 1)

Performative allyship can reflect anti-Black bias because these acts valorize minimal efforts at combating racism or prioritize white comfort over address-ing Black suffering, while not doing the hard work of uprooting white supremacy (Lopez Bunyasi & Smith, 2019). The young Black changemakers shared and expressed this type of frustration with their peers.

In sum, young Black changemakers experienced a range of positive and negative emotions – sometimes all at once – in response to the events of summer 2020. These findings speak to the complex emotional experiences of being a Black young person during summer 2020. These complex responses are expected based on what we know about how systemic racism is hugely burdensome and directly harmful (Boykin et al., 2020). Yet, movements for racial justice require hope and often come with joys, community connection, and (some argue) possibility for healing (Ginwright, 2010a). We end this section with the words of Zia (age 14, she/her), who summed up her experience of fighting in what she called "the battle" for Black racial justice by saying, "My experience has been troubling, but at the end of the day, it's worth getting that experience and gaining it."

BEING THE CHANGE

I feel like I wanna be a part of the change, not just watch the change.
Destiny

For many young Black changemakers, being part of Black resistance sparked a growth in confidence to use their voice and fight for racial justice. As previous chapters in this book have conveyed, being part of a community of change agents, especially with other Black people, can build youth power and changemaking, and summer 2020 amplified this experience. Some youth experienced more agency, reflection on systemic racism, civic action, or a combination of all three. In other words, this historic moment impacted the sociopolitical development of Black youth, prompting youth to take their civic engagement to new levels. Other research has begun to document growth in sociopolitical development in response to summer 2020 among other groups of youth, such as immigrant-origin youth (Karras et al., 2022), and research more broadly has found that young people's civic development can be shaped in substantial ways by moments of major societal change or upheaval (Dunn et al., 2022; Rogers et al., 2021).

Building Agency

Civic organizations build youth agency in different ways, as laid out in Chapter 7; major social movements or events can also build agency in transformative ways. H.E.R. (age 13, she/her) shared her heightened motivation and sense of responsibility to be civically engaged in summer 2020 in ways that intertwined with her identity as a Black girl, saying:

Because [of] everything going on right now ... a lot of people are maybe scared or just aren't into it. So, I feel like being Black pushes me because ... we're trying to meet or achieve a goal .... There's a lot of things going wrong in society that have to deal with Black lives or Black women or anybody, people of color in general. So, I feel like as a Black girl ... it's part of my job ... to be civically engaged and let people know like, "It's okay. We're gonna get through this ... we have 400 years ago. It's going to change, but we have to do something in order for it to change."

Although H.E.R. was already civically engaged before summer 2020, she felt called as a Black girl to be part of the change happening in summer 2020. James (age 16, he/him) expressed the collective power of Black youth that became more visible to the larger public through the racial justice movement of 2020. When asked what this moment means for Black youth and civic engagement, he shared that it:

Shows the power we have together. Shows that when we unite, we can pretty much accomplish anything that we set our minds to. It shows that we're able to efficiently, talk about a subject and make sense about a subject. One of the things I feel like adults tend to do is they say, kind of, "Oh, they're just kids. They don't know anything about the subject or anything about the topic." But I feel like this just shows that we can efficiently and fluently talk about a subject that makes sense and communicate a point clearly.

James' statement illustrates how, especially in summer 2020, young Black changemakers demonstrated agency and forced others to acknowledge the power and knowledge of Black young people.

NA also experienced growth in her agency as a changemaker during summer 2020. NA used to think of herself as "shy and not super confident," but this changed as she experienced the events of summer 2020. She reflected, "but now, when I see all those people that are backing me up and knowing that I have support, it gives me more confidence, which helps me to be civically engaged." Connecting back to feeling seen and inspired, support from "people on the news that are fighting for my same cause" and "a whole generation of kids behind me who also wanna help their communities" allowed NA to feel more confident. NA expressed that she had faced barriers to sustained engagement, but the current moment in time inspired her to push beyond her doubts and feel confident about her changemaking potential. She said:

Sometimes it helps when you see other people, but also, sometimes you feel alone 'cause it's hard to stay engaged in something, and what really makes it hard sometimes for me is when I feel like I'm not making a change at all, and I feel like I'm not having an impact on anybody, or I feel like . . . what I'm trying to do is useless, but then again, when I see all those people on the news, or I see people on social media, it just gives me inspiration again; there's still hope.

NA's quote brings together several different processes around agency that Black youth experienced during summer 2020. NA suggested that at times she felt disempowered and experienced challenges to staying engaged. Yet, when she witnessed the collective movement, she felt a renewed sense of hope and personal agency that she could make an impact.

Developing Critical Knowledge

Now I understand it and stuff, what's going on in the world right now.

Jaylen

Some Black youth gained a deeper awareness of racial injustices and movement organizing in summer 2020. In discussing the BLM Movement and Los Angeles protests, Soleil explained:

It's definitely educated me on some subjects that I wasn't aware about. I knew about police brutality but not to such an extent. What's happening now – it needs to happen, otherwise we won't get any attention. People haven't been taking the movement seriously . . . . The KKK is still legal to practice in the United States of America, which is ridiculous. So, it's definitely helped me become more engaged. I think before this, I wasn't really – I was involved but not at this intensity.

Soleil's increased critical knowledge deepened her engagement in the movement for racial justice. Cory's exposure to the BLM Movement made him "think more," due to the efforts of so many to raise awareness of racial injustice. He experienced a shifting awareness in critical knowledge that he then shared with others, including his family and siblings. As we described in Chapter 7, opportunities to build critical knowledge can be offered in Black-centered organizations and here, we see that these opportunities also arise from historical moments such as George Floyd's murder and the aftermath of this event. This greater shift in critical awareness gave Black youth momentum to further engage in the fight for racial justice in various ways, such as through educating others via social media and engaging in critical conversations.

Activism and Leadership

Prior to summer 2020, Black youth in our study were already changemakers with deep passions for racial justice, as we detailed in Chapter 2. During the watershed moment of summer 2020, they were drawn to political activism. Tom, once he arrived at a mass BLM protest, knew this was where he "needed to be . . . using my voice to create change." Tom also started registering people to vote for the November 2020 election as a follow-up to his participation in demonstrations and marches. The energy of the movement and his own power to make a tangible change through registering voters encouraged him. He said: "We got a lot of people, and it felt really good because . . . it's one thing to be at the protest and want change. But then, when you're really out there, watching people register to vote, that really feels like you are making a change."

Some youth furthered their activism during the current moment by taking on leadership roles. In several examples, youth began to integrate their service with advocacy or organizing through leadership. KJ described how the current moment motivated her to run for a leadership position in her service organization and bring more attention to police violence in that role. This moment helped Sara Vaughn understand how community service and politics can be integrated: "I think this has also shown me how much it's all connected. There's big national politics and people that are working on the ground every day. And there are activists and there are service workers and it all just . . . seems much more connected now." Zia also began to integrate politics into her service organization. Summer 2020 motivated her to speak out more about issues that mattered to her in Girl Scouts and led to her presenting on Juneteenth to earn a Girl Scout badge.

Some young Black changemakers who were already deeply engaged in racial justice work prior to summer 2020 felt that they gained a larger platform for leadership and movement building. Quinn described how summer 2020 expanded her reach to a "bigger audience and to more people that are finally listening." Similarly, for Unique (age 17, she/her), the moment put her existing work into the spotlight: "I was doing what I was supposed to be doing before. I think I was already engaged politically. Socially . . . I feel like . . . for anything it invents my role . . . if you is doing this, do it times 10 because now we are looking at you, like how I said before. I feel like we gotta kind of outdo ourselves." Unique's quote alludes to judgment from the public about her and other Black youth's civic engagement. As noted in Chapter 4, some Black youth worked to challenge negative stereotypes of Black youth as part of their changemaking. Unique and her peers felt like they needed to amplify their organizing and advocacy work so it would be seen in a positive light, especially given the level of public scrutiny directed toward them.

Other youth expressed a sense that the BLM Movement itself and current events encouraged conversations and actions to transform their local institutions. Some believed that they could make more tangible dents in racial justice organizing and institutional change at the local level. It has long been true that young people and communities of color gravitate toward local change to build power. For example in 2002, Shawn Ginwright and Taj James concluded about their work with urban youth of color organizers that, "Community organizing around local issues of direct concern to youth and their communities is the most central strategy that young people are using to create systemic change" (p. 38). Jen (age 15, she/her) noted that "I recently wrote a letter to [Los Angeles] Mayor Garcetti and [California] Governor Newsom about . . . my community and police brutality and how it kind of needs to stop because it's affecting me and my community." She felt sad and sick because "it's my people or I know people who have been affected by it or the people who haven't been affected by it yet or maybe will be."

In addition to writing letters and registering people to vote, youth also pressed school administrators and local government officials to make changes on long-standing racism in their schools and communities. In some of the stories shared in Chapter 3, Black youth's resistance in schools gained momentum or heightened attention in late May. Camille, for example, talked about how she challenged her school to finally accept the Black Student Union:

Yeah, and recently, something that happened just a couple of weeks ago . . ., this was really crazy, but my school on their Instagram account, they had posted something which was, the intent was to address all the protests, like for George Floyd and everything, but it was really vague and they didn't do a very good job, like they didn't even mention Black Lives Matter or Black people in general. And so basically there were thousands of comments from students, alumni, parents, and even teachers saying, like "you guys need to do a lot better than this" and sharing their experiences with racism at the school. And I think for me, it was really great to see that everybody was finally coming out and speaking about this and sharing their experiences. And so since then, the school let us have a Black Student Union, and they said that they're going to be looking to make a lot of changes on the administrative level. So I'm really happy that, [they] finally heard us and we were able to make a change within our school.

Camille went on to talk about finding her voice as a Black girl and "pushing forward" as an imperative given the current moment and "what is goin' on in the world." Her sense of agency and voice as a Black girl translated into local action.

PAVING THE WAY FOR THE NEXT GENERATION

I feel like it's our duty to carry the torch and pass it on to future generations. And then also in the midst of carrying the torch [make] more differences at the same time.

Layla

Summer 2020 reinforced and reinvigorated young Black changemakers' efforts toward their larger civic purposes, which aim to make life better for current and future generations of Black people. As we have reiterated throughout the book, these Black youth directed their changemaking efforts to the future. Unique contextualized her engagement in the racial justice movement of 2020 by saying, "I would have so many stories to tell my kids. They are going to tell their grandkids. It's just going to be so much – so I honestly feel honored." Youth's understanding that they could make an impact on future generations and their younger siblings (and eventually their own children) was important. Soleil stated:

If we wanna see a change, and we wanna make it happen, then it's something that we have to do. And life is never easy. We have to do these things in order to make sure that generations that come after us have a better experience than we do . . .. For the future of Black people because every person that fights for this, counts.

As Black youth deepened or clarified their civic purpose for racial justice, they sought to continue the legacy of fighting for racial justice and create a better future for subsequent generations. As Joe Cornell put it, a larger purpose was "making sure that change is actually sustainable and inclusive."

Paving the way for the next generation was a goal that included wanting protection for immediate family members as well as for future generations. Referencing Ahmaud Arbery, who was shot and killed by white civilians in February 2020 while jogging in a Georgia neighborhood, Amir said, "I have a sister. She's nine months old right now and I don't want her to grow up in [the] society that I'm growing up in right now, where she has to see these things and fear for her life every day. Fear that she can't go outside and jog." Martin (age 14, he/him) similarly framed efforts to enact police reform as a means of achieving a better future, stating, "In the future, if I get pulled over, I don't have to be afraid if I'm going to die there. I can just know that I'm just talking with the police officer instead of worrying if I'm going to get shot." He went on to say that Black youth have a stake in this mobilization effort to make a "better future for themselves and, maybe, their younger siblings or even their kids."

In the face of frustrations, heavy emotions, and continued structural racism, Black youth kept their civic purposes in sight and deepened their commitments to racial justice. This focus came from the belief that their efforts would pave the way for a more racially just and equitable future. They would not be a generation that sat idly by in the face of racial injustice. Across the young people's stories in this book, a signature element of young Black changemaking is working toward a better future. Young Black changemakers were engaged in freedom dreaming (Kelley, 2002), imagining a future free of struggle for Black people and actively working toward this dream with purpose.

THE TAKE-AWAYS

Young Black changemakers saw summer 2020 as a watershed moment in which real changes toward racial justice were happening. Summer 2020 connected Black youth's personal experiences of racism to a historic movement for racial justice, continuing a legacy of fighting for racial justice. Alongside profound joy, inspiration, and hope, Black youth experienced sadness, frustration, numbness, anger, and fear. We captured these youth's feelings while they were living through this momentous time, and they were still in the midst of processing the moment, their feelings, and their role in the movement. Summer 2020 activated agency, critical knowledge, and action for some, and for others, the movement advanced and solidified their purposeful commitments to racial justice now and into the future.

Contributions to Research

This chapter is among the first pieces of research, to our knowledge, to document the reflections and experiences of young Black changemakers during summer 2020. Prior research found that the first wave of the BLM Movement in 2013 prompted children of different racial and ethnic groups to become more aware of structural racism (Rogers et al., 2021) and spurred Black and Latinx college students to action (Hope et al., 2016). The lived experiences of civically engaged Black youth in summer 2020 offer valuable insights into how historical events rooted in racism shape the sociopolitical development of Black youth. This work highlights the need for more research on Black youth's emotional processing in response to racism, police violence, and racial justice movements.

The findings underscore how major historical events and periods of time can have short- and long-term impacts on youth's lives, including their civic engagement, which builds on prior research (Dunn et al., 2022; Oosterhoff et al., 2020; Wray-Lake et al., 2018). Summer 2020 shaped young Black changemakers' sociopolitical development through building agency, critical awareness of structural racism, and actions that challenge racism. This research contributes to sociopolitical development theory (Watts & Flanagan, 2007) by demonstrating that historical events can be a major catalyst for sparking or deepening critical agency, reflection, and action. In reflecting on this chapter's findings in relation to the full scope of youth's experiences, it is evident that earlier experiences in families, organizations, and schools positioned these young Black changemakers to act in response to this moment. This take-away echoes Camille's statement that "this is kinda what our whole life is leading up to." Changemakers are not developed overnight; it takes time, opportunities, and agency to grow as a changemaker, yet certain sociohistorical moments like George Floyd's murder and the racial reckoning that followed can accelerate this developmental change. We also add to sociopolitical development theory by showing that all Black youth did not respond in the same way to summer 2020. Their sociopolitical development trajectories may vary based on their past experiences, how they interpret the moment, and their opportunities and constraints for changemaking.

Black youth's reactions to summer 2020 highlighted the multifaceted emotions that Black youth experienced in this historic moment. Black youth's different emotional responses overlapped in complex ways. Admittedly, as a research team, we struggled to name some of the complex emotions in the data, such as the experience of feeling hopeful about progress toward racial justice and simultaneously feeling frustrated and disappointed that these changes took so long to come. More research should focus on complexity in and implications of Black youth's emotional responses that are part of sociopolitical development. An important body of research on Black youth's emotional development – synthesized in a recent review by Dr. Fantasy Lozada and colleagues (2022) – shows that systemic racial oppression affects the emotional development of Black youth. Likewise, our findings documented how Black youth's emotions are disregarded in many contexts such as schools, police encounters, and community spaces (see Chapters 3 and 4). We must be careful not to disregard emotional responses in studying Black youth's sociopolitical development. Recently, Drs. Jesica Fernández and Roderick Watts (2022) proposed an expansion of sociopolitical development theory that includes emotional work, and through qualitative research with youth of color in organizing spaces, concluded that emotional work is an integral part of organizing, yet needs to be more explicit in organizations' missions. More attention to emotions is an important direction for research on Black youth's sociopolitical development.

Practical Insights

For all who work with youth, these findings are an important reminder not to ignore major events of police violence, racism, and uprisings. Black youth faced substantial exposure to racial trauma, and along with hope and optimism, experienced emotional burdens of interpersonal, cultural, and institutional racism. Whether in schools, afterschool programs, families, community organizations, or other settings, failing to discuss and process these events means ignoring a large part of Black youth's lived experiences during times like these. It is important to approach conversations and actions around these moments with an anti-racist lens (Kendi, 2019) and to avoid overburdening or retraumatizing Black youth. It is also important not to assume to know how Black youth are feeling in these times, because Black youth respond differently to the same events, and instead to let Black youth speak for themselves.

Civic organizations where Black youth are already engaged are perhaps best poised to incorporate emotional support and create healing spaces to accompany racial justice efforts. Many chapters in this book have spoken to the value of Black spaces in creating feelings of safety, community, and solidarity; these spaces can support Black youth's well-being as well as collective efforts to resist racism. Some organizing spaces already emphasize healing and emotional wellness, and Black youth would benefit from more opportunities and spaces like these (Chavez-Diaz & Lee, 2015; Fernández & Watts, 2022).

These findings also add nuance to the public narrative about youth and social media that youth are addicted and social media is harmful. Our findings showed social media in a different light, as a central space for changemaking. This insight builds on other research documenting how youth, especially youth who experience oppression, create new modes of civic action that are fully youth led and initiated (Wilf & Wray-Lake, 2021). Narratives about youth, and Black youth in particular, must be multifaceted and portray all sides of youth's experiences. Social movements have been and should continue to build on the power of Black youth's voices and creativity in online spaces.

Up Next

This chapter has illustrated how the racial justice movement of summer 2020 impacted the lives and changemaking of Black youth in our study. In the next and final chapter, we end with young Black changemakers' words of hope for change, along with reflections on the major take-aways of the book from each member of the research team. Young Black changemakers give us hope for the future and also call us to action to participate in working toward a better world for Black people.

Untitled Self-Portrait by Meazi Light-Orr

9

Freedom Dreaming

LAURA WRAY-LAKE, ELAN C. HOPE, LAURA S. ABRAMS,
MARIAH BONILLA, DOMONIQUE KIANNA HENDERSON, ELENA
MAKER CASTRO, CHANNING J. MATHEWS, DOMINIQUE
MIKELL MONTGOMERY, VICTORIA MILLET, JASON ANTHONY
PLUMMER, & SARA BLOOMDAHL WILF

All of us bring light to exciting solutions never tried before
For it is our hope that implores us, at our uncompromising core,
To keep rising up for an earth more than worth fighting for.

Amanda Gorman, Earthrise

That is the promised glade,
The hill we climb, if only we dare it:
Because being American is more than a pride we inherit –
It's the past we step into, and how we repair it.

Amanda Gorman, The Hill We Climb:
An Inaugural Poem for the Country

In this concluding chapter, we begin with the words of Amanda Gorman (2018, 2021), a young Black changemaker from Los Angeles, the youngest inaugural poet in US history, and the first ever National Youth Poet Laureate. Her poetic words capture the hope and inspiration we took from the young Black changemakers featured in this book. These Black youth are "bringing light to exciting solutions" to local and national problems. Through their changemaking, they "keep rising up" for the causes they are passionate about and the communities that matter to them. These young Black changemakers are daring to climb the hill, and walk the long road, toward racial justice through many different forms of civic action and lived experiences that took them on this journey. Along the way, they provided messages and conveyed hope about how they, as leading changemakers, and we, as people and as a nation, can contribute to repairing the harms of anti-Black racism by envisioning and acting to create a new future. We end this book with messages of hope and calls to action from young Black change-makers, followed by what we – the research team – learned and took away from this work.

DREAMS FOR A WORLD FREE FROM RACISM

I always think in the back of my head I don't want racism to be a thing in the future, but it probably will be, which I don't like thinking about, 'cause it makes me really sad and hurt.

A.G.

By the time I'm 25, maybe 30, I just don't want this to be a thing to have to protest ... for Black Lives Matter. I want to be able to not fear the cops and that they'll accuse me of having a gun even though it's only my ID, and I just want it to be a world where there's no people that are like ... racist ... I want America to be great.

Amir

Basically, my goal is ... have every Black person ... literally everywhere be happy with themselves, not having to be afraid to go outside, not having to be afraid to look over their shoulder for the police or somebody shooting them just because, and just like have a voice.

Ray

I want this world to be a better place ... when my child walks into this world.

Linda

Young Black changemakers such as A.G., Amir, Ray, and Linda envision a future world where racism is eradicated. They do not want racism "to be a thing," and they do not want to live in fear of deadly police violence or people who wish them harm, treat them differently, or see them in negative terms because they are Black. They want Black people everywhere to live full, happy lives free from oppression. This freedom dreaming (Kelley, 2002) is rooted in the harms Black youth today face due to racism and the struggles against racism that generations before them have faced. Through imagining a different reality, freedom dreaming offers hope for the future. This vision of a better world for Black people served as a guiding purpose for Black youth's civic actions to uplift the Black community and challenge racial injustices. The stories that young Black changemakers shared conveyed this central message. Our approach of considering Black youth's civic actions in the context of the higher purposes they were pursuing was essential for fully capturing Black youth's experiences as changemakers.

We wonder why it is so much to ask that Black people be treated equitably and with dignity and respect, which echoes Ashley's (age 16, she/her) questions as she expressed her feelings about anti-Black racism: "Why do you feel the need to put down a race? Why do you feel the need to? What was the whole point?" We also recognize the long road ahead, given the deeply rooted nature of anti-Black racism in the institutions, culture, and interactions of society (Braveman et al., 2022; Jones, 1997; Kendi, 2019). Young Black changemakers, too, recognize that eradicating racism is a long, steep hill to climb and will take time. Yet, to follow the lead of our young Black changemakers, we hold hope that can share and embrace Black youth's freedom dreams. These young Black changemakers' stories push each of us to share in their imagining of a world free from racism, and their stories give us hope that change is on the horizon.

MESSAGES OF HOPE

Young Black changemakers' journeys give us many different reasons to be hopeful that change is coming. This book highlights numerous strengths of Black youth, their families, and their communities, and showcases Black youth as leaders on the road to racial justice. Here, we share messages from young Black changemakers to the world to underscore that they are one of our society's greatest resources and we need their leadership to challenge racism and injustice.

"We Will Fight"

That's one thing about our Generation Z. We're very, very open people. We don't care what your ... pronouns are. We don't care what your ethnicity is. We don't care about ... none of that. We just know what's right and what's wrong, and we'll fight and fight until that is shown that the world is that.

Phea

We need to stay strong for each other, you know, just to ... keep continuing the fighting, you know? From what's right, that we want our lives to matter as well.

Muffin

All I got to do is just keep my head up, keep pushing, fall a couple times, come back up, you know.

Kobe

The issues I was being passionate about are still not solved, so I feel like I have to keep pushing until they get solved.

Success with Lex

I do want to make a change in the world and until I accomplish that goal, there's no stopping and no giving up. Even if I feel like giving up, that's not a part of the plan.

Layla

Young Black changemakers have agency – they feel competent and motivated to continue pursuing racial justice and have developed the willpower to "keep pushing" with "no giving up." Young Black changemakers are driven to civic actions like helping, advocacy, and educating others by their passions for making the world better and from their own personal experiences of racism. They draw inspiration and support from family, friends, community members, and other Black changemakers, and their agency grows through opportunities and supports they experience in community-based organizations, especially those that center Black youth. The commitment and sustained dedication to racial justice of these young Black changemakers can inspire other youth and all of us, inviting us to bolster our own persistence in the fight for racial justice and draw on our own power to make positive change.

"We're Making History"

My generation's practically leading this movement for equal rights and equal justice for everyone and how ... it's literally being shown in full picture with no censoring. It's full on.

O.A.

We are the next generation, and we should be wanting to make the best for the next generation after that. And just a part of us being Black, I feel like if we all come together, we can really make a big statement.

Mea

I'm very proud and very not surprised, but wow, all these Black kids are standing up for their race and they're starting protests. They're starting petitions, they are doing all these things that ... a lot of grown adults aren't doing. Younger kids took a step up and were like, 'Oh, we're going to do this as our generation. We're going to fix our stuff.' The Black youth really stepped up with Black Lives Matter, and they're really being loud and clear [about] what they want and how they want things to go.

Creative

This is a time ... we're making history, for real, because I have never thought I would live to see somethin' like this before, pandemic-wise, and, political-wise. It's literally so much goin' on ... I would have so many stories to tell my kids. They gonna tell they grandkids. It's just gonna be so much – so I honestly feel honored, but I feel like we also have to be cautious during these times because ... the attention is on us ... people are still against us. So, I feel like we can't get caught slippin' like at no time. So, yeah, I feel honored – but still feel cautious.

Unique

Today's young Black changemakers are leading a movement for Black lives. Many of them recognized the large scale and historic nature of this movement, giving hope that lasting change is tangible and possible. As we have documented elsewhere (Chapters 1 and 8), the acceleration of the movement in 2020 led to some very real wins in Los Angeles and around the country. The young Black changemakers in our study were leading through challenging racism and whiteness in schools, sparking local policy change through organizing, and educating peers and others in their networks about racism and its harms. In harnessing the power of new social media techniques and strategies, and in drawing on collective support and identity, young Black changemakers recognized their own strengths to create change in new ways. These wins and the scope of this movement give hope that we are entering a new era of possibilities for racial justice that permeate through society's institutions – like the criminal legal system, the electoral system, and the economic system. Some refer to the new wave of Black-led racial justice activism as the Third Reconstruction, defined as a historical period beginning with the presidential election of Barack Obama in 2008 and continuing to the present (Joseph, 2022). This period has transformative potential to end structural racism and inequalities, yet Black-led and Black youth-led movements are not new. Modern movements build on past legacies such as the abolition of chattel slavery in the US in the nineteenth century and the Civil Rights Movement a century later. Young Black changemakers found inspiration, critical learning, and shared identity by drawing on the history and legacy of Black collective action to challenge racism.

Black youth today are making history for being at the forefront of change for racial justice. These narratives clearly challenge deficit-based views about Black youth that are frequently visible in the media, carceral system, schools, and other spaces that Black youth encounter daily (Adams-Bass et al., 2014; Hope & Bañales, 2019; Kohli et al., 2017). As Unique stated, Black youth still remain cautious, as the public's positive lens on their changemaking could turn negative at any time. We are hopeful that, with these stories and considerable other evidence of young Black changemaking, deficit-based notions of Black youth can be eliminated and replaced with belief in Black youth's changemaking potential. Young Black changemakers' passions and sustained actions are impressive, as is the scale of what they have achieved so far.

"So Much More to Being Black"

Just being strong in who I am to know that nothing can break me, no matter what obstacles come my way.

Layla

I want people to learn about African culture, because it's something I'm so proud of.

Cory

Everybody should just be mindful of young Black women and men, you know, treat them like they're young Black men and women and not anything less.

Harvey

There's so much more to being Black than all of this stuff that [my sister] might see on the news or on social media or whatever.

H.E.R.

An additional message of hope conveyed by the stories of young Black changemakers is that Black youth are not defined by racism. Youth in our study held great pride in being Black and often felt connected to Black communities that brought them joy and belonging. As we and many others have detailed (e.g., Hope et al., 2021; Ortega-Williams et al., 2022; Trent et al., 2019; Williams et al., 2019), racism is a harmful experience that Black youth contend with daily. Many young Black changemakers responded to these experiences by taking civic action to uplift the Black community and challenge racial injustice. Black youth respond in many other ways to racism, as well (Hope & Spencer, 2017). The stories in this book underscore how Black youth have very different lived experiences. If you haven't already, we recommend reading Appendix C, which briefly summarizes each young Black changemaker's unique story. Black youth are full human beings navigating everything else that other teenagers do, such as schoolwork, sports and hobbies, emotions, identity, family and peer relationships, and more. Especially given that we – the authors – share an interest in young people's development and optimizing their chances to thrive, we want to emphasize that Black youth are children growing up, with all that entails, and these strivings are part of their lives in addition to struggles against racism and changemaking efforts. These young Black changemakers' stories share the message of hope that Black youth can truly be seen, appreciated, and valued fully for who they are, especially if we all take the chance to listen to their experiences.

CALLS TO ACTION

We ended each chapter with next steps for research to better understand and uplift Black sociopolitical development across contexts that support and hinder changemaking. We offered practical insights by noting how adults who interact with and make decisions that affect Black youth – including family members, educators, policymakers, and media – could use our findings to make tangible changes that benefit Black youth's changemaking and well-being. Here, we do not reiterate all of the actionable implications of our study. Instead, we end with a few calls to action voiced directly by young Black changemakers in this study.

A Call to White People: "Black People Aren't Oppressin' Ourselves"

Black people aren't oppressin' ourselves, you know. We are getting oppressed, so the oppressor, that's the one who's gonna be able to create the real lasting change.

Tom

White kids our age are opening their eyes and seeing the privilege and what is really going on. So, I think that there can be change.

Creative

Being racist to each other and ... being a bigot towards someone is ... not gonna help anything. We should learn to get along and stuff.

Nicole

What I'm hoping is that there's gonna be some more policy changes ... making the police a bit better at de-escalating situations and using less forceful tactics.

Martin

These words, and Black youth's stories shared throughout this book, offer a clear message for non-Black people. As Tom put it, "Black people aren't oppressin' ourselves." And, as we discussed in Chapters 1 and 3, white supremacy is a root cause of racism. Thus, the call to action is for white people, and other non-Black people, to critically self-reflect on white privileges and the ways in which they – knowingly or not – uphold white supremacy and allow anti-Black racism to continue. Non-Black people need to be part of the change by challenging racism and oppression, including when they are complicit in it. We are certainly not the first to call for white people and others to embrace anti-racism (Helms, 2020; Kendi, 2019), and we echo this call with urgency.

Change needs to go beyond changing attitudes and sentiments toward Black people. Policies need to change, as Martin articulated, such as policing. Systemic racism leads to racial inequalities and disproportionately negative impacts on Black people in many different spheres of life (Feagin, 2013). The Black Lives Matter Movement has a policy change agenda that charts a course for anti-racist policy change, and other scholars and advocates are also actively putting forth innovative ideas for reimagining social institutions (see for example Kaepernick, 2021).

This call to white people to challenge racism in themselves and other white people is, we recognize, not that popular of an idea among white people. White backlash in response to Black racial justice movement successes has been evident in many forms, such as in the January 6, 2021 riot on the Capital led by white supremacist groups; the rampant spread of policies that ban books and discussions about race and racism from schools; voter suppression in largely Black communities; and policies that limit the rights of protesters (Brennan Center for Justice, 2022; Holloway, 2021; Johnson et al., 2022; R. Ray, 2021; Schwartz, 2022). In an entangled irony, white discomfort with naming white privilege and supremacy is a defining feature of white privilege and supremacy (DiAngelo, 2018; Helms, 2020). Despite the considerable obstacles to getting oppressors to "create the real, lasting change," hearing about Black youth's experiences of racism – and their unending passion to stop it – should be enough to drive us all to make change. How can we let this continue to happen to Black young people?

A Call for Investment in Black Youth

These different spaces that may not be, you know, historically designed to be a safe space or be a space that's . . . for Black individuals.

Joe Cornell

They [Black youth] don't have the resources or the things that they need to actually do stuff to impact the world.

Damian

I feel like my voice is louder now . . .. Because . . . people who are not of color are finally realizing that all this is going on and that we need to be heard.

Jen

Schools can invest in Black youth by offering them safe spaces where they feel welcome, understood, and can be themselves. Black Student Unions and other Black affinity groups are crucial Black spaces for ensuring safety and building solidarity, and Black youth need and deserve these spaces within schools. Additionally, school administrators and staff must listen to Black youth's views with sincerity and respect and take appropriate, tangible actions in response. Investing in Black youth also includes investing in Black educators and staff who can help Black students feel like they belong through representation in school spaces.

Community-based civic organizations can invest in Black youth by strengthening opportunities for Black youth to develop agency. These action steps require investments of time, resources, and staff. Organizations must also be committed to listening to and involving Black youth in decision-making and leadership within and outside of the organization. Civic organizations also have an opportunity to recognize and build on the power of Black families and their role in creating and supporting young Black changemakers in various ways such as family-focused initiatives.

Anyone with financial resources can invest in the causes Black youth are passionate about, the organizations that serve and support Black youth's changemaking, and Black youth-led movements. Young Black changemakers in our study came from different socioeconomic backgrounds but were all able to access community, family, or other resources to support their growth as changemakers. As Damian pointed out, not all Black youth have equal access to these resources, and this book identifies a host of opportunities that help Black youth initiate and sustain changemaking that are worthy of investment.

Anyone can invest in Black youth by listening to them. Young Black changemakers shared with us how they are often not listened to at school, by policymakers, and by other adults in their lives. Giving Black youth space to speak and be heard – and to not be judged or disrespected – is a simple action that any person can take and one that can make a tangible difference in the lives of Black youth.

A Call for Collective Action: "We Can All Come Together As One"

I feel like improving the community is not something that I can only do by myself, so … if I had more help, then maybe yeah.

Bree

So, we have a direct, main goal. If we can all come together as one, for everybody to be on the same page.

KJ

It's so many ways you can reach out and be a part of something right now … there is no excuse to not … do anything about this cause right now.

Destiny

What matters is that you care and you're tryin' to do something about it.

Soleil

Young Black changemakers sometimes engaged in civic actions on their own, but more often they recognized the power of collective action for making lasting change in their communities or on a large scale. This is a call to action for collective power building; they need other people to join them. Their stories can inspire other Black youth to follow their footsteps as they come of age and recognize their power to challenge these injustices. Non-Black young people can and are joining in solidarity with Black youth to challenge racial injustices in their families, in schools, and elsewhere (e.g., Lee et al., 2022). Adults can also play many different supportive roles in youth-led changemaking, especially when careful to not overstep or replace Black youth's visions with their own (Clay & Turner, 2021; Gordon, 2007). Black youth shared with us how allies can benefit and also harm their changemaking efforts. Regardless of who we are, young Black changemakers appeal to us to join collectively in the work of making the world better for Black people. As Destiny so clearly stated, "there is no excuse to not do anything about this cause right now."

REFLECTIONS FROM THE AUTHORS

We end with personal reflections from each author on how we approached the project, what it meant to us, and what insights we are taking away from these young Black changemakers. It may seem strange to end with introducing ourselves, but we felt strongly that we needed to lead with youth's stories, and in doing qualitative research, it is also important that we name our positionalities. Positionalities consist of our identities, personal life histories, experiences, and views that shape how we approached the research, consciously or not (Holmes, 2020). We start with reflections from the Black authors on our team and then follow with reflections from the non-Black authors.

Dominique Mikell Montgomery: On the Faith and Hope of Black Youth and a Call to End Stereotyping

Participating in dialogues with Black youth who were deeply dedicated to and involved in changemaking during a time in which the fight for Black humanity was so central to our public consciousness led to insights that are profoundly important for scholarship, practice, and policy. In addition, as a Black woman who was struggling to process the violence and disdain segments of our country were showing toward the Black community during summer 2020, participating in this project became a way for me to heal in ways that ventured outside my expectations.

The faith that tomorrow could be a better day for the Black community that seemed to motivate the actions of many of the youth we interviewed deeply moved and inspired me. This resistant sense of hopefulness, despite being in the midst of a period defined by the viral distribution of a video of a modern-day lynching of a Black man, is perhaps the most significant takeaway for me in this study. To be clear, the Black changemakers we interviewed were not blindly optimistic. Youth spoke candidly about their intimate understandings of Black individuals' racial oppression in the United States. These understandings were often based on personal experiences of discrimination at the hands of peers, school staff, and police or discrimination of others they had witnessed firsthand. I will never forget the stories of youth who were beaten by school police, called the N-word by peers, or worried that their fathers might become the next victims of racial violence. Youth who participated in this study understood and spoke clearly about how anti-Blackness has cost innocent people who looked like them their lives.

Nevertheless, these youth were optimistic that things could be different and they could play a hand in changing things. They worked daily to create change for themselves, their families, and the larger Black community. These youth recognized that our country was at a tipping point and saw themselves as actors who could and would shape the future of this country. Youth imagined themselves becoming a governor who defended civil rights, a doctor who served low-income communities, and a titan of industry who invested in the low-income community in which he was born. While youth varied in terms of their pathways, they sought to create change, and the changes they aimed to make almost universally displayed high amounts of investment into creating a better tomorrow, particularly for the Black community.

For this reason, it is essential that practitioners, policymakers, and researchers stop blanketly categorizing Black youth from specific communities as at-risk or disengaged and to call out others that make these stereotypical statements. Instead, we should begin to categorize our schools, our programs, our policies, and our society as at-risk of extinguishing the passion, power, and optimism of Black youth and at-risk of not benefiting from the changemaking capabilities of these youth. We need to change our systems so that they are incubators for Black youth's vision for themselves, their communities, and the world.

Jason Anthony Plummer: On Helping Black Youth Transform Their Communities

I was part of the coding team on a project that was a precursor to this one, an investigation of civically engaged urban youth of color that used qualitative methods. I had zero experience in qualitative work. My research training was in statistical methods; however, I did have a willingness to learn and had experience in youth civic engagement. Working on that first project made me appreciate how community programs and services are a part of youth's childhood experiences. The things adults do to and for youth influence how they see and act in the world. As a Black, first-generation American, cisgender male who also did community work as a teen, I felt connected to that project and this one as well. It is rare for research to see and value Black youth as assets to their community.

I hope readers of this book understand that for Black youth, civic engagement is not always an extracurricular activity. In working on this project, I was reminded of my own civic engagement journey. What motivated me to participate and what kept me going was my belief that my community deserved to have nice things and I was able to be someone that could make that happen. With that said, I think, in terms of implications for practice, recruiting Black youth into service organizations needs to emphasize how being a part of that organization helps Black youth transform their communities.

Victoria Millet: On Black Youth's Families and Friends and Centering Black Youth Voices

As a then first-year Master of Social Welfare student at UCLA, a conversation with my academic adviser, Dr. Laura Wray-Lake, reignited my interest in research and led me to joining the Young Black Changemakers' team. Prior to graduate school, I was involved in research focused on Black families impacted by the prison industrial complex, so I was eager to broaden my experience to civically engaged Black youth.

From my perspective as a Black woman, a significant take-away from the research was how highly the youth spoke of their friends and the strong influence their families had on their civic engagement journeys. Youth are typically portrayed to be peer pressured by their friends and dismissive of family, however, the youth in our study contradicted these very narratives. Their friends inspired them to join organizations and speak out on social media. While also incredibly aware of how their families, particularly their moms, instilled in them a sense of responsibility to themselves, their families, and the Black community.

In terms of the implementation for social work practice, it begins with acceptance and centering Black youth's voices when developing civic engagement curricula, programs, and organizations. In order to effectively grow and benefit those who are most impacted by the system, it will be necessary to not only invite youth to the table but include them in imagining a more equitable and inclusive future. They bring fresh insight and complex understanding to conversations and social justice progress in a constantly evolving political landscape.

During my time on this project, I have been able to learn far more than I anticipated from the youth and the brilliant scholars who all contributed to the book. The youth opened up my mind into their world and the realities of growing up in a highly racialized and politicized moment in time. In addition to navigating school, a social life, in the midst of a global pandemic, I commend them for their courage, tenacity, and boldness. As a student, collaborating with scholars with various areas of expertise challenged me to expand my thinking. Now, as I begin my career as a social worker, I will take the lessons I've learned from each person who has shared their mind and lives with me in the creation of this book.

Channing J. Mathews: On Black Identities and Being Seen

I joined this project as a postdoctoral scholar seeking to stay connected to the roots of my research interests through the study of Black youth activism. Dr. Elan Hope pulled me in on the team as writing and thought-partner support, and I didn't want to miss the opportunity to learn from brilliant qualitative and mixed-methods scholars. As someone who entered the work toward the end of the project (i.e., engaged in data analysis and active writing), I was deeply encouraged by the stories of these young Black changemakers. They remind me of why I do this work, even when it's hard and frustrating; to help amplify the joy, success, and resilience of Black youth despite the obstacles they face.

The young Black changemakers remind me of what I craved as a Black girl growing up in the deep South attending a predominantly white school: to be seen and heard. Though my parents were always exposing me to the brilliance and activist legacy of Black people, in school I felt alone and unable to speak to the injustices I experienced, being one of five Black people in my high school. Seeing the fearlessness of these young Black changemakers, driven by the love of family and community and a context of racial injustice, makes that little Black girl smile and grounds me in my scholarly work.

My key take-away from the young Black changemakers is the ways that racialized experiences, whether through engaging in rich cultural experiences or responding to racism and discrimination, shape Black youth's understanding of what it means to be Black. And because our experiences vary across our integrated social identities (such as class, sexual orientation, immigration status, geography), there is no one experience that defines Black culture or what Blackness means. The beauty of these young Black changemakers lies in the ways they highlight, through their experiences, the multidimensional and layered aspects of their experiences that challenge the narrative of Blackness as a monolith. Their experiences and voices push society to have broader representations of Blackness that move beyond stereotypes and center Black brilliance as a fundamental truth.

Domonique K. Henderson: On Black Youth Voices and How to Support Them

When Dr. Wray-Lake asked if I was interested in joining this team, I knew this study would contribute to the Black community's journey toward creating a future where Black voices and bodies are valued. As someone who actively participated in protests when our community lost Tamir Rice, Freddie Gray, Trayvon Martin, Michael Brown, Philando Castile, George Brown, Breonna Taylor, and Ahmaud Arbery, there was an overwhelming sense of responsibility I felt toward this project. Fighting for future generations of Black people must happen on multiple fronts, and I believed that going on this journey with the researchers on this team was another way to support my community.

As a Black woman from Compton, California, I personally remember advocating for the Black community and other important causes during my youth. I also remember adults from schools, clubs, and organizations who both supported and discouraged my efforts, which is similar to many youth we described in this book. Ruby Bridges, Angela Davis, Mari Copeny, Thandiwe Abdullah, and so many more all began their journey of revolutionizing racial equality for the Black community during their youth. Similarly, each Black changemaker in this study began their journey of activism during their youth and shared a powerful story and experience of pursuing racial justice and equality. After absorbing Black youth's truths from this book, the key messages I hope readers walk away with are that Black youth's voices should be heard and respected; Black youth should be encouraged to lead and advocate for racial justice rather than expected to take on these responsibilities, especially when adults in these spaces have the power to influence change in these settings; school staff should make genuine and intentional efforts to create an inclusive school environment for Black students; and Black families must continue to play an essential role in cultivating our Black leaders of tomorrow. Centralizing Black youth's voices and emphasizing their humanity is not something that happens enough across various contexts. However, by amplifying Black youth's voices, I believe this book has the power to influence policy and practice in schools, nonprofits, and other contexts where Black youth's voices are often rendered insignificant and invisible. Despite the weight placed on these Black youth, it is my hope that they continue to show up and show out! There is no one who can dim their light or minimize their voice. They are our ancestors' pride and joy.

Elan Hope: On Moving from Being Black Youth to Parenting Black Youth

When Dr. Laura Wray-Lake invited me to this project, I was ecstatic. I study Black kids and their families. I was Black kids. I now have Black kids. I get excited thinking about the hope and possibility of young Black changemakers. It's a privilege to be a part of hearing and sharing the stories of young Black changemakers; an opportunity that I could not let pass me by. I came to the work of young Black changemakers from my own past being one. I engaged in many of the ways of changemaking that we described in Chapter 2, and my parents instilled values and supported changemaking in many of the ways we described in Chapter 5 on families. My identity as a Black woman was and is shaped by racism and the matrix of domination and that motivated and continues to motivate my own changemaking as we illustrated in Chapter 4. Even still, the joy, the fortitude, the tenacity, and creativity of Black communities has been just as powerful, if not a more powerful motivator.

The key message that I take from these young Black changemakers is that Black lives are worth fighting for. Black lives are worth loving for. Black lives are worth living for. Black lives are worth sacrificing for. Black lives are worth joy. Black lives are worth anger. Black lives are worth vindication. This worth is not earned or measured. I take these lessons into my own changemaking and into how I go on to raise and mentor changemakers. These young Black changemakers remind me, remind us, that the environments they grow up in are not created equal. They traverse dangerous and challenging roads in schools, in communities, and even in the organizations where they pursue justice. They also remind us that they carry the legacies of the ancestors before them and walk this road with pride, love, joy, and righteous anger for justice.

Mariah Bonilla: On the Burdens on and Resistance of Young Black Changemakers

As a Latina woman who was born and raised in Los Angeles, I was immediately interested in joining this project because it would allow me to explore the experiences of young Black changemakers in my city. I joined this project as an eager sophomore in college. As an undergraduate student, I was really excited to learn about research and social welfare. Working alongside Laura Wray-Lake and our amazing team has inspired me to pursue a career in research. This project has bolstered my interest in racial and social justice work. I was immediately attracted to this project because as a high schooler, I participated in community organizing among Latinx and Black neighborhoods in Los Angeles. Learning about young Black changemakers' experiences of organizing was eye-opening and humbling.

The stories of the young Black changemakers in this book have taught me the significant ways in which Black youth are involved in changemaking. The Black changemakers interviewed were extremely insightful, reflective, and inspiring. Their passion, optimism, inquiry, and resistance have deepened my understanding of changemaking among Black youth and their understanding of racism and social justice.

One major take-away for me was the experiences of young Black changemakers in schools. Frequently, Black youth are expected to take on the labor of educating their peers about their racism. Experiencing everyday hostility from peers while simultaneously feeling unheard by staff was prevalent among the youth interviewed. Hearing this, I was disappointed, but sadly not surprised. I hope this book can influence educators and organizers to support Black youth by better promoting civic education and centering the voices of civically engaged Black youth. I hope organizations will center Black voices and support young Black changemakers in their efforts to support their community and selves.

Laura S. Abrams: On Young Black Changemaking as Imperative for Survival

When I joined forces with Laura Wray-Lake on this project in 2019, I did so as follow up to our work published in the *Monographs of the Society for Research on Child Development* on civically engaged urban youth and as an opportunity to build knowledge about Black youth and civic engagement. I came to this work as a white woman whose primary scholarship is on youth and the carceral state. Working with Laura Wray-Lake gave me an opportunity to work on a project that uses a strengths and empowerment perspective that is often lacking in my other research endeavors.

In 2019, there was no way of knowing how meaningful and impactful this work would become in the wake of the murder of George Floyd. While we were in the middle of this large social movement, my personal and professional life were also quite affected. I found myself going back and forth between working with Black students at UCLA's Luskin School of Public Affairs to address anti-Blackness in social work in a meaningful way, while also trying to educate my white family and friends about racism and anti-Blackness. My own children were high school aged at the time, and I took them to protests as young white men and tried to educate them about racial justice and injustice. In the midst of all of this, of course, we were still collecting data and working together on the Young Black Changemakers Project.

I learned a lot from this time period and working with the data and this team, both personally and professionally. Personally, I came to a greater understanding that for my community and my children, civic engagement is "optional" – a choice; for the young Black changemakers, it's imperative and part of community survival. This is an important lesson for me, and one that I am still seeking to understand on a deeper level. I hope to share these lessons with others in the future.

Moreover, at the onset, conducting a project with Black youth as the center of the conversation – as two white female principal investigators who acted on an opportunity to secure grant funding for this project – didn't sit right from the start. I really appreciate how Laura Wray-Lake thoughtfully brought Elan Hope, a Black researcher and expert in youth sociopolitical development onto the project leadership team. Laura also ensured that we hired all Black interviewers and made a very intentional effort to center the voices of Black researchers and community collaborators. She created a model that I believe other white researchers can build upon in doing research pertaining to the Black community.

In regard to the findings, we have so many layers of interesting material; it was hard to imagine how we would pull this all together. For me, the biggest take-aways from this book are the tenacity and courage of the young people that took part in our study; the strong and enduring ties to family and cultural traditions, and overall, the inspiration that I was able to glean for the future of our country. It is my hope that our readers can take interest in the many ways that young Black changemakers are building a better world for all of us; now it is time to join with them to engage and support these efforts.

Sara Bloomdahl Wilf: On Black Youth-Led Movements and the Tolls of Changemaking

I was really thrilled to join this project. First, I was excited to focus on uplifting the changemaking potential of young people in high school – when I was in high school, I felt like my voice wasn't taken as seriously and I wasn't given that many opportunities to be a changemaker. So, I wanted to explore whether that was also true for youth in the study who, in addition to being high school age, likely faced racial and other forms of discrimination that I did not encounter. Second, I grew up hearing inspirational stories about Black-led social movements to challenge racial injustice – the Civil Rights Movement was very prominent in my school curriculum, as it is in many liberal areas across the US, and my dad is from Philadelphia so I also remember him telling me about the Black Panthers and the state-sponsored violence they faced (like the MOVE bombing). I remember feeling inspired by Black leaders in these movements, especially because most of them were young people. Dr. Martin Luther King Jr. was only in his thirties throughout much of the movement, and many prominent leaders in the Student Nonviolent Coordinating Committee and the Black Panthers were in their early twenties. When we started this study in 2020, the Black Lives Matter Movement had also more recently instigated national conversations about police brutality and racial injustice, and I was inspired by Black youth across the country who had protested the murders of Black people by police and white supremacist violence. I was interested in how the strong legacy of changemaking in the Black community, particularly leadership by Black youth, might affect Black youth changemaking today. When I joined this project, I felt excited and honored to be part of a team uplifting the unique changemaking experiences of Black youth, who both historically and contemporaneously have had an outsized impact on social movements in the US and around the world.

Looking back at my own evolution throughout the project, I can say now that my view of Black youth's involvement and leadership in these movements was through rose-colored glasses. For example, I lionized the Freedom Riders' courage and the Black Panthers' creativity in creating their own community-based infrastructure without considering the impacts that constant violence, surveillance, and dehumanizing rhetoric must have had on their psychological well-being and mental health. Another example is that during the Black Lives Matter resurgence in May 2020 following George Floyd's murder, until I read through the interview transcripts from this study, I just didn't realize how much of a toll the violence, particularly graphic videos of Ahmaud Arbery's and others' murders, were having on Black youth. These are examples of how my own positionality as a white woman, who had never experienced racial discrimination or violence, created a blind spot in my research. This realization made me reflect on what I was taught in school, and how my (all white) teachers never brought up the psychological harms that Black people in these movements must have endured. I am grateful for youth's willingness to be open about their experience with our team, including the challenges to their mental health and well-being. The interviewers' expertise and empathy helped in making youth feel more comfortable sharing as well.

For me, the research team community we created throughout this project – including uplifting each other's achievements, check-ins during rough times when we were all struggling, and providing lots of space for reflection and debate – was core to our ability to deeply engage with youth's experiences. I'm grateful for the process of inductive analysis, memoing, and weekly discussions, which took a lot of time (significantly more than in other qualitative projects I've worked on) but ultimately led to a much fuller and richer view into Black youth's changemaking journeys and experiences. I am proud of how together, we stayed true to youth's voices and experiences and produced a book that uplifts Black youth changemaking while highlighting the unique challenges they face, with practical applications for schools and community settings. Ultimately, I have learned so much from this project – from youth themselves, community organizations who we presented our findings to, and the research team members – that I will carry with me for the rest of my research career. I hope this book makes young Black changemakers feel seen and heard and celebrated for the incredible work they are doing!

Elena Maker Castro: On the Personal Nature of Young Black Changemaking and Translation of Findings to Schools

I joined this project as a first-year doctoral student at UCLA. As someone intent on pursuing research on civic engagement, and as someone hoping to expand our understanding of what civic engagement looks like across youth of different ethnic and racial backgrounds, I vividly remember seeing the call for research assistants and immediately dismissing all other responsibilities to apply. I am so grateful I did, because this project taught me so much more than I ever could have anticipated.

Working on this project has been a humbling experience on multiple levels. First and foremost, I am most humbled by the work being done by the young Black changemakers featured in this book. While I often look fondly back on my own history of civic action as a young person, I also see how surface-level my approach was. As a young white person in an upper middle-class community, my civic endeavors focused on service, largely via mentoring and teaching younger children. I enjoyed the privilege of pursuing civic action because I liked giving back, uninhibited by a racial context that allowed me to see my whiteness, my existence, as "normal." In leading the analysis for Chapter 2, I was struck by how deeply personal changemaking is for Black youth, and this has led me to believe that it is all the more imperative to understand and support Black youth in their civic work. To that end, I leave the project deeply impressed, and also sobered, by the civic work young Black changemakers are doing.

I was also humbled by the research team conducting this study. At every turn, members of this team were rigorous, thoughtful, and committed to doing justice to the youth we had the opportunity to interview. As the project took on yet greater salience as our interviews occurred in tandem with the 2020 Black Lives Matter uprising, our team responded with new questions and more space for youth to process the intense emotions and experiences of the moment. As we then came out of the interview phase and began analyzing the data, it became clear that our findings would have meaning, and potentially more impact, for a broader audience than a traditional academic publication. Writing a book of this type was no easy endeavor and required a great deal of patience, deliberation, and dedication. I am grateful to have observed the leaders and members of this team chart this course, and I hope that we can continue to find ways to share findings.

In particular, as a former social studies teacher, I often think about how the findings across this book can translate into school and classroom-based practices. While I did not end up working on Chapter 3, I was deeply struck by the ways in which Black youth worked to navigate non-Black school spaces. I hope readers will especially take note of the incredible unpaid and often thankless labor Black youth are putting into often hostile and unwelcoming school spaces, and make strident efforts to offer more support and opportunities to listen to, and follow the lead of, Black youth. Moreover, while I am admittedly becoming more removed from the classroom with each passing year, I remain sensitive to the civic education crisis threatening our democracy and our students' right to information and civic expression. Black youth will surely bear the brunt of this attack on civic history and civic information, and they will undoubtedly be on the frontlines of resistance. As schools grapple with how to better foster civic education and engagement for their students, I hope they turn to books like this one that center Black youth's voices. Black youth in this book, just as the many Black youth of generations past, are the ones envisioning and leading the type of change we need to cultivate a more just and equitable society.

Laura Wray-Lake: On Black Lives Mattering and Hope for the Future

I initiated this project to understand the journeys of young Black changemakers in Los Angeles. I was passionate about doing this work because academic research needed much more attention on Black youth and their civic engagement, and the public needed to hear Black youth's stories of changemaking. Black youth have so much wisdom and power to share with the world, and I wanted to do my part to elevate and amplify their voices. However, as a white female academic researcher, I knew I could not and should not do this work alone. I can never fully understand the lived experiences of Black youth. What I brought to the project was years of experience doing research on young people's civic engagement across a variety of backgrounds, racial and ethnic identities, and neighborhoods. I also brought my own history growing up in the rural South surrounded by anti-Black racism, but of course, never as its target. Witnessing the daily injustices of anti-Black racism toward my Black peers, friends, and community members growing up made me angry and still does. It has taken me years to learn the language and tools to challenge racism that I witness and that I internalized from my environment, and I am still learning. A third thing I brought to this project was an amazing team of 10 other scholars of different ages, from different racial and ethnic backgrounds, and with different lived experiences. In our collaborative work, I learned from their expertise, I took their direction and feedback, and we made decisions together. In fact, it was not originally my idea to write a book, but other scholars on the team felt that this was the best way to tell the young people's stories, so that is what we did, and I have truly enjoyed it. Every step of the way, we centered the voices and experiences of the young people in the study.

Each chapter is full of important insights about Black youth's lived experiences as changemakers, but if I had to boil it down to a single take-away message, it would be that Black lives matter. This phrase has been uttered millions of times since it was posted on Facebook by Alicia Garza in July 2013 in response to the acquittal of George Zimmerman who killed Trayvon Martin. For me, this simple phrase still holds so much power and layers of meaning that align with the take-aways of this book: Black Lives Matter is a response to the dehumanization of Black people; an assertion of the value of Black youth and their experiences; and a call to action to challenge racial injustice. The young Black changemakers in this study matter, and their changemaking matters for creating a better world for Black people. They help us imagine what the world might look like if everyone truly and fully believed that Black lives matter.

Appendix A

Study Methodology

Data for this book came from a qualitative study conducted in Los Angeles (LA) between February and August 2020. This project was initially conceptualized by Drs. Laura Wray-Lake and Laura Abrams as part of a grant funded by AmeriCorps (Grant No. 17REHCA001). The overall goal of the study was to understand the lived experiences and developmental journeys of young Black changemakers. We understood that our own lens and expertise as two white women would be inadequate to carry out this study with cultural integrity or depth of understanding. So, in assembling our research team, we prioritized Black scholars. We invited Dr. Elan Hope, a leading Black scholar of youth sociopolitical development, to join the leadership team early in the process and hired all Black interviewers, some of whom became co-authors of the book. This group consisted of scholars at all levels of academia (undergraduates to PhDs). This team is represented across the authorship of the chapters that comprise this book, and as the last chapter details, offered a range of perspectives.

RECRUITMENT AND SAMPLING

The study was approved by UCLA's Institutional Review Board. We began to recruit Black young people for this study in fall 2019 by reaching out to LA-based organizations that work with youth volunteers and activists, prioritizing organizations that worked with Black youth. We spent a few months contacting and meeting with organizations to identify organizations with whom we would partner. We planned to interview young Black changemakers in a handful of organizational spaces, and were prepared to do that starting in February. However, after conducting five interviews in person, the COVID-19 pandemic commenced, and we had to pivot our recruitment strategy. Our team created a website, study flier, and a Google form where young people could indicate their interest in the study. The organizations we had originally identified, along with others, helped to circulate our flier. Approximately half of the sample of 43 youth were recruited via eight organizational partners that work with Black youth in LA, and the remaining youth were recruited via broader circulation efforts. When a young person signed up, we confirmed their eligibility via their Google form responses. To be eligible, young people had to self-identify as Black and as a changemaker, live in LA County, and be between the ages of 13–18 years. We obtained verbal parental consent via phone calls with parents or guardians, except for 18-year-olds, who provided their own consent. We obtained youth assent at the start of the interviews for youth aged 13–17 years.

The sample of 43 Black youth was 65.1% female, and between the ages of 13–18, with a modal age of 16 years. This sample reflects considerable diversity in racial and ethnic backgrounds, with 41.9% identifying as another race or ethnicity in addition to Black, and 20.9% being born outside of the US. The sample included diversity in civic involvement, as youth were involved in numerous civic organizations and activities. The sample also spanned a variety of school and neighborhood contexts, as youth were enrolled in 37 different high schools across LA. They came from different socioeconomic backgrounds, with 57.7% of youth having at least one parent with a college degree or higher, and 37.2% of youth reporting that their family had just enough money to meet basic needs or a hard time meeting financial needs. This sample variability is a study strength that allowed us to describe different lived experiences of young Black changemakers.

Youth selected a pseudonym of their choice for the book. Readers can follow the thread of individual young people across the book through our use of pseudonyms. This practice of youth-selected pseudonyms gave youth ownership over how they were represented and allowed us to protect the identities of individuals and organizations in the study. Our general practice through the chapters was to ground youth's quotes in the context of their background and experiences, as relevant.

DATA COLLECTION

Black interviewers conducted one-on-one interviews with self-identified, highly civically engaged Black youth that lasted for approximately 45 minutes. A consistent semi-structured interview protocol was used across the interviews (described in full below). We conducted five interviews in person with youth before the COVID-19 pandemic hit in March 2020, and the remaining interviews were conducted virtually. We interviewed 18 youth before the next national crisis hit on May 25th: the brutal police murder of George Floyd. After pausing the study for several weeks to allow youth and our own research team to grieve, process, and respond to unfolding events, we restarted the study with several changes. We added an additional interview prompt with four sub-questions to elicit youth's feelings and experiences related to this historical moment. With this updated protocol and primarily online recruitment, we interviewed 25 youth. We also re-contacted the initial 18 youth for a second interview to ask these additional questions about their experiences in the current moment. We completed 10 follow-up interviews, each lasting approximately 30 minutes. We stopped data collection at the end of summer 2020, after collectively determining we had reached saturation in youth's comments across interview questions.

INTERVIEW PROTOCOL

The interview questions were developed iteratively as a research team and refined after several pilot interviews with Black young adults in the research team's network. The interview protocol was organized by seven larger goals that served as guideposts for interviewers. Goal 1 was for interviewers to introduce themselves to the young person, establish rapport, and make the young person comfortable. Goal 2 was to briefly introduce youth to the study purpose to set the stage for the interview.

Goal 3 was to learn about young people's civic activities. To do this, interviewers utilized a civic engagement checklist, shown in its entirety in Appendix B. Youth were presented with a long list of possible ways to be civically engaged, which were derived from our previous research with Black youth and other youth of color (Wray-Lake & Abrams, 2020). Youth indicated which of the civic actions on the list they had taken, and were then prompted to share other ways they were civically engaged that did not appear on the list. In the process of examining the list, youth were asked to "tell me about some of these activities and how you're engaged" (Interview Question #1). A second main interview question asked youth to "tell me a story of a time when you were civically engaged" (Interview Question #2). Various follow-up questions were posed to gather youth's experiences in different civic activities, the meaning these experiences held for them, and the passions that drove their civic actions.

Our first five interviews did not use this checklist as a jumping off point. We found that establishing some shared examples of changemaking helped youth have a frame for conveying their own views of changemaking. Interviews without this beginning sometimes led to initial confusion from youth about what we wanted to hear about, and some underestimating or undersharing of the variety of civic actions young people took, which came out later through prodding.

Goal 4 was to understand youth's journey to civic engagement. The primary interview question asked in this section was, "We're interested in understanding how you became so civically engaged. Walk me through your own journey of becoming engaged" (Interview Question #3). Interviewers asked various follow-up questions to gather information about youth's journeys but made sure to cover (a) launching points, or what got them started on their journeys and (b) sustaining factors, or "what makes you stay involved?"

Goal 5 was to learn about how youth connect racial identity and civic engagement. Interviewers asked three main questions in this section: "What is unique about civic engagement for Black youth?" (Interview Question #4); "I think of you as a young Black changemaker: How does being Black matter for your civic engagement?" (Interview Question #5); and "All of us have a different combination of personal identities. What other identities (aside from Black identity) do you hold that connect to your civic engagement?" (Interview Question #6). Interviewers used a variety of follow-up questions, as relevant, to probe more about youth's identity and civic engagement and influences on this process.

Goal 6 was to learn how youth connect the current moment of political action and their civic engagement. This section was added to interviews that occurred after George Floyd's murder (June–August, 2020). The primary interview question was "Tell me what this current moment of political action means to you" (Interview Question #7). Potential prompts included: (a) "How are you feeling?"; (b) "How are you being impacted?"; (c) "Has it changed anything about your civic engagement going forward?"; and (d) "What do you think this moment means for Black youth and civic engagement?"

Goal 7 was to capture youth's final thoughts ("Is there anything else we should know about your experiences?" Interview Question #8). Youth were asked how they felt about the interview and then picked their pseudonym.

The interview protocol for the 10 follow-up interviews began with reintroducing young people to the study, its purpose, and the reason for the follow up. Then, the interviewers asked the same question as #7 above, "Tell me what this current moment of political action means to you." The list of follow-up questions included the same four as listed in (a)–(d) above, with the additional questions of "Have you been involved in the current political movement for racial justice?" and "Has this moment changed how you view your role in the world? In your community?" Then, the interview transitioned to asking: "How does being Black matter for your civic engagement in the current political moment?"; "What do you think this moment means for Black youth and civic engagement in general?"; and "What other identities do you hold that connect to your civic engagement right now?" The interview then captured youth's final thoughts as described above.

ANALYSIS AND WRITING

Coding

Our analytic process was multistep, involved our entire team, and took over two years. First, we transcribed all interviews verbatim; about half were transcribed by our research team, and the other half of transcriptions were outsourced for expediency. For the 10 young people we interviewed twice, we consolidated their transcripts into a single document for coding and analysis. Although the transcripts were analyzed verbatim, for this book publication, we removed all ums, uhs, repeated words, and unnecessary "likes" without noting where we did this. We consider these edits an important professional ethic and courtesy to be used with any speaker. If we removed two or more words that were unnecessary for the interpretation of the quote, we added an ellipses (. . .); these often included false starts or speech errors, but sometimes contained other content. We did not change grammar because this captures the style of how youth talked and sounded, and this is part of hearing their voices. If we needed to add a word or change a part of speech to enhance readability of the quote, we added that information in brackets.

Our coding process was sequential, iterative, and collaborative. We used an inductive method, grounded in thematic analysis (Braun & Clarke, 2012), to identify codes, clusters, themes, and higher-order concepts through a systematic team process. We began with line-by-line coding of three complete transcripts. The research team reviewed and discussed the line-by-line codes, which resulted in a set of focused codes. The remaining analyses were conducted using Dedoose software. In the next iteration, focused codes were applied to eight randomly selected complete transcripts. Each transcript was discussed by the same two coders and broader questions and ideas were discussed by the whole research team. With each pass, we added, merged, or redefined codes as needed to capture youth's perspectives. At this point, we realized ways to streamline our coding scheme and eliminate overlaps, and this major revision reduced our coding scheme from 143 to 89 codes.

Next, two coders applied the new codes to three transcripts sequentially, and this process led to clarifications in code definitions, further code refinement, and in a few cases, merging of codes (leading to the elimination of seven codes). Then, pairs of researchers coded the same transcript and discussed discrepancies to ensure shared understanding and reasonably similar application of codes across researchers. At this stage, we also wrote memos for each young person and included these in our coding database. These memos considered each transcript holistically and captured themes and salient experiences for each young person, to be examined in analyses alongside coded excerpts. This rigorous multistep coding process offered a strong and comprehensive foundation for the analysis and themes as outlined below.

The transcripts were fully coded using the finalized coding scheme. In total, 82 codes were organized under six categories: ways of being civically engaged; influences and consequences of civic engagement; worldviews and identity; Black experiences and culture; contexts; and developmental processes. The latter two categories of codes were cross-cutting, meaning that they were intentionally overlaid with other codes to understand the contexts and developmental processes at play. A full codebook is available upon request from Laura Wray-Lake. The three-person coding team was Laura Wray-Lake, Dominique Mikell Montgomery, and Elena Maker Castro. Other members of the research team engaged in coding checks for 10 transcripts. The purpose of the code-checking process was to make sure the codes and code applications were inclusive of different perspectives and interpretations. Code checkers added codes to excerpts where needed but did not remove code applications from the original coders; code checkers also wrote their own holistic memos to enhance the interpretation of interviews. We only conducted 10 such checks, given the high level of alignment in code applications and interpretations across the team.

Analysis

Once the transcripts were fully coded and checked, the team began analysis. To determine how to prioritize topics for analysis, we reviewed the holistic memos that were written for each young person. There were 43 primary memos and 10 additional holistic memos that came from the code-checking process. Parts of the youth profiles in Appendix C were also derived from these memos. Reviewing these memos gave us a bigger picture view of the data and youth's changemaking journeys, in addition to the in-depth view of the data that we gained from conducting the coding.

Each team member examined the 53 memos and reflected on the major ideas and organizing concepts we saw. As a group, we used an online platform called Padlet to share thoughts about main ideas and organizing concepts. We met over several weeks to discuss, arrange, and rearrange these major organizing concepts. This organizing framework was loose and malleable at the time, but roughly mirrors what are now the chapters of this book.

Once we had a set of main ideas that cut across the data, we determined smaller teams that would conduct analyses and write up findings. Laura Wray-Lake created a schema of authorship roles and responsibilities, so that research team members could consider what roles they wanted and were able to assume. Analysis teams were established, as reflected in the author list for each chapter. We also decided on sets of codes that were most applicable for each topic, which offered a starting point for analyses.

Analysis teams wrote analytic memos on codes and clusters of codes and their meanings within their topic area, for example, on the idea of "community helping" or "Black identity." When the code content spanned too much ground, it was broken down into smaller units for memo writing. To construct these memos, we used Dedoose to pull excerpts associated with a given code. In memos, team members reflected on the meanings and experiences that were shared and divergent for young people and wrote about potential themes to capture the main ideas from the given set of excerpts. Memo writers aimed to stay open to what was coming out of the data and mindful of when and how personal views and experiences were shaping interpretation. Memos included reflection on noticeable patterns, relationships, or connections in the data, as well as exemplary quotes that illustrated key concepts and relationships.

Memo writers circulated their memos to the entire research team, and in weekly meetings, team members took turns presenting and discussing the memos. These frequent group discussions were a signature aspect of our analysis. New insights on themes and integration across themes emerged from these discussions, allowing findings to transcend beyond any single researcher's perspective on the data and encompass viewpoints from across the team. Memo writers took notes that were used to revise memos, and as needed, revisit the data for clarity or to reground the findings in youth's words. Particularly in cases of questions or disagreement over interpretation, data were reexamined and interpretations were clarified.

As analyses deepened, more advanced analyses were conducted as warranted. This included examining code co-occurrence frequencies in Dedoose to identify significant overlaps and examine excerpts of relevant code co-occurrences (e.g., "helping others" x "having social connections"). We eventually used the collection of analytic memos to construct detailed chapter outlines, including both content, themes, and relevant quotes. Some memos were used across chapters, but we made sure to delineate and parcel out the organizing principles to avoid overlap. These detailed outlines were then discussed with the team to decide on direction of the chapter and overall thematic cohesiveness within and across chapters.

The analytic process continued throughout the writing of the book. This was a large team effort that is not common among qualitative projects, but the process represented and integrated the authors' different expertise and viewpoints. Laura Wray-Lake was actively involved in all analytic and writing teams in order to have a comprehensive understanding of the project process and findings, and to facilitate having a shared voice and style across the chapters. Once all of the chapters were complete, the three lead authors, Wray-Lake, Hope, and Abrams, edited the book for cohesiveness and consistency.

Appendix B

Civic Engagement Checklist

What Is Civic Engagement Anyway?

There are SO many ways to be civically engaged. CIRCLE any ways that YOU are civically engaged from the list below:

Helping family
Helping neighbors
Helping others in need
Improving the community
Bettering myself to better my community
Speaking out against injustice or unfairness
Mentoring younger children or peers
Conserving resources to protect the environment
Volunteering for an organization or cause
Contacting a government official
Campaigning for a cause or candidate
Protesting or demonstrating an injustice
Organizing or advocating for a policy
Participating in a group, club, or team
Participating in religious programs or services
Participating in music or art that shares an important message
Organizing community events or activities
Expressing opinions about a social issue
Following the news and staying informed about issues
Educating others or creating awareness of an issue
Posting on social media about social issues

There may be other forms of civic engagement as well! Young people often create their own unique ways of being engaged. Write any other ways you are civically engaged in the space below.

Appendix C

Young Black Changemaker Profiles

A.G. was a 15-year-old in the ninth grade who preferred to be called African American instead of Black. A.G. described herself as a mostly B student whose Black identity was somewhat important to her. She was dedicated to working with the Black community for social change. Her primary forms of engagement were through a Black service organization and Black Lives Matter protests with her family. Both spaces were impactful for her, given that she attended a predominately white (49%), private Christian school and had few school-based opportunities to interact with Black peers. A.G. planned to attend a four-year college or university upon completing high school (*pages 105, 109–110, 132, 148, 161*).

Amir was a 13-year-old Black male in the eighth grade. He described himself as a mostly B student and attended an elite private school whose population was 70% white. His experiences of racial discrimination from white peers motivated him to join his school's Black Student Alliance, where he served as its president. Amir was driven to challenge anti-Blackness to create a better world for his little sister and credited his mother for fostering his interest in civic engagement. Amir planned to attend a four-year college or university upon graduating from high school (*pages 19, 37–39, 46, 68, 82, 102–103, 128–129, 148, 155, 161*).

Ashley was a 16-year-old Black female in the eleventh grade. She described herself as a mostly A student whose Black identity was extremely important to her. Ashley's engagement was rooted in her experiences at church where the practice of Christian faith was integrated with engagement in social justice. Her church facilitated numerous engagement activities, including screening documentaries on Black issues, planning events for graduating students during COVID-19, organizing toy drives for children with incarcerated parents, and interviewing community members about

Channing Mathews led the compilation of these profiles

political action. Ashley's civic engagement, coupled with her family's emphasis on the importance of fighting for Black communities, drove her consistent efforts to uplift Black people. Ashley attended a private, Catholic, and predominately white (62%) high school. She planned to attend a four-year college or university (*pages 104–105, 119, 122, 161*).

Bree was a 15-year-old Black female in the tenth grade. Bree described herself as a mostly A student whose Black identity was extremely important to her. She held a communal orientation to supporting Black people, with particular focus on uplifting the experiences of Black people. Though she saw the value in changemaking through protest, she felt that engaging in critical conversations about race and building relationships were more tenable routes for her to engage social change. Bree attended a public, predominately white (40%), and Hispanic (35%) high school where she was a leader in the Black Student Union. She planned to attend a two-year or junior college upon graduating high school (*pages 29, 48, 64, 148, 168*).

Camille was a 15-year-old, Black and white (French) biracial female in the eleventh grade. She described herself as a mostly A student whose Black identity was extremely important to her and who was motivated to work with other Black people to change unfair laws. Her civic engagement was grounded in her work with a Black service organization, where she gained clarity on her role in creating social change. This recognition translated into her efforts to implement a Black Student Union at her school to create a more supportive environment for Black students. Camille attended a racially diverse private, Catholic all-girls high school. She planned to attend a four-year college or university upon completing high school (*pages 35, 40–42, 44–46, 48, 50, 58, 65, 126, 140–141, 145, 154–155, 157*).

CJ was an 18-year-old who identified as a Black male in the eleventh grade at an alternative high school and used they/them pronouns. They described themselves as a mostly B student, whose Black identity was moderately important to them. CJ's civic engagement centered on the role of music in Black movements and Black healing. They used music to speak their mind and create. Beyond music, CJ was also a primary caretaker for their father who had multiple sclerosis, but also found time to participate in sports teams and group activities at school. They were unsure of their plans after high school (*pages 87–88, 108*).

Cory was a 15-year-old Nigerian American male in the tenth grade. He described himself as a mostly B student who was involved in several school leadership activities. Cory's Nigerian American identity informed his motivation for civic engagement, as he brought the perspective of being both Black and an immigrant. He was deeply engaged in two organizations that emphasized critical education, participatory action research, and organizing to challenge racial injustice. He attended a public magnet school that was predominately Hispanic (72%), where he participated in several social justice initiatives that included uplifting the Black community. He planned to attend a four-year college or university upon graduating high school (*pages 21, 23, 88, 100, 102, 117–119, 128, 130–131, 145, 153, 164*).

Creative was an 18-year-old Black female in the twelfth grade who described herself as a mostly B student. Creative had Caribbean roots (in Belize) and her Black identity was very important to her. She used dance to facilitate awareness and appreciation of Black culture. Creative's engagement coincided with awareness of her privilege as she worked with youth in foster care and youth in neighborhoods plagued with gang violence. Although she was not allowed to participate in Black Lives Matter protests, she did participate through social media. Creative attended a racially diverse public charter school and planned to attend a four-year college or university upon graduation (*pages 100, 163, 166*).

Damian was an 18-year-old biracial Black and Hispanic male in the twelfth grade. He described himself as a mostly B student whose Black identity and connectedness to Black issues was important to him. His civic engagement was rooted in mentoring and conducting research on social issues that impacted his neighborhood. His work on social justice issues educated him on several issues that impacted the Black community, including how incarceration affected college matriculation rates for Black people. His goal was to start a cycle of success within his own family and to create a safe environment for members of the Black community. He attended a predominately Hispanic (81%) public school. Damian planned to attend a four-year college or university (*pages 70, 72, 85, 109–110, 112, 122–124, 128, 167*).

Destiny was a 16-year-old Black female in the eleventh grade. She described herself as a mostly B student. Her Black identity was extremely important to her, and she worked to build Black pride in community with other Black youth. She married art with her civic engagement, using dance to spread awareness about injustice. Destiny was also passionate about protesting and educating youth about police violence after being held at gunpoint by officers in her neighborhood. She encouraged Black youth to know their rights and how to protect themselves during police interactions. Destiny attended an all-girls, racially diverse high school. She planned to attend a four-year college or university and join the military (*pages 20, 25–26, 67–68, 74–75, 124, 149, 151, 168*).

Harvey was an 18-year-old Black female in the eleventh grade who attended an alternative school. She described herself as a mostly A student whose Black identity was extremely important to her. She focused her civic engagement on supporting the children's choir at her family church. She was also passionate about women's issues and involved in Black Lives Matter protests. Her experiences as a Black woman deeply informed the ways she understood sociopolitical issues related to race and gender in the current sociopolitical moment. Upon completing school, she planned to attend junior college (*pages 16, 62, 69, 164*).

H.E.R. was a 13-year-old Black female in the ninth grade. She described herself as a mostly A student whose Black identity was extremely important to her. Her key form of civic engagement was mentoring children, and she focused on addressing racial inequity and fostering Black pride. She attended a predominately white (40%) and Hispanic (35%) high school. H.E.R.'s experiences, coupled with the service orientation of her family, led her to be active in her school's Black Student Alliance, where she built community with other Black youth to combat negative stereotyping. She planned to attend a four-year college or university upon completing high school (*pages 47, 71–72, 151, 164*).

James was a 16-year-old Black male in the eleventh grade. He described himself as a mostly A student whose Black identity and connection to Black community issues were important to him. James was deeply motivated by an ethic of care that was cultivated in his school and church environments. He emphasized a desire to help the less fortunate, and he felt good when helping others. However, James also highlighted the challenges of civic engagement, including his exhaustion and feeling underqualified for various leadership positions, particularly when called to speak about racial injustices at school. James attended a private, predominately white (57%) high school, but lived in a predominantly Black neighborhood. He planned to attend a vocational school or a four-year college or university (*pages 24, 35, 47, 53–54, 107–108, 151–152, 154*).

Jaylen was a 15-year-old Black male in the tenth grade. He described himself as a mostly C student, heavily involved in school clubs and sports such as basketball. His civic engagement activities were diverse; from developing meaningful art to helping others within the community, Jaylen sought to improve the lives of others while supporting his personal growth. Jaylen named his Black identity as very important to him, which manifested in his focus on challenging deficit narratives of Black communities being disengaged. He attended a predominately Black (75%), public magnet school. He planned to attend a two-year college or junior college after high school (*pages 81–83, 85, 107–108, 152*).

JD was a 13-year-old Black boy in eighth grade, engaged in a variety of civic engagement activities. He focused his civic engagement on issues related to South Central LA and the Black community, educating himself and others about improving the experiences of Black people. JD was inspired by the late musical artist Nipsey Hussle's investment in Black community building and focused on intergenerational uplift. He believed that Black youth were inspired to action by seeing the Black community struggle with violence and wanting to bring the Black community together. JD found it very important to work with other members of the Black community to create social change through law and policy. He described himself as a mostly C student and attended a public middle school where 91% of students received free and reduced-price lunches. Upon graduating from high school, JD planned to join the military. He was born outside of the US (*pages 19, 87, 107–108, 112*).

Jen was a 15-year-old Black female in the eleventh grade. She was born outside of the US. Jen described herself as a mostly B student whose Black identity was extremely important to her. Her Black identity was deeply integrated with her gender identity, and she was committed to amplifying Black women's voices. She noted that her civic engagement changed over the years, particularly during the election of Donald Trump. She had primarily been engaged through a Black service organization and Girl Scouts; Donald Trump's election pushed her engagement outside of formal civic organizations. She had leadership experience in service organizations. She attended a racially diverse public all-girls high school. After high school, she planned to attend a four-year college or university (*pages 104–106, 154, 167*).

Joe Cornell was a 17-year-old Black male. He described himself as a mostly B student whose Black identity was very important to him. His civic engagement journey was rooted in his challenges in finding his voice and claiming his space as a student in a non-Black space. Mentors of color such as his dean and his adviser helped him to self-advocate, a skill he then used to advocate for Black and other students of color. He attended a private school that was predominately white (49%), where he worked to hold the school accountable to be proactive, rather than reactive to anti-racist policy. He planned to attend a four-year college or university after high school (*pages 1–2, 7, 9–10, 13, 35–38, 45–47, 49, 50, 52–55, 72, 148, 155, 167*).

Kevin was a 17-year-old Black male in the twelfth grade. He described his Black identity and connection to Black social issues as very important to him. Civic organizations facilitated Kevin's engagement, giving him opportunities to participate in lobbying campaigns against police violence and hold space for community voices to be heard. School fostered his civic activity, particularly as he built more positive peer relationships and developed strong mentoring relationships with his teachers. He attended a public school that was predominately Hispanic (81%). He planned to attend a two-year or junior college after high school (*pages 21, 73, 90, 123–124, 130–132*).

KJ was a 16-year-old Black female in the eleventh grade. She described herself as a mostly B student whose Black identity was extremely important to her. While a Black service organization served as an entry point for her civic engagement, she expanded her reach by using social media as a platform to speak out on events of the current sociopolitical moment. She used her social media as a space to emphasize her Black pride, garner awareness around Black issues, and organize people around issue of racial justice. KJ attended a private, Catholic, and predominately white (62%) high school, where she participated in her school's Black Student Union. She planned to attend a four-year college or university after high-school graduation (*pages 27, 33–34, 36, 38, 46, 49, 51, 103, 125–126, 150, 153, 168*).

Kobe was a 17-year-old Black male in the twelfth grade. He described himself as a mostly B student and attended an alternative high school. He was deeply impacted by his incarceration experience and focused on mentoring his younger sister to thrive in a world that was not designed to ensure her success. In mentoring his sister, he sought to improve his self-reliance and commitment to his family. Kobe planned to attend a two-year college or junior college after graduating (*pages 29, 87, 108–110, 162*).

Layla was a 16-year-old Black female in the eleventh grade. She described herself as a mostly B student whose Black identity was extremely important to her. Her civic engagement included involvement in her church, staying informed via the news, and supporting her family and community. She was building toward her future goal of starting a non-profit focused on mentoring Black youth around entrepreneurship. Layla attended a private Christian school that was predominately Black (92%). She planned to attend a four-year college or university (*pages 15–16, 22, 29, 72–73, 75, 86–88, 155, 162, 164*).

Lee was an 18-year-old Black male and recent high-school graduate. His civic engagement centered on his family, helping his immediate community, and educating himself and others on Black issues. Lee saw his civic engagement as critical to his personal development, particularly to be a petter person. He recognized the ways Black people are connected through shared trauma, particularly after being mistaken for a police suspect in his own backyard. He described his Black identity and connection to Black social issues as very important to him. He planned to attend a two-year or junior college (*pages 4, 141, 149*).

Linda was a 13-year-old biracial Black and Chinese girl going into the ninth grade. She was engaged in organizations that focused on the experiences of Black girls, and actively sought civic spaces where she was not seen as an outsider given her Chinese identity. She spoke passionately against police brutality and had attended Black Lives Matter protests. Her civic purpose included making the world a better place for her children. She described herself as a mostly A student and attended a public middle school where 57% of students received free and reduced-price lunches. She helped create the Black Student Union at her school and described her Black identity as very important to her. She planned to attend a four-year college or university upon graduating from high school (*pages 120, 149, 161*).

Martin was a 14-year-old Black male with Antiguan roots. He described himself as a mostly A student. Though he believed that Black people have always had to fight for their rights, he did not feel that his civic engagement had been shaped by his Black identity or experiences of discrimination. He was engaged in service activities, partly to complete a community service requirement at his school, but also due to his general enjoyment of helping and being educated about community issues. He was also motivated by his father, who encouraged him to attend protests and participate in volunteer opportunities. Martin attended a diverse school with a slight majority of Black students (40%). He planned to attend a four-year college or university after high school (*pages 74, 100, 102, 105–106, 156, 166*).

Mea was a 16-year-old Black female in the eleventh grade. She described herself as a mostly A student whose Black identity was extremely important to her. Her primary source of civic engagement was participating in a Black service organization, where activities such as feeding the homeless shaped her understanding of her socioeconomic privilege and Black identity. While she reported no personal experience of discrimination, her Black identity was a central lens through which she saw the world. Mea attended a private, Catholic, and predominately white (62%) high school. After high school, she planned to attend a two-year or junior college (*pages 19, 65, 106–107, 110, 142, 163*).

Mia was a 16-year-old Black female in the eleventh grade with Caribbean roots. She described herself as a mostly A student whose Black identity was extremely important to her. Mia expressed a deep passion for health equity and leadership. She was driven by her own passions and personal experiences of inequity and influenced by the mentorship and modeling she received from upperclassmen at her school. She was committed to facilitating teens' access to mental health services and girls' access to affordable menstrual products in school. Mia attended a public, predominately Hispanic (62%) high school, which influenced her desire to show how Black youth can be leaders in non-Black spaces. She planned to attend a four-year college or university upon graduating high school (*pages 18, 21, 45, 69, 92, 120*).

Muffin was a 16-year-old Black female in the eleventh grade. She was born outside of the US, and described herself as a mostly A student whose Black identity was extremely important to her. She was motivated by a desire for connection with Black community and wanted to exemplify Black people thriving. Muffin's civic engagement was driven by the desire to help others and to stay socially connected to others through service. Muffin attended a public and predominately Hispanic (59%) high school. She planned to attend a two-year college or junior college (*pages 83, 122, 129, 132, 162*).

NA was a 13-year-old Black girl in the eighth grade. She was highly engaged in her family and school contexts and focused on bettering herself and her environment through large and small acts. She was proud to be Black and dedicated to service through a Black service organization, where she learned about and engaged in social issues affecting the Black community. She recognized the current moment as a major turning point for herself and racial justice more broadly. She described herself as a mostly A student and attended an elite private school whose population was 56% white. NA wanted

Black people to work together to change laws they found unfair. After high school, she planned to attend a four-year college or university (*pages 36, 44, 119–120, 129–130, 142–144, 152*).

Nicole was an 18-year-old biracial Black and white female in the twelfth grade. She participated in a wide range of civic activities and was motivated by an ethic of care and helping others. She grew up participating in community service with her grandmother and was active in church. She was dedicated to supporting the mental health of others, particularly in the face of bullying. She experienced race-based bullying from peers due to being biracial. She described herself as a mostly B student and attended a predominately Hispanic (87%) public school. She planned to attend a four-year college or university after high school (*pages 53, 101, 107–108, 166*).

O.A. was a 15-year-old Nigerian American female in the tenth grade. She described herself as a mostly A student whose experiences as a first-generation Nigerian immigrant informed values to strive for academic success. O.A.'s civic journey was deeply intertwined with her personal development, as she sought to become a better person through civic engagement. She was active in community service and saw her civic engagement as an opportunity to challenge negative stereotypes about Black youth, particularly in her predominately white (37%) public high school where she was involved in the Black Student Union. She felt inspired by the ways others were speaking up about race and racism. Upon finishing high school, she planned to attend a four-year college or university (*pages 19, 44, 51, 122, 163*).

Phea was a 17-year-old Senegalese and Nicaraguan Black female who had just begun attending a racially diverse junior college. She described herself as a mostly B student whose Black identity was extremely important to her. She participated in almost every civic activity on our list and more. She was especially involved in informal helping, service organizations, and political engagement in campaigns and protests. She balanced her civic work with entrepreneurship with a beauty product business. She was passionate about racial justice in incarceration, immigration, and mental health in schools. She planned to finish college and pursue her business career (*pages 28, 86, 88, 150, 162*).

Quinn was a 16-year-old Black female in the eleventh grade. She described herself as a mostly B student whose Black identity was extremely important to her. Quinn's civic engagement centered on policy changes in her school district to help bring better resources to students like her. She aspired to be a politician to bring about impactful policy change. Quinn's civic engagement was inspired by personal encounters with police violence and meaning making around how the Black Lives Matter Movement has been taken up by non-Black communities. Quinn attended a public, predominately Black (67%) high school and planned to attend a two-year or junior college (*pages 22–25, 63, 69, 73–74, 85, 93, 111, 122, 124, 126, 131–132, 145–146, 149, 154*).

Ray was a 17-year-old Panamanian Black female in the twelfth grade. She described herself as a mostly A student whose Black identity was extremely important to her. Her civic engagement was rooted in her family, as she served as caretaker to her grandmother and younger brother who had special needs. She mentored children at her aunt's day care. She was also passionate about issues related to Black people given her experiences with racial discrimination and witnessing the rise of the Black Lives Matter Movement after the death of George Floyd in 2020. Her goal was to cultivate spaces that support Black joy and dissipate Black fear. Ray attended a predominately Hispanic (67%) public charter school. She planned to attend a four-year college or university and to get a full-time job (*pages 38, 48, 108, 110, 149, 161*).

Sa'Myah was an 18-year-old Black female attending a predominately Hispanic (63%) junior college. She described herself as a mostly B student. Her Black identity and connection to Black issues were very important to her, given her experiences in school. Mentorship was a powerful influence on Sa'Myah's civic engagement. She credited a high-school mentor for preventing her drop out and helping her to attend college. After a community member was killed by the police on the day of her graduation, Sa'Myah engaged in the subsequent protest movement to demand safety and care for her people (*pages 18, 26, 53, 91, 93, 120*).

Sara Vaughn was a 15-year-old tenth-grade female who identified as Black with strong Cajun roots. She described herself as a mostly A student. Her Black identity and activism were important to her, and she was highly engaged in service and leadership in a Black service organization. Her motivation for civic engagement overlapped with her social class identity, as her parents emphasized the importance of using their resources to create social change. She attended a private all-girls school that was predominately white (67%), where she actively negotiated her identity as one of few Black girls in the space. She planned to attend a four-year college or university after high school (*pages 51–52, 60–61, 65, 67–68, 75, 104, 123, 145, 153*).

Sean was a 16-year-old Black male in the tenth grade. He described himself as a mostly A student whose Black identity was very important to him. Sean's civic engagement centered on education and information; he sought to stay informed through the news and shared his thoughts and opinions about social issues on social media with his friends. He wanted to improve the lives of others by being an example of success. Sean attended a public high school that was predominately Black (67%) and planned to attend a four-year college or university after graduation (*pages 19, 29, 76*).

Soleil was a 13-year-old biracial Black girl in the ninth grade. She was deeply committed to justice, particularly with respect to race, gender, and LGBTQIA+ identities. Soleil emphasized the importance of safety within the Black community in the face of everyday racism. Her mother was a deep inspiration for her changemaking, particularly as she navigated the current sociopolitical moment. She described herself as a mostly A student and attended a public charter school where 85% of students received free and reduced-priced lunches. The school population was 86% Hispanic. She served as school president in the fifth grade. Soleil planned to attend a four-year college or university after high school (*pages 72, 102–103, 113, 133, 143, 147, 147–148, 152–153, 155, 168*).

Success with Lex was an 18-year-old Black female who was attending a predominately Hispanic junior college and was a mostly A student. She was passionate about addressing police brutality, creating supports for the formerly incarcerated, and improving the lived experiences of the community in South LA. She was motivated to improve the environment and participated in beach cleanups and painting murals in her community. Success with Lex's connection to civic engagement was generational; her grandmother and aunt were involved with the Black Power Movement of the 1970s. Rooted in her family's legacy of Black civic engagement, Success with Lex's Black identity was very important to her and drove her to support Black communities to ultimately manifest generational change. She was born outside of the US and planned to attend a four-year college or university (*pages 23, 39, 41, 50, 65, 68, 74, 86, 112, 143–144, 162*).

T was a 17-year-old Black male in the twelfth grade. He was born outside of the US. He described himself as a mostly B student and attended an alternative high school. T focused on bettering himself and youth around him who had struggled to excel at traditional schools. He wanted to break the cycle of young people not getting the support they needed to thrive, particularly when coming from a neighborhood plagued with violence and gang activity. T planned to attend a two-year college or junior college after high school (*pages 18, 133*).

Tom was a 17-year-old biracial Black and white male in the eleventh grade. He described himself as a mostly B student whose Black identity was very important to him. His motivations for civic engagement transformed over time, as he was initially driven by encouragement from family and friends, but became more aware of the impact of his own power. He was engaged in various civic activities including volunteering at a homeless shelter and mentoring young Black men. The Black Lives Matter protests in summer 2020 were an important turning point for Tom, as he attended several protests and used his creativity to design a T-shirt for a voter registration event. He credited his mother for supporting and inspiring him. He attended a public charter school that was predominately Hispanic (40%). He planned to attend a four-year college or university after high school (*pages 18, 20, 24–25, 37, 43, 71, 83–85, 101–102, 113, 130, 143, 153, 165–166*).

Tsehai was a 14-year-old Ethiopian female in the tenth grade who was born outside of the US and adopted by white parents. She described herself as a mostly A student whose Black identity was moderately important to her. Tsehai grounded her civic engagement in her homeland roots by supporting a rural school in Ethiopia through her mother's foundation. She actively participated in her school's Black Student Alliance to address the struggles with racial equality at her school. She attended an elite, predominately white (60%) private school where she actively created affirming spaces for Black students. She planned to attend a four-year college or university after high school (*pages 36–38, 42, 44, 51, 53–54, 70, 90, 121–122, 142–143, 149*).

Unique was a 17-year-old Black female in the eleventh grade. She described herself as "unapologetically Black" and as a mostly B student whose Black identity was extremely important to her. Unique was strongly connected to civic organizations and benefited from family influences. Given her family history with civic engagement, Unique demonstrated clarity around the "long game" of civic engagement – that it takes sustained effort and time. Unique attended a predominately Black (67%) public school, where she organized around racial and economic inequities. She planned to attend a four-year college or university (*pages 60, 62–64, 66, 87–90, 101–102, 119, 122–123, 154–155, 163–164*).

Zia was a 14-year-old biracial Black and Filipina female in the tenth grade. She described herself as a mostly A student. Her biracial and female identity informed how she perceived and challenged racial and gender oppression. Participating in Girl Scouts was critical to her development of agency. She credited her family for cultivating her openness to diverse cultures and helping her navigate the racism she experienced as a Black and Filipina youth. She attended a public charter school that was predominately Hispanic (77%). Upon graduating from high school, she planned to attend a four-year college or university (*pages 62, 98, 102, 125–127, 133, 151, 153–154*).

REFERENCES

Adams, V. N., & Stevenson, H. C. (2012). Media socialization, Black media images and Black adolescent identity. In D. T. Slaughter-Defoe (Ed.), *Racial stereotyping and child development contributions to human development* (pp. 28–46). Karger.

Adams-Bass, V. N., Bentley-Edwards, K. L., & Stevenson, H. C. (2014). That's not me I see on TV. . .: African American youth interpret media images of Black females. *Women, Gender, and Families of Color, 2*(1), 79–100. https://doi.org/10.5406/womgenfamcol.2.1.0079

Adams-Bass, V. N., & Henrici, E. J. (2018). Hardly ever, I don't see it: Black youth speak about positive media images of Black men. In O. O. Banjo (Ed.), *Media across the African diaspora* (pp. 147–162). Routledge.

Akiva, T., Cortina, K. S., & Smith, C. (2014). Involving youth in program decision-making: How common and what might it do for youth? *Journal of Youth and Adolescence, 43*, 1844–1860. https://doi.org/10.1007/s10964-014-0183-y

Aldana, A., Bañales, J., & Richards-Schuster, K. (2019). Youth anti-racist engagement: Conceptualization, development, and validation of an anti-racism action scale. *Adolescent Research Review, 4*(4), 369–381. https://doi.org/10.1007/s40894-019-00113-1

Allen, R. L. (1995). Racism, sexism and a million men. *The Black Scholar, 25*(4), 24–26. https://www.jstor.org/stable/41069990

American Psychological Association. (2009). *Civic engagement.* Retrieved from https://www.apa.org/education-career/undergrad/civic-engagement

Anderson, E. (2021). *Black in white spaces: The enduring impact of color in everyday life.* The Chicago University Press.

Anderson, R. E., & Stevenson, H. C. (2019). RECASTing racial stress and trauma: Theorizing the healing potential of racial socialization in families. *American Psychologist, 74*(1), 63–75. https://doi.org/10.1037/amp0000392

Annamma, S. A., Anyon, Y., Joseph, N. M., Farrar, J., Greer, E., Downing, B., & Simmons, J. (2019). Black girls and school discipline: The complexities of being overrepresented and understudied. *Urban Education, 54*(2), 211–242. https://doi.org/10.1177/0042085916646610

Anyiwo, N., Bañales, J., Rowley, S. J., Watkins, D. C., & Richards-Schuster, K. (2018). Sociocultural influences on the sociopolitical development of African American youth. *Child Development Perspectives*, *12*(3), 165–170. https://doi.org/10.1111/cdep.12276

Anyiwo, N., Watkins, D. C., & Rowley, S. J. (2022). "They can't take away the light": Hip-hop culture and Black youth's racial resistance. *Youth & Society*, *54*(4), 611–634. https://doi.org/10.1177/0044118X211001096

Anyon, Y., Bender, K., Kennedy, H., & Dechants, J. (2018). A systematic review of youth participatory action research (YPAR) in the United States: Methodologies, youth outcomes, and future directions. *Health Education & Behavior*, *45*(6), 865–878. https://doi.org/10.1177/1090198118769357

Assari, S., & Caldwell, C. H. (2018). Teacher discrimination reduces school performance of African American youth: Role of gender. *Brain Sciences*, *8*(10), 183. https://doi.org/10.3390/brainsci8100183

Astuto, J., & Ruck, M. (2017). Growing up in poverty and civic engagement: The role of kindergarten executive function and play predicting participation in 8th grade extracurricular activities. *Applied Developmental Science*, *21*(4), 301–318. https://doi.org/10.1080/10888691.2016.1257943

Augsberger, A., Collins, M. E., & Gecker, W. (2018). Engaging youth in municipal government: Moving toward a youth-centric practice. *Journal of Community Practice*, *26*(1), 41–62. https://doi.org/10.1080/10705422.2017.1413023

Ballard, P. J., Malin, H., Porter, T. J., Colby, A., & Damon, W. (2015). Motivations for civic participation among diverse youth: More similarities than differences. *Research in Human Development*, *12*(1–2), 63–83. http://doi.org/10.1080/15427609.2015.1010348

Ballonoff Suleiman, A., Ballard, P. J., Hoyt, L. T., & Ozer, E. J. (2021). Applying a developmental lens to youth-led participatory action research: A critical examination and integration of existing evidence. *Youth & Society*, *53*(1), 26–53. https://doi.org/10.1177/0044118X19837871

Banaji, M. R., Fiske, S. T., & Massey, D. S. (2021). Systemic racism: Individuals and interactions, institutions and society. *Cognitive Research: Principles and Implications*, *6*(1), 82. https://doi.org/10.1186/s41235-021-00349-3

Bañales, J., Aldana, A., & Hope, E. C. (2023). Critical race consciousness: Conceptualizing a race-specific model of youth critical consciousness. In E. B. Godfrey & L. J. Rapa (Eds.), *Developing critical consciousness in youth: Contexts and settings* (pp. 195–231). Cambridge University Press.

Bañales, J., Aldana, A., Richards-Schuster, K., Flanagan, C. A., Diemer, M. A., & Rowley, S. J. (2021). Youth anti-racism action: Contributions of youth perceptions of school racial messages and critical consciousness. *Journal of Community Psychology*, *49*(8), 3079–3100. https://doi.org/10.1002/jcop.22266

Bañales, J., Hoffman, A. J., Rivas-Drake, D., & Jagers, R. J. (2020). The development of ethnic-racial identity process and its relation to civic beliefs among Latinx and Black American adolescents. *Journal of Youth and Adolescence*, *47*(3), 1–14. https://doi.org/10.1007/s10964-020-01254-6

Bañales, J., Hope, E. C., Rowley, S. J., & Cryer-Coupet, Q. R. (2021). Raising justice-minded youth: Parental ethnic-racial and political socialization and Black youth's critical consciousness. *Journal of Social Issues*, *77*(4), 964–986. https://doi.org/10.1111/josi.12486

Bañales, J., Mathews, C., Hayat, N., Anyiwo, N., & Diemer, M. A. (2020). Latinx and Black young adults' pathways to civic/political engagement. *Cultural Diversity and Ethnic Minority Psychology*, 26(2), 176–188. https://doi.org/10.1037/cdp0000271

Barnes, C. Y., & Hope, E. C. (2017). Means-tested public assistance programs and adolescent political socialization. *Journal of Youth and Adolescence*, 46, 1611–1621. https://doi.org/10.1007/s10964-016-0624-x

Barroso, A., & Minkin, R., (2020, June 24). *Recent protest attendees are more racially and ethnically diverse, younger than Americans overall*. Pew Research Center. https://www.pewresearch.org/fact-tank/2020/06/24/recent-protest-attendees-are-more-racially-and-ethnically-diverse-younger-than-americans-overall/

Baumeister, R. (2012). Need-to-belong theory. In P. A. M. Van Lange, A. W. Kruglanski, & E. T. Higgins (Eds.), *Handbook of theories of social psychology, volume 2*, (pp. 121–140). SAGE Publications.

Belgrave, F. Z., & Allison, K. W. (2018). *African American psychology: From Africa to America*. SAGE Publications.

Bell, C. (2020). "Maybe if they let us tell the story I wouldn't have gotten suspended": Understanding Black students' and parents' perceptions of school discipline. *Children and Youth Services Review*, 110, 104757. https://doi.org/10.1016/j.childyouth.2020.104757

Bell, K. E., Orbe, M. P., Drummond, D. K., & Camara, S. K. (2000). Accepting the challenge of centralizing without essentializing: Black feminist thought and African American women's communicative experiences. *Women's Studies in Communication*, 23(1), 41–62. https://doi.org/10.1080/07491409.2000.11517689

Bery, S. (2014). Multiculturalism, teaching slavery, and white supremacy. *Equity & Excellence in Education*, 47(3), 334–352. https://doi.org/10.1080/10665684.2014.933072

Blay, Z. (2019, April 4). Nipsey Hussle's work in the Black community went deeper than you think. *HuffPost*. https://www.huffpost.com/entry/nipsey-hussle-black-community-activism_n_5ca4ba20e4b0798240256d96

Bogel-Burroughs, N., Eligon, J., & Wright, W. (2021, March, 29). L.A.P.D severely mishandled George Floyd protests, report finds. *The New York Times*. https://www.nytimes.com/2021/03/11/us/lapd-george-floyd-protests.html

Bonilla-Silva, E. (2018). *Racism without racist: Color-blind racism and the persistence of racial inequality in America* (5th Ed.). Rowman and Littlefield.

Boykin, A. W. (1986). The triple quandary and the schooling of Afro-American children. In U. Neisser (Ed.), *The school achievement of minority children* (pp. 57–92). Erlbaum.

Boykin, C. M., Brown, N. D., Carter, J. T., Dukes, K., Green, D. J., Harrison, T., Hebl, M., McCleary-Gaddy, A., Membere, A., McJunkins, C. A., Simmons, C., Singletary Walker, S., Smith, A. N., & Williams, A. D. (2020). Anti-racist actions and accountability: Not more empty promises. *Equality, Diversity and Inclusion*, 39(7), 775–786. https://doi.org/10.1108/EDI-06-2020-0158

Braun, V., & Clarke, V. (2012). *Thematic analysis*. American Psychological Association.

Braveman, P. A., Arkin, E., Proctor, D., Kauh, T., & Holm, N. (2022). Systemic and structural racism: Definitions, examples, health damages, and approaches to dismantling. *Health Affairs, 41*(2), 171–178. https://doi.org/10.1377/hlthaff.2021 .01394

Brennan Center for Justice. (2022). *The impact of voter suppression on communities of color.* Retrieved from https://www.brennancenter.org/our-work/research-reports/impact-voter-suppression-communities-color

Brooms, D. R., & Davis, A. R. (2017). Staying focused on the goal: Peer bonding and faculty mentors supporting Black males' persistence in college. *Journal of Black Studies, 48*(3), 305–326. https://doi.org/10.1177/0021934717692520

Brown v. Board of Education, 347 U.S. 483 (1954).

Brown, K. T., & Ostrove, J. M. (2013). What does it mean to be an ally? The perception of allies from the perspective of people of color. *Journal of Applied Social Psychology, 43*(11), 2211–2222. https://doi.org/10.1111/jasp.12172

Brown, S. L. (2009). Student Non-Violent Coordinating Committee (SNCC). *The International Encyclopedia of Revolution and Protest,* 1–3. https://doi.org/10 .1002/9781405198073.wbierp1411

Bucholtz, M. (2014). Black feminist theory and African American women's linguistic practice. In V. L. Bergvall, J. M. Bing, & A. F. Freed (Eds.). *Rethinking language and gender research: Theory and practice* (pp. 267–290). Routledge.

Bunn, C. (2022, March 3). Black people are still killed by police at a higher rate than other groups. *NBC News.* https://www.nbcnews.com/news/nbcblk/report-black-people-are-still-killed-police-higher-rate-groups-rcna17169

Burns, M. D., & Granz, E. L. (2022). "Sincere White people, work in conjunction with us": Racial minorities' perceptions of White ally sincerity and perceptions of ally efforts. *Group Processes & Intergroup Relations,* Advanced online publication. https://doi.org/10.1177/13684302211059699

Butler-Barnes, S. T., Williams, T. T., & Chavous, T. M. (2012). Racial pride and religiosity among African American boys: Implications for academic motivation and achievement. *Journal of Youth and Adolescence, 41*(4), 486–498. https://doi .org/10.1007/s10964-011-9675-1

Calhoun-Brown, A. (2000). Upon this rock: The Black church, nonviolence, and the civil rights movement. *PS: Political Science & Politics, 33*(2), 169–174. https://doi .org/10.2307/420886

California Department of Education. (2019). *Data Quest.* Retrieved from https://dq .cde.ca.gov/dataquest/

Carey, R. L. (2019). Imagining the comprehensive mattering of Black boys and young men in society and schools: Toward a new approach. *Harvard Educational Review, 89*(3), 370–396. https://doi.org/10.17763/1943-5045-89.3.370

Carter, D. (2008). Achievement as resistance: The development of a critical race achievement ideology among Black achievers. *Harvard Educational Review, 78* (3), 466–497. https://doi.org/10.17763/haer.78.3.83138829847hw844

Carter Andrews, D. J., Brown, T., Castro, E., & Id-Deen, E. (2019). The impossibility of being "perfect and white": Black girls' racialized and gendered schooling experiences. *American Educational Research Journal, 56*(6), 2531–2572. https:// doi.org/10.3102/0002831219849392

Case, A. D., & Hunter, C. D. (2012). Counterspaces: A unit of analysis for understanding the role of settings in marginalized individuals' adaptive responses to oppression. *American Journal of Community Psychology, 50*(1–2), 257–270. https://doi .org/10.1007/s10464-012-9497-7

Chan, S., & Maxouris, C. (2022, April 1). City of Los Angeles agrees to provide thousands of beds in homelessness crisis lawsuit settlement. *CNN.* https://www .cnn.com/2022/04/01/us/los-angeles-homeless-population-settlement/index.html

Chapel, B. (2021, June 25). Derek Chauvin is sentenced for 22 1/2 years for George Floyd's murder. *National Public Radio.* https://www.npr.org/sections/trial-over-killing-of-george-floyd/2021/06/25/1009524284/derek-chauvin-sentencing-george-floyd-murder

Chapman-Hilliard, C., Hunter, E., Adams-Bass, V., Mbilishaka, A., Jones, B., Holmes, E., & Holman, A. C. (2022). Racial identity and historical narratives in the civic engagement of Black emerging adults. *Journal of Diversity in Higher Education, 15*(2), 230–240. https://doi.org/10.1037/dhe0000251

Chavez-Diaz, M., & Lee, N. (2015). *A conceptual mapping of healing centered youth organizing: Building a case for healing justice.* Urban Peace Institute. http://urbanpeacemovement.org/wp-content/uploads/2014/02/HealingMapping_FINALVERSION.pdf

Christens, B. D. (2012). Toward relational empowerment. *American Journal of Community Psychology, 50,* 114–128. https://doi.org/10.1007/s10464-011-9483-5

Christens, B. D. (2019). *Community power and empowerment.* Oxford University Press.

Christens, B. D., & Kirshner, B. (2011). Taking stock of youth organizing: An interdisciplinary perspective. *New Directions for Child and Adolescent Development, 2011*(134), 27–41. https://doi.org/10.1002/cd.309

Christens B. D., Peterson, N. A., & Speer, P. W. (2011). Community participation and psychological empowerment: Testing reciprocal causality using a cross-lagged panel design and latent constructs. *Health Education & Behavior, 38*(4), 339–347. https://doi.org/10.1177/1090198110372880

Christophe, N. K., Martin Romero, M. Y., Hope, E., & Stein, G. L. (2022). Critical civic engagement in Black college students: Interplay between discrimination, centrality, and preparation for bias. *American Journal of Orthopsychiatry, 92*(2), 144–153. https://doi.org/10.1037/ort0000600

City Council of the City of Culver City. (2021). Acknowledging the racial history of Culver City, Resolution no. 2021-R066. https://www.culvercity.org/files/content/public/city-hall/get-involved/race-and-equity/2021-06-17_resolution-2021-r066_acknowledging-racial-history-of-culver-city_signed.pdf

City News Service. (2021, March 19). Homelessness rising in Los Angeles amid record number of people rehoused, agency says. *ABC 7 Eyewitness News.* https://abc7 .com/homeless-los-angeles-homelessness-rehoused/10432710/

Clay, K. L., & Turner III, D. C. (2021). "Maybe you should try it this way Instead": Youth activism amid managerialist subterfuge. *American Educational Research Journal, 58*(2), 386–419. https://doi.org/10.3102/0002831221993476

Cohen, A. K., Littenberg-Tobias, J., Ridley-Kerr, A., Pope, A., Stolte, L. C., & Wong, K. K. (2018). Action civics education and civic outcomes for urban youth:

An evaluation of the impact of Generation Citizen. *Citizenship Teaching & Learning, 13*(3), 351–368. https://doi.org/10.1386/ctl.13.3.351_1

Collins, P. H. (1990). Black feminist thought in the matrix of domination. *Black Feminist Thought: Knowledge, Consciousness, and the Politics of Empowerment, 138,* 221–238.

Collins, P. H. (2000). Gender, Black feminism, and Black political economy. *The Annals of the American Academy of Political and Social Science, 568*(1), 41–53. https://www.jstor.org/stable/1049471

The Combahee River Collective. (1977). Combahee River Collective Statement. United States. [Web Archive] Retrieved from the Library of Congress, https://www.loc.gov/item/lcwaN0028151/

Conner, J. O., Ober, C. N., & Brown, A. S. (2016). The politics of paternalism: Adult and youth perspectives on youth voice in public policy. *Teachers College Record, 118*(8), 1–48. https://doi.org/10.1177/016146811611800805

County of Los Angeles. (n.d.) *Alternatives to incarceration initiative.* Chief Executive Office. Retrieved from https://ceo.lacounty.gov/ati/measure-j-history/

Cox, K., & Tamir, C. (2022, April 14). *Family history, slavery and knowledge of Black history.* Pew Research Center. https://www.pewresearch.org/race-ethnicity/2022/04/14/black-americans-family-history-slavery-and-knowledge-of-black-history/

Crenshaw, K. (1991). Mapping the margins: Intersectionality, identity politics, and violence against women of color. *Stanford Law Review, 43*(6), 1241–1299. https://doi.org/dn82xw

Crockett, L. J., Carlo, G., & Schulenberg, J. E. (Eds.). (2023). *APA handbook of adolescent and young adult development.* American Psychological Association. https://doi.org/10.1037/0000298-000

Cross Jr, W. E., Parham, T. A., & Helms, J. E. (1991). The stages of Black identity development: Nigrescence models. In R. L. Jones (Ed.), *Black psychology* (pp. 319–338). Cobb & Henry Publishers.

Damon, W., Menon, J. L., & Bronk, K. C. (2003). The development of purpose during adolescence. *Journal of Applied Developmental Science, 7*(3), 119–128. https://doi.org/10.1207/S1532480XADS0703_2

Davis, N. D., Marchand, A. D., Moore, S. S., Greene, D., & Colby, A. (2021). We who believe in freedom: Freedom Schools as a critical context for the positive, sociopolitical development of Black youth. *Race Ethnicity and Education,* Advanced online publication. https://doi.org/10.1080/13613324.2021.1969901

Davis, S. (2020). Socially toxic environments: A YPAR project exposes issues affecting urban Black girls' educational pathway to STEM careers and their racial identity development. *The Urban Review, 52*(2), 215–237. https://doi.org/10.1007/s11256-019-00525-2

Dawes, N. P., & Larson, R. (2011). How youth get engaged: Grounded-theory research on motivational development in organized youth programs. *Developmental Psychology, 47*(1), 259–269. https://doi.org/10.1037/a0020729

DeCuir-Gunby, J. T. (2009). A review of the racial identity development of African American adolescents: The role of education. *Review of Educational Research, 79*(1), 103–124. https://doi.org/10.3102/0034654308325897

Del Toro, J., Jackson, D. B., & Wang, M. T. (2022). The policing paradox: Police stops predict youth's school disengagement via elevated psychological distress. *Developmental Psychology*, *58*(7), 1402–1412. https://doi.org/10.1037/devo001361

Delta Sigma Theta Sorority, Inc. (2022). *Delta Sigma Theta, Incorporated.* https://www.deltasigmatheta.org/about-delta/

DiAngelo, R. (2018). *White fragility: Why it's so hard for white people to talk about racism.* Beacon Press.

Diemer, M. A., & Rapa, L. J. (2016). Unraveling the complexity of critical consciousness, political efficacy, and political action among marginalized adolescents. *Child Development*, *87*(1), 221–238. https://doi.org/10.1111/cdev.12446

Dunn, D., Wray-Lake, L., & Plummer, J. A. (2022). Youth are watching: Adolescents' sociopolitical development in the Trump era. *Child Development*, *93*(4), 1044–1060. https://doi.org/10.1111/cdev.13762

Education Commission of the States. (2022). *50-State Comparison: State Policies for Service-Learning.* Retrieved from https://www.ecs.org/state-policies-for-service-learning/

Egalite, A. J., Kisida, B., & Winters, M. A. (2015). Representation in the classroom: The effect of own-race teachers on student achievement. *Economics of Education Review*, *45*, 44–52. https://doi.org/10.1016/j.econedurev.2015.01.007

Ellison, R. (1952). *Invisible man.* Random House.

Ellithorpe, M. E., & Bleakley, A. (2016). Wanting to see people like me? Racial and gender diversity in popular adolescent television. *Journal of Youth and Adolescence*, *45*(7), 1426–1437. https://doi.org/10.1007/s10964-016-0415-4

English, D., Lambert, S. F., Tynes, B. M., Bowleg, L., Zea, M. C., & Howard, L. C. (2020). Daily multidimensional racial discrimination among Black U.S. American adolescents. *Journal of Applied Developmental Psychology*, *66*, 101068. https://doi.org/10.1016/j.appdev.2019.101068

Feagin, J. (2013). *Systemic racism: A theory of oppression.* Routledge.

Felker-Kantor, M. (2018). *Policing Los Angeles: Race, resistance, and the rise of the LAPD.* UNC Press Books.

Fernández, J. S., & Watts, R. J. (2022). Sociopolitical development as emotional work: How young organizers engage emotions to support community organizing for transformative racial justice. *Journal of Adolescent Research*, Advanced online publication. https://doi.org/10.1177/07435584221091497

Fisher v. University of Texas, 579 U.S. 365 (2016).

Flanagan, C. A. (2013). *Teenage citizens: The political theories of the young.* Harvard Press.

Flanagan, C. A., Syvertsen, A. K., Gill, S., Gallay, L. S., & Cumsille, P. (2009). Ethnic awareness, prejudice, and civic commitments in four ethnic groups of American adolescents. *Journal of Youth and Adolescence*, *38*(4), 500–518. https://doi.org/10.1007/s10964-009-9394-z

Freire, P. (1970). *Pedagogy of the oppressed.* Continuum.

Frey, S. R. (2020). *Water from the rock: Black resistance in a revolutionary age.* Princeton University Press.

Garza, A. (2020). *The purpose of power: How we come together when we fall apart.* One World Publishing.

Gasman, M., Spencer, D., & Orphan, C. (2015). "Building bridges, not fences": A history of civic engagement at private Black colleges and universities, 1944–1965. *History of Education Quarterly, 55*(3), 346–379. https://www.jstor .org/stable/24481716

Gillion, D. Q. (2020). *The loud minority: Why protests matter in American democracy.* Princeton University Press.

Ginwright, S. A. (2010a). *Black youth rising: Activism and radical healing in urban America.* Teachers College Press.

Ginwright, S. A. (2010b). Peace out to revolution! Activism among African American youth: An argument for radical healing. *Young, 18*(1), 77–96. https://doi.org/10 .1177/110330880901800106

Ginwright, S. (2015). *Hope and healing in urban education: How urban activists and teachers are reclaiming matters of the heart.* Routledge.

Ginwright, S., & James, T. (2002). From assets to agents of change: Social justice, organizing, and youth development. *New Directions for Youth Development, 96,* 27–46. https://doi.org/10.1002/yd/25

Godfrey, E. B., & Burson, E. (2018). Interrogating the intersections: How intersectional perspectives can inform developmental scholarship on critical consciousness. In C. E. Santos & R. B. Toomey (Eds.), Envisioning the Integration of an Intersectional Lens in Developmental Science. *New Directions for Child and Adolescent Development, 161,* 17–38. https://doi.org/10.1002/cad.20246

Gomez, M. (2021, February 16). L.A. school board cuts its police force and diverts funds for Black student achievement. *Los Angeles Times.* https://www.latimes .com/california/story/2021-02-16/lausd-diverting-school-police-funds-support-black-students

Gordon, H. R. (2007). Allies within and without: How adolescent activists conceptualize ageism and navigate adult power in youth social movements. *Journal of Contemporary Ethnography, 36*(6), 631–668. https://doi.org/10.1177/ 0891241606293608

Gorman, A. (2018, August 18). *Earthrise.* Delivered at the Los Angeles Climate Reality Leadership Training. Retrieved from the North American Association for Environmental Education, https://eepro.naaee.org/eepro/blog/earthrise-poem-amanda-gorman

Gorman, A. (2021). *The hill we climb: An inaugural poem for the country.* Viking Books.

Gorski, P. C., & Erakat, N. (2019). Racism, whiteness, and burnout in antiracism movements: How white racial justice activists elevate burnout in racial justice activists of color in the United States. *Ethnicities, 19*(5), 784–808. https://doi.org/ 10.1177/1468796819833871

Gould, J., Jamieson, K. H., Levine, P., McConnell, T., & Smith, D. B. (2011). *Guardian of democracy: The civic mission of schools.* Philadelphia: Lenore Annerberg Institute for Civics of the Annenberg Public Policy Center at the University of Pennsylvania. https://www.carnegie.org/publications/guardian-of-democracy-the-civic-mission-of-schools/

Gray, D. L., Hope, E. C., & Byrd, C. M. (2020). Why Black adolescents are vulnerable at school and how schools can provide opportunities to belong to fix it. *Policy*

Insights from the Behavioral and Brain Sciences, 7(1), 3–9. https://doi.org/10 .1177/2372732219868744

Gray, D. L., Hope, E. C., & Matthews, J. S. (2018). Black and belonging at school: A case for interpersonal, instructional, and institutional opportunity structures. *Educational Psychologist*, 114(2), 97–113. https://doi.org/10.1080/00461520.2017.1421466

Greer, T. M., & Cavalhieri, K. E. (2019). The role of coping strategies in understanding the effects of institutional racism on mental health outcomes for African American men. *Journal of Black Psychology*, 45(5), 405–433. https://doi.org/10 .1177/0095798419868105

Hagerman, M. A. (2018). *White kids: Growing up with privilege in a racially divided America*. New York University Press.

Haggler, P. (2018). From the Black church basement to the public pavement: Grassroots alliances, the Sunday school, organized youth activism, and a public theology of education. *Religious Education*, 113(5), 464–476. https://doi.org/10 .1080/00344087.2018.1492289

Hanisch, C. (2017, November 14). *The personal is political: The women's liberation movement classic with a new explanatory introduction*. Retrieved from http:// www.carolhanisch.org/CHwritings/PIP.html

Harrison, T., Moore, M., Rogers, B., Booker, A., Smith, M., & Rono, M. (2020). The sanctity of Black spaces: Why high school Black student unions are necessary. *Black History Bulletin*, 83(1), 5–11. https://doi.org/10.1353/bhb.2020.0006

Heard-Garris, N., Boyd, R., Kan, K., Perez-Cardona, L., Heard, N. J., & Johnson, T. J. (2021). Structuring poverty: How racism shapes child poverty and child and adolescent health. *Academic Pediatrics*, 21(8), S108–S116. https://doi.org/10 .1016/j.acap.2021.05.026

Heberle, A. E., Rapa, L. J., & Farago, F. (2020). Critical consciousness in children and adolescents: A systematic review, critical assessment, and recommendations for future research. *Psychological Bulletin*, 146(6), 525–551. https://doi.org/10.1037/ bul0000230

Helms, J. E. (1990). *Black and white racial identity: Theory, research, and practice*. Praeger.

Helms, J. E. (2020). *A race is a nice thing to have: A guide to being a white person or understanding the white persons in your life*. Cognella.

Herndon, A. (2020, September 26). How a pledge to dismantle the Minneapolis police collapsed. *New York Times*. https://www.nytimes.com/2020/09/26/us/politics/ minneapolis-defund-police.html

Hernández, K. L. (2017). *City of inmates: Conquest, rebellion, and the rise of human caging in Los Angeles, 1771–1965*. UNC Press Books.

Hill, R. B. (1999). *The strengths of African American families: Twenty-five years later*. University Press of America.

Hipolito-Delgado, C. P., Stickney, D., Zion, S., & Kirshner, B. (2022). Transformative student voice for sociopolitical development: Developing youth of color as political actors. *Journal of Research on Adolescence*, 32(3), 1098–1108. https:// doi.org/10.1111/jora.12753

Hochschild, A. R. (1983). *The managed heart: Commercialization of human feeling*. University of California Press.

Holloway, K. (2021, July 19). Our racial reckoning is turning out to be a white lie. *The Nation.* https://www.thenation.com/article/society/black-lives-matter-back lash-2/

Holmes, A. G. D. (2020). Researcher positionality – A consideration of its influence and place in qualitative research – A new researcher guide. *International Journal of Education, 8*(4), 1–10. https://doi.org/10.34293/education.v8i4.3232

hooks, b. (1981). *Ain't I a woman: Black women and feminism.* Routledge.

Hope, E. C. (2016). Preparing to participate: The role of youth social responsibility and political efficacy on civic engagement for Black early adolescents. *Child Indicators Research, 9*(3), 609–630. https://doi.org/10.1007/s12187-015-9331-5

Hope, E. C., & Bañales, J. (2019). Black early adolescent critical reflection of inequitable sociopolitical conditions: A qualitative investigation. *Journal of Adolescent Research, 34*(2), 167–200. https://doi.org/10.1177/0743558418756360

Hope, E. C., Brinkman, M., Hoggard, L. S., Stokes, M. N., Hatton, V., Volpe, V. V., & Elliot, E. (2021). Black adolescents' anticipatory stress responses to multilevel racism: The role of racial identity. *American Journal of Orthopsychiatry, 91*(4), 487–498. https://doi.org/10.1037/ort0000547

Hope, E. C., Cryer-Coupet, Q. R., & Stokes, M. N. (2020). Race-related stress, racial identity, and activism among young Black men: A person-centered approach. *Developmental Psychology, 56*(8), 1484–1405. https://doi.org/10.1037/dev0000836

Hope, E. C., Gugwor, R., Riddick, K. N., & Pender, K. N. (2019). Engaged against the machine: Institutional and cultural racial discrimination and racial identity as predictors of activism orientation among Black youth. *American Journal of Community Psychology, 63*(1–2), 61–72. https://doi.org/10.1002/ajcp.12303

Hope, E. C., Keels, M., & Durkee, M. I. (2016). Participation in Black Lives Matter and deferred action for childhood arrivals: Modern activism among Black and Latino college students. *Journal of Diversity in Higher Education, 9*(3), 203. https://doi.org/10.1037/dhe0000032

Hope, E. C., Mathews, C. J., Briggs, A. S., & Alexander, A. R. (2023). The quest for racial justice: An overview of research on racism and critical action for youth of color. In E. B. Godfrey & L. J. Rapa (Eds.), *Developing critical consciousness in youth: Contexts and settings.* Cambridge University Press.

Hope, E. C., Pender, K. N., & Riddick, K. N. (2019). Development and validation of the Black Community Activism Orientation Scale. *Journal of Black Psychology, 45*(3), 185–214. https://doi.org/10.1177/0095798419865416

Hope, E. C., Smith, C. D., Cryer-Coupet, Q. R., & Briggs, A. S. (2020). Relations between racial stress and critical consciousness for Black adolescents. *Journal of Applied Developmental Psychology, 70,* 101184. https://doi.org/10.1016/j.appdev.2020.101184

Hope, E. C., & Spencer, M. B. (2017). Civic engagement as an adaptive coping response to conditions of inequality: An application of phenomenological variant of ecological systems theory (PVEST). In N. J. Cabrera, & B. Leyendecker (Eds.), *Handbook on positive development of minority children and youth* (pp. 421–435). Springer. https://doi.org/10.1007/978-3-319-43645-6_25

Howard, T. C. (2013). How does it feel to be a problem? Black male students, schools, and learning in enhancing the knowledge base to disrupt deficit frameworks. *Review of Research in Education*, *37*(1), 54–86. https://doi.org/10.3102/0091732X12462985

Hughes, D., Rodriguez, J., Smith, E. P., Johnson, D. J., Stevenson, H. C., & Spicer, P. (2006). Parents' ethnic-racial socialization practices: A review of research and directions for future study. *Developmental Psychology*, *42*, 747–770. https://doi.org/10.1037/0012-1649.42.5.747

Jefferies, K. (2022). The strong Black woman: Insights and implications for nursing. *Journal of the American Psychiatric Nurses Association*, *28*(4), 332–338. https://doi.org/10.1177/10783903209839 00

Johansson, A., & Vinthagen, S. (2020). *Conceptualizing 'everyday resistance': A transdisciplinary approach*. Routledge.

Johnson, Jr., S. L., Bishop, J. P., Howard, T. C., James, A., Rivera, E., Noguera, P. A. (2021). *Beyond the schoolhouse, digging deeper: COVID-19 & reopening schools for Black students in Los Angeles*. Center for the Transformation of Schools, School of Education & Information Studies, University of California, Los Angeles. https://transformschools.ucla.edu/research/beyond-the-schoolhouse-digging-deeper/

Johnson, T. R., Gold, E., & Zhao, A. (2022). *How anti-critical race theory bills are taking aim at teachers*. Fivethirtyeight. https://fivethirtyeight.com/features/how-anti-critical-race-theory-bills-are-taking-aim-at-teachers/

Jones, J. M. (1997). *Prejudice and racism* (2nd ed.). McGraw Hill Companies.

Jones, J. M. (2021). The dual pandemics of COVID-19 and systemic racism: Navigating our path forward. *School Psychology*, *36*(5), 427–431. https://doi.org/10.1037/spq0000472

Jones, M. K., Hill-Jarrett, T. G., Latimer, K., Reynolds, A., Garrett, N., Harris, I., Joseph, S., & Jones, A. (2021). The role of coping in the relationship between endorsement of the strong Black woman schema and depressive symptoms among Black women. *Journal of Black Psychology*, *47*(7), 578–592. https://doi.org/10.1177/00957984211021229

Jones, S. C., Anderson, R. E., & Stevenson, H. C. (2021). Not the same old song and dance: Viewing racial socialization through a family systems lens to resist racial trauma. *Adversity and Resilience Science*, *2*, 225–233. https://doi.org/10.1007/s42844-021-00044-8

Jones, V. A., & Reddick, R. J. (2017). The heterogeneity of resistance: How Black students utilize engagement and activism to challenge PWI inequalities. *The Journal of Negro Education*, *86*(3), 204–219. https://doi.org/10.7709/jnegroeducation.86.3.0204

Joseph, P. E. (2022). *The third reconstruction: America's struggle for racial justice in the 21st century*. Basic Books.

Kaepernick, C. (2021). *Abolition for the people*. Kaepernick Publishing.

Karras, J., Astuto, J., Niwa, E., & Ruck, M. D. (2020). Trajectories of civic socialization in context: Examining variation among children in African American and Black immigrant families. *Developmental Psychology*, *56*(12), 2293–2308. https://doi.org/10.1037/dev0001116

Karras, J. E., Maker Castro, E., & Emuka, C. (2022). Examining the sociopolitical development of immigrant-origin youth during a season of social unrest. *Journal of Research on Adolescence*, *32*(3), 1042–1063. https://doi.org/10.1111/jora.12777

Kaste, M. (2021, November 3). Minneapolis voters reject a measure to replace the city's police department. *National Public Radio*. https://www.npr.org/2021/11/02/1051617581/minneapolis-police-vote

Keels, M. (2019). *Campus counterspaces: Black and Latinx students' search for community at historically White universities*. Cornell University Press.

Kelley, R. D. (2002). *Freedom dreams: The Black radical imagination*. Beacon Press.

Kelly, B. T., Gardner, P. J., Stone, J., Hixson, A., & Dissassa, D.-T. (2021). Hidden in plain sight: Uncovering the emotional labor of Black women students at historically White colleges and universities. *Journal of Diversity in Higher Education*, *14*(2), 203–216. https://doi.org/10.1037/dhe0000161

Kelly, D. C. (2009). The civic legacy of the civil rights era: Exploring the values of a movement. *Smith College Studies in Social Work*, *83*(4), 427–445. https://doi.org/10.1080/00377317.2013.834731

Kendi, I. X. (2019). *How to be an antiracist*. One World.

Kilgo, D. (2021). Media bias delegitimizes Black-rights protesters. *Nature Briefing*, *593*, 315. https://doi.org/10.1038/d41586-021-01314-2

King, J. E. (2006). "If justice is our objective": Diaspora literacy, heritage knowledge, and the praxis of critical studyin' for human freedom. *Teachers College Record*, *108*(14), 337–360. https://doi.org/10.1177/016146810610801418

Kirshner, B. (2015). *Youth activism in an era of education inequality* (Vol. 2). New York University Press.

Kirshner, B., & Ginwright, S. (2012). Youth organizing as a developmental context for African American and Latino adolescents. *Child Development Perspectives*, *6*(3), 288–294. https://doi.org/10.1111/j.1750-8606.2012.00243.x

Kishi, R., Stall, H., Wolfson, A., & Jones, S. (2021). *A year of racial justice protests: Key trends in demonstrations supporting the BLM Movement*. Armed Conflict Location and Event Data Project (ACLED). https://acleddata.com/acleddatanew/wp-content/uploads/2021/05/ACLED_Report_A-Year-of-Racial-Justice-Protests_May2021.pdf

Kohli, R. (2014). Unpacking internalized racism: Teachers of color striving for racially just classrooms. *Race Ethnicity and Education*, *17*(3), 367–387. https://doi.org/10.1080/13613324.2013.832935

Kohli, R., Pizarro, M., & Nevárez, A. (2017). The "new racism" of K–12 schools: Centering critical research on racism. *Review of Research in Education*, *41*(1), 182–202. https://doi.org/10.3102/0091732X16686949

Lamont, A. (2021). *Guide to allyship: An open source starter guide to help you become a more thoughtful and effective ally*. Retrieved from https://guidetoallyship.com/license/

Lane, P. (2022). *A multi-site, embedded case study of Black Student Unions: Bridging and buffering Black student experiences* (Doctoral Dissertation). California State University, Bakersfield.

Leath, S., Mathews, C., Harrison, A., & Chavous, T. (2019). Racial identity, racial discrimination, and classroom engagement outcomes among Black girls and boys in predominantly Black and predominantly White school districts. *American Educational Research Journal*, 56(4), 1318–1352. https://doi.org/10.3102/0002831218816955

Lee, H., Lei, Q., Su, G., & Zhang, S. (2022). Acknowledging anti-Blackness, overlooking anti-Asian racism: Missed developmental opportunities for Chinese American youth. *Journal of Research on Adolescence*, 32(3), 1064–1082. https://doi.org/10.1111/jora.12749

Lee, N. J., Shah, D. V., & McLeod, J. M. (2013). Processes of political socialization: A communication mediation approach to youth civic engagement. *Communication Research*, 40(5), 669–697. https://doi.org/10.1177/0093650212436712

Lerner, R. M., Johnson, S. K., Wang, J., Ferris, K. A., & Hershberg, R. M. (2015). The study of the development of civic engagement within contemporary developmental science: Theory, method, and application. *Research in Human Development*, 12(1–2), 149–156. https://doi.org/10.1080/15427609.2015.1013759

Levine, P. (2022). *What should we do? A theory of civic life.* Oxford University Press.

Levy, B. L. (2018). Youth developing political efficacy through social learning experiences: Becoming active participants in a supportive model United Nations club. *Theory & Research in Social Education*, 46(3), 410–448. https://doi.org/10.1080/00933104.2017.1377654

Linder, C., Quaye, S. J., Lange, A. C., Roberts, R. E., Lacy, M. C., & Okello, W. K. (2019). "A student should have the privilege of just being a student": Student activism as labor. *The Review of Higher Education*, 42(5), 37–62. https://doi.org/10.1353/rhe.2019.0044.

Lindsay-Dennis, L., Cummings, L., & McClendon, S. C. (2011). Mentors' reflections on developing a culturally responsive mentoring initiative for urban African American girls. *Black Women, Gender & Families*, 5(2), 66–92. https://muse.jhu.edu/article/454243

Lodi, E., Perrella, L., Lepri, G. L., Scarpa, M. L., & Patrizi, P. (2021). Use of restorative justice and restorative practices at school: A systematic literature review. *International Journal of Environmental Research and Public Health*, 19(1), 96–130. https://doi.org/10.3390/ijerph19010096

Lopez Bunyasi, T. & Smith, C. W. (2019). *Stay woke: A people's guide to making all Black lives matter.* New York University Press.

Lott, M. (2017). The relationship between the "invisibility" of African American women in the American Civil Rights Movement of the 1950s and 1960s and their portrayal in modern film. *Journal of Black Studies*, 48(4), 331–354. https://doi.org/10.1177/0021934717696758

Love, B. (2019). *We want to do more than survive: Abolitionist teaching and the pursuit of educational freedom.* Beacon Press.

Lozada, F. T., Jagers, R. J., Smith, C. D., Bañales, J., & Hope, E. C. (2017). Prosocial behaviors of Black adolescent boys: An application of a sociopolitical development theory. *Journal of Black Psychology*, 43(5), 493–516. https://doi.org/10.1177/0095798416652021

Lozada, F. T., Riley, T. N., Catherine, E., & Brown, D. W. (2022). Black emotions matter: Understanding the impact of racial oppression on black youth's emotional development: Dismantling systems of racism and oppression during adolescence. *Journal of Research on Adolescence, 32*(1), 13–33. https://doi.org/10.1111/jora.12699

Maker Castro, E., Wray-Lake, L. & Cohen, A. K. (2022). Critical consciousness and wellbeing in adolescents and young adults: A systematic review. *Adolescent Research Review, 7*, 499–522. https://doi.org/10.1007/s40894-022-00188-3

Malin, H., Ballard, P. J., & Damon, W. (2015). Civic purpose: An integrated construct for understanding civic development in adolescence. *Human Development, 58*(2), 103–130. https://doi.org/10.1159/000381655

Mannheim, K. (1952). The problem of generations. In K. Mannheim (Ed.), *Essays on the sociology of knowledge* (pp. 276–321). Routledge & Kegan Paul.

Mathews, C. J., Durkee, M., & Hope, E. C. (2022). Critical action and ethnic racial identity exploration: Tools of racial resistance at the college transition. *Journal of Research on Adolescence, 32*(3), 1083–1097. https://doi.org/10.1111/jora.12790

Mathews, C. J., Medina, M. A., Bañales, J., Pinetta, B. J., Marchand, A. D., Agi, A. C., Miller, S. M., Hoffman, A. J., Diemer, M. A., & Rivas-Drake, D. (2020). Mapping the intersections of adolescents' ethnic-racial identity and critical consciousness. *Adolescent Research Review, 5*(4), 363–379. https://doi.org/10.1007/s40894-019-00122-0

Maxie-Moreman, A. D., & Tynes, B. M. (2022). Exposure to online racial discrimination and traumatic events online in Black adolescents and emerging adults. *Journal of Research on Adolescence, 32*(1), 254–269. https://doi.org/10.1111/jora.12732

Mayorga-Gallo, S. (2019). The white-centering logic of diversity ideology. *The American Behavioral Scientist, 63*(13), 1789–1809. https://doi.org/10.1177/0002764219842619

McClain, D. (2019, March 28). As a Black mother, my parenting is always political. *The Nation.* https://www.thenation.com/article/archive/Black-motherhood-family-parenting-dani-mcclain/

McIntosh, H., Hart, D. & Youniss, J. (2007) The influence of family political discussion on youth civic development: Which parent qualities matter? *PS: Political Science and Politics, 40*(3), 495–499. https://doi.org/10.1017/s1049096507070758

Morrison, T. (2019). *The pieces I am.* [Documentary film.] Produced by Timothy Greenfield-Sanders. Magnolia Pictures.

Mosley, D. V., Hargons, C. N., Meiller, C., Angyal, B., Wheeler, P., Davis, C., & Stevens-Watkins, D. (2021). Critical consciousness of anti-Black racism: A practical model to prevent and resist racial trauma. *Journal of Counseling Psychology, 68*(1), 1–16. https://doi.org/10.1037/cou0000430

Murry, V. M., Butler-Barnes, S. T., Mayo-Gamble, T. L., & Inniss-Thompson, M. N. (2018). Excavating new constructs for family stress theories in the context of everyday life experiences of Black American families. *Journal of Family Theory & Review, 10*(2), 384–405. https://doi.org/10.1111/jftr.12256

Naples, N. (1992). Activist mothering: Cross-Generational continuity in the community work of women from low-income urban neighborhoods. *Gender and Society,* 6(3), 441–463. https://doi.org/10.1177/089124392006003006

National Center for Education Statistics. (2020). *Race and ethnicity of public school teachers and their students.* Retrieved from https://nces.ed.gov/pubs2020/2020103/index.asp

Neblett, E. W., Rivas-Drake, D., & Umaña-Taylor, A. J. (2012). The promise of racial and ethnic protective factors in promoting ethnic minority youth development. *Child Development Perspectives,* 6(3), 295–303. https://doi.org/10.1111/j.1750-8606.2012.00239.x

Nesbit, R. (2013). The influence of family and household members on individual volunteer choices. *Nonprofit and Voluntary Sector Quarterly,* 42(6), 1134–1154. https://doi.org/10.1177/0899764012450365

Offidani-Bertrand, C., Velez, G., Benz, C., & Keels, M. (2022). "I wasn't expecting it": High school experiences and navigating belonging in the transition to college. *Emerging Adulthood,* 10(1), 212–224. https://doi.org/10.1177/2167696819882117

Oosterhoff, B., Wray-Lake, L., Palmer, C. A., & Kaplow, J. B. (2020). Historical trends in concerns about social issues across four decades among U.S. adolescents. *Journal of Research on Adolescence,* 30(2), 485–498. https://doi.org/10.1111/jora.12493

Ortega-Williams, A., Booth, J., Fussell-Ware, D., Lawrence, Y., Pearl, D., Chapman, N., Allen, W., Reid-Moore, A., & Overby, Z. (2022). Using ecological momentary assessments to understand Black youths' experiences of racism, stress, and safety. *Journal of Research on Adolescence,* 32(1), 270–289. https://doi.org/10.1111/jora.12733

Palmer, G., Fernández, J. S., Gordon, L., Masud, H., Hilson, S., Tang, C., Thomas, D., Clark, L., Guzman, B., & Bernal, I. (2019). Oppression and power. In L. A. Jason, O. Glantsman, J. O'Brien, & K. Ramian, (Eds.), *Introduction to community psychology: Becoming an agent of change.* https://press.rebus.community/introductiontocommunitypsychology/

Pearce, N. J., & Larson, R. W. (2006). How teens become engaged in youth development programs: The process of motivational change in a civic activism organization. *Applied Developmental Science,* 10(3), 121–131. https://doi.org/10.1207/s1532480xads1003_2

Pearson, J. C., Semlak, J. L., Western, K. J., & Herakova, L. L. (2010). Answering a call for service: An exploration of family communication schemata and ethnic identity's effect on civic engagement behaviors. *Journal of Intercultural Communication Research,* 39 (1), 49–68. https://doi.org/10.1080/17475759.2010.520838

Pender, K., Hope, E., & Sondel, B. (2022). Reclaiming "Mydentity": Counterstorytelling to challenge injustice for racially and economically marginalized emerging adults. *Journal of Community and Applied Social Psychology,* Advanced online publication. https://doi.org/10.1002/casp.2662

Pinckney IV, H. P., Outley, C., Blake, J. J., & Kelly, B. (2011). Promoting positive youth development of Black youth: A rites of passage framework. *Journal of Park & Recreation Administration,* 29(1), 98–112.

Plummer, J. A., Wray-Lake, L., Alvis, L., Metzger, A., & Syvertsen, A. K. (2022). Assessing the link between adolescents' awareness of inequality and civic engagement across time and racial/ethnic groups. *Journal of Youth and Adolescence, 51,* 428–442. https://doi.org/10.1007/s10964-021-01545-6

Pope, R. J., & Flanigan, S. T. (2013). Revolution for breakfast: Intersections of activism, service, and violence in the Black Panther Party's community service programs. *Social Justice Research, 26*(4), 445–470. https://doi.org/10.1007/s11211-013-0197-8

Quimby, D., Richards, M., Santiago, C. D., Scott, D., & Puvar, D. (2018). Positive peer association among Black American youth and the roles of ethnic identity and gender. *Journal of Research on Adolescence, 28*(3), 711–730. https://doi.org/10.1111/jora.12363

Ray, J. (2021, December 27). Los Angeles fatal shootings: By the numbers. *Los Angeles Times.* https://www.latimes.com/california/newsletter/2021-12-27/los-angeles-police-department-fatal-shootings-by-the-numbers-essential-california

Ray, R. (2021). *How we rise: What the Capitol insurgency reveals about white supremacy and law enforcement.* Brookings Institute. https://www.brookings.edu/blog/how-we-rise/2021/01/12/what-the-capitol-insurgency-reveals-about-white-supremacy-and-law-enforcement/

Reitsma, M. B., Claypool, A. L., Vargo, J., Shete, P. B., McCorvie, R., Wheeler, W. H., Rocha, D. A., Myers, J. F., Muray, E. L., Bregman, B., Dominguez, D. M., Nguyen, A. D., Porse, C., Fritz, C. L., Jain, S., Watt, J. P., Salomon, J. A., & Goldhaber-Fiebert, J. D. (2021). Racial/Ethnic disparities in COVID-19 exposure risk, testing, and cases at the subcounty level in California. *Health Affairs, 40*(6), 870–878. https://doi.org/10.1377/hlthaff.2021.00098

Richards-Schuster, K., & Dobbie, D. (2011) Tagging walls and planting seeds: Creating spaces for youth civic action. *Journal of Community Practice, 19*(3), 234–251. https://doi.org/10.1080/10705422.2011.595283

Rivas-Drake, D., Syed, M., Umaña-Taylor, A., Markstrom, C., French, S., Schwartz, S. J., Lee, R., Cross, W. E., Knight, G. P., Quintana, S. M., Seaton, E., Sellers, R. M., & Yip, T. (2014). Feeling good, happy, and proud: A meta-analysis of positive ethnic-racial affect and adjustment. *Child Development, 85*(1), 77–102. https://doi.org/10.1111/cdev.12175

Rivas-Drake, D., & Umaña-Taylor, A. J. (2019). *Below the surface: Talking with teens about race, ethnicity, and identity.* Princeton University Press

Roberts, L. M., & Grayson, M. (2021, June 1). Businesses must be accountable for their promises on racial justice. *Harvard Business Review.* https://hbr.org/2021/06/businesses-must-be-accountable-for-their-promises-on-racial-justice

Rodriguez, C. (2016). Mothering while Black: Feminist thought on maternal loss, mourning and agency in the African diaspora. *Transforming Anthropology, 24*(1), 61–69. https://doi.org/10.1111/traa.12059

Rogers, L. O., Rosario, R. J., Padilla, D., & Foo, C. (2021). "[I]t's hard because it's the cops that are killing us for stupid stuff": Racial identity in the sociopolitical context of Black Lives Matter. *Developmental Psychology, 57*(1), 87–101. https://doi.org/10.1037/dev0001130

Rogers, L. O., & Way, N. (2016). "I have goals to prove all those people wrong and not fit into any one of those boxes": Paths of resistance to stereotypes among Black adolescent males. *Journal of Adolescent Research, 31*(3), 263–298. https://doi.org/10.1177/0743558415600071

Ross, R. (2022, July 21). California beachfront land taken from Black family returned in ceremony. *Reuters.* https://www.reuters.com/world/us/california-beachfront-land-taken-black-family-returned-ceremony-2022-07-20/

Ruby, M. (2020). Tokenism. In Z. A. Casey (Ed.), *Encyclopedia of critical whiteness studies in education* (pp. 675–680). Brill.

Santos, C. E. (2020). Themes in political development: Considering the potential of an intersectionality lens. *Journal of Applied Developmental Psychology, 71,* 101211. https://doi.org/10.1016/j.appdev.2020.101211

Schelbe, L., Chanmugam, A., Moses, T., Saltzburg, S., Williams, L. R., & Letendre, J. (2015). Youth participation in qualitative research: Challenges and possibilities. *Qualitative Social Work, 14*(4), 504–521. https://doi.org/10.1177/1473325014556792

Schiff, M. (2018). Can restorative justice disrupt the 'school-to-prison pipeline?' *Contemporary Justice Review, 21*(2), 121–139. https://doi.org/10.1080/10282580.2018.1455509

Schulz, W., Ainley, J., Fraillon, J., Kerr, D., & Losito, B. (2010). *ICCS 2009 International Report: Civic knowledge, attitudes, and engagement among lower-secondary school students in 38 countries.* International Association for the Evaluation of Educational Achievement. https://www.iea.nl/sites/default/files/2019-04/ICCS_2009_International_Report.pdf

Schwartz, S. (2022, September 28). Map: Where critical race theory is under attack. *Education Week.* https://www.edweek.org/policy-politics/map-where-critical-race-theory-is-under-attack/2021/06

Scott, J., Moses, M. S., Finnigan, K. S., Trujillo, T., & Jackson, D. D. (2017). *Law and order in school and society: How discipline and policing policies harm students of color, and what we can do about it.* National Education Policy Center. https://nepc.colorado.edu/publication/law-and-order

Seaton, E. K., Scottham, K. M., & Sellers, R. M. (2006). The status model of racial identity development in African American adolescents: Evidence of structure, trajectories, and well-being. *Child Development, 77*(5), 1416–1426. https://doi.org/10.1111/j.1467-8624.2006.00944.x

Seider, S., & Graves, D. (2020). *Schooling for critical consciousness: Engaging Black and Latinx youth in analyzing, navigating, and challenging racial injustice.* Harvard Education Press.

Sellers, R. M., Smith, M. A., Shelton, J. N., Rowley, S. A., & Chavous, T. M. (1998). Multidimensional model of racial identity: A reconceptualization of African American racial identity. *Personality and Social Psychology Review, 2*(1), 18–39. https://doi.org/10.1207/s15327957pspr0201_2

Sevon, M. A. (2022). Schooling while Black: Analyzing the racial school discipline crisis for behavior analyst. *Behavior Analysis in Practice,* Advanced online publication. https://doi.org/10.1007/s40617-022-00695-8

Shehata, A. (2016). News habits among adolescents: The influence of family communication on adolescents' news media use—Evidence from a three-wave panel study. *Mass Communication and Society, 19*(6), 758–781. https://doi.org/10.1080/15205436.2016.1199705

Shiller, J. T. (2013). Preparing for democracy: How community-based organizations build civic engagement among urban youth. *Urban Education, 48*(1), 69–91. https://doi.org/10.1177/0042085912436761

Shuster, K. (2018, January 31). *Teaching hard history.* Southern Poverty Law Center. https://www.splcenter.org/20180131/teaching-hard-history

Smith, C. D., & Hope, E. C. (2020). "We just want to break the stereotype": Tensions in Black boys' critical social analysis of their suburban school experiences. *Journal of Educational Psychology, 112*(3), 551–566. https://doi.org/10.1037/edu0000435

Solórzano, D. G. & Perez Huber, L. (2020). *Racial microaggressions: Using critical race theory to respond to everyday racism.* Teachers College Press.

Solórzano, D. G., & Yosso, T. J. (2002). Critical race methodology: Counter-storytelling as an analytical framework for education research. *Qualitative Inquiry, 8*(1), 23–44. https://doi.org/10.1177/107780040200800103

Sondel, B., Kretchmar, K., & Dunn, A. H. (2019). "Who do these people want teaching their children?" White saviorism, colorblind racism, and anti-blackness in "no excuses" charter schools. *Urban Education, 57*(9), 1621–1650. https://doi.org/10.1177/0042085919842618

Stattin, H., & Russo, S. (2022). Youth's own political interest can explain their political interactions with important others. *International Journal of Behavioral Development, 46*(4), 297–307. https://doi.org/10.1177/01650254221095843

Sue, D. W. (2006). The invisible whiteness of being: Whiteness, white supremacy, white privilege, and racism. In M. G. Constantine & D. W. Sue (Eds.), *Addressing racism: Facilitating cultural competence in mental health and educational settings* (pp. 15–30). John Wiley & Sons, Inc.

Sullivan, L. Y. (1997). Hip-hop nation: The undeveloped social capital of Black urban America. *National Civic Review, 86*(3), 235–244. https://doi.org/10.1002/ncr.4100860309

Tatum, Beverly Daniel. (2003). *Why are all the Black kids sitting together in the cafeteria? And other conversations about race.* Basic Books.

Taylor, K. Y. (2016). *From #BlackLivesMatter to Black liberation.* Haymarket Books.

Taylor, U. (1998). The historical evolution of Black feminist theory and praxis. *Journal of Black Studies, 29*(2), 234–253. https://www.jstor.org/stable/2668091

Terriquez, V. (2015). Intersectional mobilization, social movement spillover, and queer youth leadership in the immigrant rights movement. *Social Problems, 62*(3), 343–362. https://doi.org/10.1093/socpro/spv010

Terriquez, V., Brenes, T., & Lopez, A. (2018). Intersectionality as a multipurpose collective action frame: The case of the undocumented youth movement. *Ethnicities, 18*(2), 260–276. https://doi.org/10.1177/1468796817752558

Thelamour, B., George Mwangi, C., & Ezeofor, I. (2019). "We need to stick together for survival": Black college students' racial identity, same-ethnic friendships, and campus connectedness. *Journal of Diversity in Higher Education*, 12(3), 266–279. https://doi.org/10.1037/dhe0000104

Thomas, D., & Horowitz, J. M. (2020, September 16). *Support for Black Lives Matter has decreased since June but remains strong among Black Americans*. Pew Research Center. https://www.pewresearch.org/fact-tank/2020/09/16/support-for-black-lives-matter-has-decreased-since-june-but-remains-strong-among-black-americans/

Tichavakunda, A. A. (2021). Black joy on white campuses: Exploring Black students' recreation and celebration at a historically white institution. *The Review of Higher Education*, 44(3), 297–324. https://doi.org/0.1353/rhe.2021.0003

Trent, M., Dooley, D. G., Dougé, J., Section on Adolescent Health, Council on Community Pediatrics, Committee on Adolescence, Cavanaugh, R. M., Lacroix, A. E., Fanburg, J., Rahmandar, M. H., Hornberger, L. L., Schneider, M. B., Yen, S., Chilton, L. A., Green, A. E., Dilley, K. J., Gutierrez, J. R., Duffee, J. H., Keane, V. A., … Wallace, S. B. (2019). The impact of racism on child and adolescent health. *Pediatrics*, 144(2), e20191765. https://doi.org/10.1542/peds.2019-1765

Tuck, E., & Yang, K. W. (2014). *Youth resistance research and theories of change*. Routledge.

Turner III, D. C. (2021). The (good) trouble with Black boys: Organizing with Black boys and young men in George Floyd's America. *Theory Into Practice*, 60(4), 422–433. https://doi.org/10.1080/00405841.2021.1983317

Turner, E. A., Harrell, S. P., & Bryant-Davis, T. (2022). Black Love, Activism, and Community (BLAC): The BLAC model of healing and resilience. *Journal of Black Psychology*, 48(3–4), 547–568. https://doi.org/10.1177/00957984211018364

Uslaner, E. M., & Conley, R. S. (2003). Civic engagement and particularized trust: The ties that bind people to their ethnic communities. *American Politics Research*, 31 (4), 331–360. https://doi.org/10.1177/1532673X03031004001

Van Goethem, A., Van Hoof, A., Orobio de Castro, B., Van Aken, M., & Hart, D. (2014). The role of reflection in the effects of community service on adolescent development: A meta-analysis. *Child Development*, 85(6), 2114–2130. https://doi.org/10.1111/cdev.12274

Variety. (2020, September 18). Two in three Black Americans don't feel properly represented in media, study finds. *NBC News*. https://www.nbcnews.com/news/nbcblk/two-three-black-americans-don-t-feel-properly-represented-media-n1240438

Verba, S., Burns, N., & Schlozman, K. L. (2003). Unequal at the starting line: Creating participatory inequalities across generations and among groups. *The American Sociologist*, 34(1–2), 45–69. https://doi.org/10.1007/s12108-003-1005-y

Verba, S., Schlozman, K. L., & Brady, H. E. (1995). *Voice and equality: Civic voluntarism in American politics*. Harvard University Press.

Vincent, C., Inglish, J., Girvan, E., Van Ryzin, M., Svanks, R., Springer, S., & Ivey, A. (2021). Introducing restorative practices into high schools' multi-tiered systems of support: Successes and challenges. *Contemporary Justice Review*, 24(4), 409–435. https://doi.org/10.1080/10282580.2021.1969522

Voight, A., & King-White, D. (2021). School counselors' role in supporting student voice initiatives in secondary schools. *Multicultural Learning and Teaching*, 16 (1), 63–79. https://doi.org/10.1515/mlt-2020-0003

Watts, R. J., Diemer, M. A., & Voight, A. M. (2011). Critical consciousness: Current status and future directions. *New Directions for Child and Adolescent Development, 2011*(134), 43–57. https://doi.org/10.1002/cd.310

Watts, R. J., & Flanagan, C. (2007). Pushing the envelope on youth civic engagement: A developmental and liberation psychology perspective. *Journal of Community Psychology, 35*(6), 779–792. https://doi.org/10.1002/jcop.20178

Watts, R., & Guessous, O. (2006). Sociopolitical development: The missing link in research and policy on adolescents. In S. Ginwright, P. Noguera, & J. Cammarota (Eds.), *Beyond Resistance! Youth activism and community change: New democratic possibilities for practice and policy for America's youth.* Routledge.

Watts, R. J., & Halkovic, A. (2022). Further theorizing on sociopolitical development. *Journal of Research on Adolescence, 32*(4), 1270–1279. http://doi.org/10.1111/jora.12811

Watts, R. J., & Hipolito-Delgado, C. P. (2015). Thinking ourselves to liberation? Advancing sociopolitical action in critical consciousness. *The Urban Review, 47,* 847–867. https://doi.org/10.1007/s11256-015-0341-x

Watts, R. J., Williams, N. C., & Jagers, R. J. (2003). Sociopolitical development. *American Journal of Community Psychology, 31*(1–2), 185–194. https://doi.org/10.1023/A:1023091024140

Webster, N. (2021). Acknowledging the historical contributions of Black youth's civic engagement in society. *Sociology Compass, 15*(5), e12871. https://doi.org/10.1111/soc4.12871

Wellman, M. L. (2022). Black squares for Black lives? Performative allyship as credibility maintenance for social media influencers on Instagram. *Social Media & Society, 8*(1), 1–10. https://doi.org/10.1177/205630512210804

Wells-Barnett, Ida B. (1997). *Southern horrors and other writings: The anti-lynching campaign of Ida B. Wells, 1892–1900.* Bedford Books.

White, E. S., & Mistry, R. S. (2016). Parent civic beliefs, civic participation, socialization practices, and child civic engagement. *Applied Developmental Science, 20*(1), 44–60. https://doi.org/10.1080/10888691.2015.1049346

White-Johnson, R. L. (2012). Prosocial involvement among African American young adults: Considering racial discrimination and racial identity. *Journal of Black Psychology, 38*(3), 313–341. https://doi.org/10.1177/0095798411420429

Wikipedia. (2022, November 29). *List of George Floyd protests outside the United States.* https://en.wikipedia.org/wiki/List_of_George_Floyd_protests_outside_the_United_States

Wilf, S., & Wray-Lake, L. (2021). "That's how revolutions happen": Psychopolitical resistance in youth's online civic engagement. *Journal of Adolescent Research,* Advanced online publication. https://doi.org/10.1177/07435584211062121

Williams, D. R. (2018). Stress and the mental health of populations of color: Advancing our understanding of race-related stressors. *Journal of Health and Social Behavior, 59*(4), 466–485. https://doi.org/10.1177/0022146518814251

Williams, D. R., Lawrence, J. A., & Davis, B. A. (2019). Racism and health: Evidence and needed research. *Annual Review of Public Health, 40,* 105–125. https://doi.org/10.1146/annurev-publhealth-040218-043750

Williams, M. G. (2022). "They never told us that Black is beautiful": Fostering Black joy and pro-Blackness pedagogies in early childhood classrooms. *Journal of Early Childhood Literacy*, 22(3), 357–382. https://doi.org/10.1177/14687984221121163

Wilson, B. L. (2020). I'm your Black friend, but I won't educate you about racism. That's on you. *The Washington Post*. https://www.washingtonpost.com/outlook/2020/06/08/black-friends-educate-racism/

Witherspoon, D. P., Wray-Lake, L., & Halgunseth, L. C. (2022). Black lives matter! Adolescent research incrementally dismantles racism and systems of oppression. *Journal of Research on Adolescence*, 32(1), 4–12. https://doi.org/10.1111/jora.12736

Wray-Lake, L. (2019). How do young people become politically engaged? *Child Development Perspectives*, 13(2), 127–132. https://doi.org/10.1111/cdep.12324

Wray-Lake, L., & Abrams, L. S. (2020). Pathways to civic engagement among urban youth of color. *Monographs of the Society for Research in Child Development*, 85(2), 7–154. https://doi.org/10.1111/mono.12415

Wray-Lake, L., & Ballard, P. J. (2023). Civic engagement across adolescence and early adulthood. In L. J. Crockett, G. Carlo, & J. E. Schulenberg (Eds.), *APA handbook of adolescent and young adult development* (pp. 573–593). American Psychological Association. https://doi.org/10.1037/0000298-035

Wray-Lake, L., Gneiwosz, B., Benavides, C., & Wilf, S. (2021). Youth civic engagement: Exploring micro and macro social processes. In A. Kostic & D. Chadee (Eds.), *Positive psychology: An international perspective* (pp. 152–176). Wiley.

Wray-Lake, L., Halgunseth, L., & Witherspoon, D. (2022). "Good trouble, necessary trouble": Dismantling oppression through resistance and activism. *Journal of Research on Adolescence*, 32(3), 949–958. https://onlinelibrary.wiley.com/toc/15327795/2022/32/3

Wray-Lake, L., Metzger, A., & Syvertsen, A. K. (2017). Testing multidimensional models of youth civic engagement: Model comparisons, measurement invariance, and age differences. *Applied Developmental Science*, 21(4), 266–284. http://doi.org/10.1080/10888691.2016.1205495

Wray-Lake, L., & Syvertsen, A. (2011). The developmental roots of social responsibility in childhood and adolescence. In C. Flanagan & B. Christens (Eds.), Youth development: Work at the cutting edge. *New Directions for Child and Adolescent Development*, 134, 1–25. https://doi.org/10.1002/cd.308

Wray-Lake, L., Wells, R., Alvis, L., Delgado, S., Syvertsen, A. K., & Metzger, A. (2018). Being a Latinx adolescent under a Trump presidency: Analysis of Latinx youth's reactions to immigration politics. *Children and Youth Services Review*, 87, 192–204. https://doi.org/10.1016/j.childyouth.2018.02.032

Youniss, J., & Yates, M. (1999). Youth service and moral-civic identity: A case for everyday morality. *Educational Psychology Review*, 11(4), 361–376. https://doi.org/10.1023/A:1022009400250

Zeldin, S., Gauley, J., Krauss, S. E., Kornbluh, M., & Collura, J. (2017). Youth adult partnership and youth civic development. *Youth & Society*, 49, 851–878. https://doi.org/10.1177%2F0044118X15595153

INDEX

Milton Keynes UK
Ingram Content Group UK Ltd.
UKHW010630070224
437407UK00008B/53

9 781009 244213